BELOVED MAMA

Private Correspondence of
Queen Victoria and the German Crown Princess

1878–1885

Private Correspondence of
Queen Victoria and the German Crown Princess

Earlier volumes in the series
DEAREST CHILD   1858–1861
DEAREST MAMA   1861–1864
YOUR DEAR LETTER   1865–1871
DARLING CHILD   1871–1878

Queen Victoria and Princess Beatrice, May 1879.

BELOVED MAMA

Private Correspondence of
Queen Victoria and the German Crown Princess

1878–1885

Edited by

ROGER FULFORD

Evans Brothers Limited London

Published by
EVANS BROTHERS LIMITED
Montague House, Russell Square, London WC1B 5BX

This selection © Roger Fulford 1981

First published 1981

British Library Cataloguing in Publication Data

Victoria, *Queen of Great Britain*
    Beloved mama.
    1. Victoria, *Queen of Great Britain*
    2. Victoria, *Empress, consort of Friedrich III,*
    Emperor of Germany
    I. Title   II. Victoria, *Empress, consort of*
    Friedrich III, Emperor of Germany
    III. Fulford, Roger
    941.08'13'0924   DA552

ISBN 0-237-44997-8

Set in 11 on 12 point Bembo
and printed in Great Britain by
Butler & Tanner Limited, Frome and London

PRA 7140

CONTENTS

Preface   *page* xi

Introduction   1

Familiar Names used in this Correspondence   13

The Battenberg Family   18

The Correspondence, 1878–1885   21

Index   197

— v —

ILLUSTRATIONS

Queen Victoria and Princess Beatrice, 1879   *frontispiece*

The Grand Duke and Duchess of Hesse with
  their family, 1878   *facing page* 34

Queen Victoria with the Grand Duke of Hesse and his
  children, 1879   34

Prince Waldemar of Prussia with his sisters, 1878   35

Prince Henry of Prussia, 1883   35

The Hereditary Prince and Princess of Saxe-Meiningen,
  1879   50

Prince William of Prussia and Princess Victoria of
  Schleswig-Holstein, 1880   50

The children of the Duke of Edinburgh, 1881   51

The Queen at Balmoral, 1882   51

The Prince of Wales and his brothers, 1881   82

The Emperor William I with his son, grandson and
  great-grandson, 1882   83

The Duke of Connaught, 1882   98

The Duke and Duchess of Connaught with their children,
  1883   98

The Princess of Saxe-Meiningen with her daughter, 1879   99

Prince William of Prussia with his son, 1883   99

The Duchess of Albany with her children   130

Grand Duke and Grand Duchess Serge of Russia, Prince
and Princess Louis of Battenberg and the Grand Duke
of Hesse, 1884   131

Queen Victoria with the Duchess of Edinburgh and her
daughters, the Crown Princess, Princess Victoria of
Prussia and Princess Beatrice, 1884   146

Queen Victoria with Princess Victoria of Wales, Princess
Victoria of Prussia, Princess Victoria Melita of
Edinburgh and the Crown Princess, 1884   147

Alexander, Prince of Bulgaria (Sandro)   170

The Duchess of Connaught in her wedding dress, 1879
The Duchess of Albany in her wedding dress, 1882
between pages 170/171

The wedding of Princess Beatrice to Prince Henry of
Battenberg, 1885   171

All the illustrations, except that facing page 170, are reproduced
by gracious permission of Her Majesty Queen Elizabeth II.

THE ROYAL FAMILY TREE

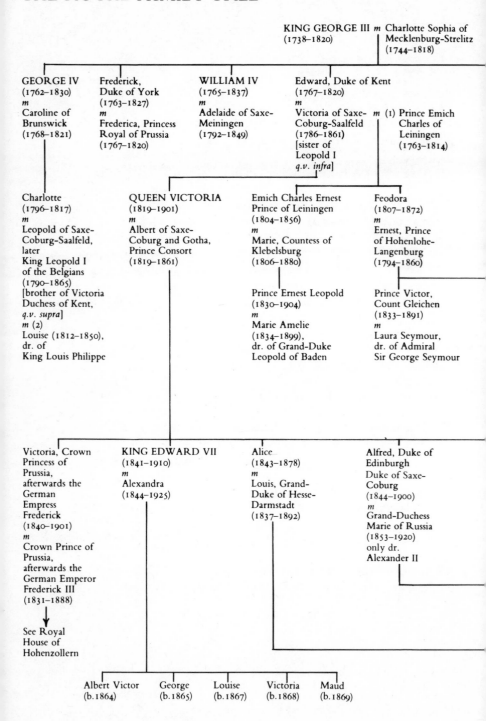

KING GEORGE III *m* Charlotte Sophia of
(1738–1820)   Mecklenburg-Strelitz
(1744–1818)

GEORGE IV   Frederick,   WILLIAM IV   Edward, Duke of Kent
(1762–1830)   Duke of York   (1765–1837)   (1767–1820)
m   (1763–1827)   *m*   *m*
Caroline of   *m*   Adelaide of Saxe-   Victoria of Saxe- *m* (1) Prince Emich
Brunswick   Frederica, Princess   Meiningen   Coburg-Saalfeld   Charles of
(1768–1821)   Royal of Prussia   (1792–1849)   (1786–1861)   Leiningen
             (1767–1820)   [sister of   (1763–1814)
                                            Leopold I
                                            q.v. infra]

Charlotte   QUEEN VICTORIA   Emich Charles Ernest   Feodora
(1796–1817)   (1819–1901)   Prince of Leiningen   (1807–1872)
m   *m*   (1804–1856)   *m*
Leopold of Saxe-   Albert of Saxe-   *m*   Ernest, Prince
Coburg-Saalfeld,   Coburg and Gotha,   Marie, Countess of   of Hohenlohe-
later   Prince Consort   Klebelsburg   Langenburg
King Leopold I   (1819–1861)   (1806–1880)   (1794–1860)
of the Belgians
(1790–1865)
[brother of Victoria   Prince Ernest Leopold   Prince Victor,
Duchess of Kent,   (1830–1904)   Count Gleichen
q.v. supra]   *m*   (1833–1891)
m (2)   Marie Amelie   *m*
Louise (1812–1850),   (1834–1899),   Laura Seymour,
dr. of   dr. of Grand-Duke   dr. of Admiral
King Louis Philippe   Leopold of Baden   Sir George Seymour

Victoria, Crown   KING EDWARD VII   Alice   Alfred, Duke of
Princess of   (1841–1910)   (1843–1878)   Edinburgh
Prussia,   *m*   *m*   Duke of Saxe-
afterwards the   Alexandra   Louis, Grand-   Coburg
German   (1844–1925)   Duke of Hesse-   (1844–1900)
Empress   Darmstadt   *m*
Frederick   (1837–1892)   Grand-Duchess
(1840–1901)   Marie of Russia
m   (1853–1920)
Crown Prince of   only dr.
Prussia,   Alexander II
afterwards the
German Emperor
Frederick III
(1831–1888)

See Royal
House of
Hohenzollern

Albert Victor   George   Louise   Victoria   Maud
(b.1864)   (b.1865)   (b.1867)   (b.1868)   (b.1869)

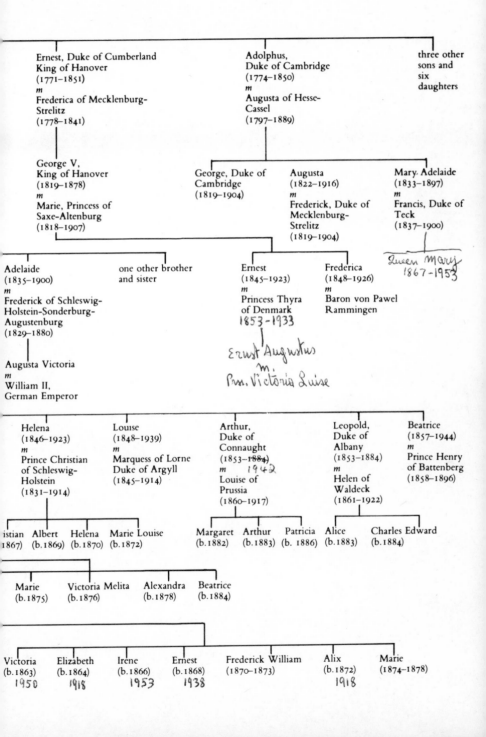

Ernest, Duke of Cumberland
King of Hanover
(1771–1851)
m
Frederica of Mecklenburg-
Strelitz
(1778–1841)

Adolphus,
Duke of Cambridge
(1774–1850)
m
Augusta of Hesse-
Cassel
(1797–1889)

three other
sons and
six
daughters

George V,
King of Hanover
(1819–1878)
m
Marie, Princess of
Saxe-Altenburg
(1818–1907)

George, Duke of
Cambridge
(1819–1904)

Augusta
(1822–1916)
m
Frederick, Duke of
Mecklenburg-
Strelitz
(1819–1904)

Mary Adelaide
(1833–1897)
m
Francis, Duke of
Teck
(1837–1900)

Queen Mary
1867-1953

Adelaide
(1835–1900)
m
Frederick of Schleswig-
Holstein-Sonderburg-
Augustenburg
(1829–1880)

Augusta Victoria
m
William II,
German Emperor

one other brother
and sister

Ernest
(1845–1923)
m
Princess Thyra
of Denmark
1853-1933

Frederica
(1848–1926)
m
Baron von Pawel
Rammingen

Ernst Augustus
m.
Pm. Victoria Luise

Helena
(1846–1923)
m
Prince Christian
of Schleswig-
Holstein
(1831–1914)

Louise
(1848–1939)
m
Marquess of Lorne
Duke of Argyll
(1845–1914)

Arthur,
Duke of
Connaught
(1853–1884)
m 1942
Louise of
Prussia
(1860–1917)

Leopold,
Duke of
Albany
(1853–1884)
m
Helen of
Waldeck
(1861–1922)

Beatrice
(1857–1944)
m
Prince Henry
of Battenberg
(1858–1896)

istian   Albert   Helena   Marie Louise
1867)   (b.1869) (b.1870) (b.1872)

Margaret Arthur   Patricia   Alice   Charles Edward
(b.1882) (b.1883) (b. 1886) (b.1883) (b.1884)

Marie   Victoria Melita   Alexandra   Beatrice
(b.1875)   (b.1876)   (b.1878)   (b.1884)

Victoria   Elizabeth   Irene   Ernest   Frederick William   Alix   Marie
(b.1863)   (b.1864)   (b.1866)   (b.1868)   (1870–1873)   (b.1872)   (1874–1878)
1950   1918   1953   1938   1918

PREFACE

The correspondence between Queen Victoria and her eldest child, the German Crown Princess and Princess Royal of England, started in 1858 when the Princess married the future Emperor, Frederick III, and it continued until the start of the present century. The Queen's last letter was written on January 6, 1901, and in that year both correspondents died. The Queen's letters were, as the book-sellers would say, "neatly bound" in dark blue cloth by the year though sometimes two volumes were needed to cover the whole of one year. They amount to some 60 volumes. The letters from the Crown Princess are more handsomely bound in leather and are in the Archives at Windsor Castle. They too run to about 60 volumes of roughly 400 pages each. At the end of the life of the Crown Princess (or the Empress Frederick as she had become) both sides of the correspondence were at Friedrichshof—the house near Frankfurt which she had built to the memory of her husband. There is no evidence why she sent for her own letters from Windsor; it is possible that she wanted to use them for a biography of the Emperor and it is possible that she wanted to remove certain passages which she knew would be offensive to her son, the Kaiser. She returned them to Windsor shortly before she died.

The son of one of the Empress's oldest friends, Lady Ponsonby, edited and published some of these letters in 1928 in a single volume so that his book was only a fraction of the whole, and roughly a quarter was devoted to the illness and death of the Emperor Frederick. With one or two exceptions the English Royal Family received the book with indignation and the ex-Kaiser attempted to stop publication. Unsuccessful in this he bought the German rights making it a condition that he should write an introduction. He wrote "she was very sensitive and everything wounded her;

she saw everything in shadows, everything hostile, saw want of sympathy and coolness where there was only a helpless silence".

After this rather explosive start the correspondence was undisturbed until the close of the Second World War. The Empress had made her youngest daughter, the Landgravine of Hesse, her literary executor; the Landgravine therefore had the custody of Queen Victoria's letters which were kept at Friedrichshof. The American invading troops were showing some rather unwelcome curiosity about the contents of Friedrichshof and King George VI sent his Librarian to bring back the letters to Windsor. After a few years they were returned to the Landgravine; she wanted them back so that Count Corti could use some of the material for his biography of the Empress which was published by Cassell in 1954 under the title *The English Empress*. Queen Victoria's letters, therefore, are at Friedrichshof (though the copyright belongs to the Queen) and the Empress's letters are at Windsor. Yet whatever the disturbances of the past it is true that history affords few instances where a complete correspondence of this kind has been preserved intact.

I wish to express my gratitude to Her Majesty the Queen for her gracious permission to edit the correspondence and to reproduce certain pictures and photographs from the Royal Collection.

I am very greatly indebted to the Empress's family at Friedrichshof for their constant help to me. I am saddened that her eldest grandson, the Landgrave, died before this book was finished. With a fine appreciation for the arts—no doubt in part inherited from his grandmother—he collected the family treasures and arranged them at the Schloss Faisanerie at Fulda. Many of them came from other properties of the Hesse family which had been damaged or made uninhabitable by the war. Of especial interest to English visitors are the possessions of Princess Mary, the youngest daughter of King George II. These include a fine library of English books which she brought over when she married the Landgrave Frederick II. She was described by Horace Walpole as "the mildest and gentlest of her race". The Schloss was further enriched by the fine collection of classical sculptures formed by the Landgrave; his kindness in spending a day to take me round Fulda is an experience which I shall not forget. His brother, Prince Wolfgang, has helped me with constant kindness and understanding which from the start have been of the greatest encouragement to me.

I can never adequately express my gratitude to Miss Cuthbert of the Royal Archives. She helped me with difficult passages in the Queen's writing both in English and in German. She and Miss Langton spent days—I do not like to calculate how many—in reading my final version, drawing attention to words which were dubious and phrases which needed an explanation—in short putting a finish on what was slovenly. I thank them both.

The Queen's Librarian, Sir Robin Mackworth Young has, as always, been constant in guidance and encouragement.

Mrs. Willy Rous interpreted my trumpetings on the dictating machine into a splendidly coherent typescript. Mrs. Jones of the Lonsdale Staff Bureau at Kendal and her team did the final draft for the printer and helped in countless ways.

Threading my way through the maze of German Royal Families—reigning, mediatised and morganatic—I acknowledge my indebtedness to the *Book of Kings* edited by the late Arnold McNaughton and to Lady Longford's admirable biography of the Queen. As always the London Library has proved a staunch helper.

I owe a particular debt to my publishers and their chairman, John Browning. I do not think that the book could have found its way into print without the stimulating zeal of Audrey White, a Director of the firm. I thank her with affection and gratitude.

INTRODUCTION

The seven years covered by this collection of letters between Queen Victoria and her eldest daughter reveal the characters, the courage and the true natures of mother and daughter more exactly, more graphically than from any other source. Both were compelled to pass through the shadows of sorrow. For the Crown Princess these years saw the death of her favourite son, the rapid retreat from liberal thought in Germany and the undisguised contempt for her and for her opinions shown by Bismarck and his *claque*, and indeed by her own eldest children. Repeatedly the Queen assures her daughter that the only way to face tribulations is to accept them as the will of God. What the Queen felt is summed up by a verse from that celebrated hymn by Charlotte Elliott which was Princess Alice's personal favourite.

> "Though dark my path, and sad my lot,
> Let me be still and murmur not,
> Or breathe the prayer divinely taught
> Thy will be done."

Among these seven years there is perhaps only one—1882—free from sorrow. In November 1878 the Queen's grand-daughter, Princess Mary of Hesse, died as a result of diphtheria, and a few weeks afterwards on the anniversary of the Prince Consort's death, Princess Alice—the Queen's second daughter—died, also from diphtheria.

In the long letter which the Crown Princess wrote to her mother after the Princess's death she was obviously afraid that her mother would slide back into the dark corridors of grief from which she had only begun to emerge some ten years earlier. But she did not. She attended the Memorial Service at Windsor sustained by the courage which Princess Alice had shown, and strengthened by the realisation of the deep affection felt for their sovereign by the British people.

At the end of March the Crown Princess had to watch the death of her favourite son, Prince Waldemar aged 11, from diphtheria. News of the boy's serious illness reached the Queen when she was travelling to Darmstadt for the confirmation of two of her grandchildren, and she wrote to the Crown Princess: "Are we never to have any more relief from anxiety? This is really too terrible." (See page 38.)

Later in the same year came the news that the Prince Imperial—the only child of the Emperor Napoleon III—had been killed. The young Prince joined the staff of Lord Chelmsford who had been appointed to the Imperial Command in South Africa. At the beginning of 1879 Chelmsford invaded Zululand and suffered a serious defeat at Isandhlwana. In February the Prince was allowed to join the British forces, but only as a spectator. Just before the British victory at Ulundi in June the Prince was killed in a skirmish with the Zulu forces. The Prince was on terms of friendship with the Queen and her two youngest children and for a quarter of a century the Queen had been an affectionate friend of the Empress. What made this blow the more painful was that the Queen was mortified to feel that the Prince had been inadequately safeguarded by British troops. She wrote to her daughter that it was "a disgrace which fills me with grief unspeakable". (See page 52.)

In 1881 Lord Beaconsfield died; it was an event whose likelihood the Queen had been reluctant to face. When it came she wrote: "To me the blow is terrible ... Lord Beaconsfield was the truest, kindest friend and wisest counsellor and he too is gone. I feel much crushed by it." (See page 99.)

In 1883 came the cruellest and most personal blow of all. After a short illness John Brown died on March 27. Mr. Gladstone referred to the loss of an intelligent domestic, a phrase which the Queen would not have liked, but then went on to speak of "the sense of serious loss in the Queen's closely occupied life". This was of course the heart of the matter and the Queen missed John Brown's solicitude and loyalty at every hour of the day. What he meant to her may perhaps be illustrated by a very trifling detail. At the end of her life she invited Lord Esher to tea at Windsor; when tea was brought in she said plaintively "none of my favourite biscuits—do see to it". We may be certain that if Brown had been alive it would not have been necessary for the Queen to say anything. The influence and authority of Brown were much disliked by the Queen's elder children, and it will be noticed that even the Crown Princess, most sympathetic and affectionate of the Queen's elder children, could only send a rather formal message about "dear Brown". (See page 136.) The elder sons were undoubtedly rather unwise in what they said about Brown and set gossip sailing away before a fair breeze. This gave rise to stories which, as the author of a recent book on King George I has shrewdly said, "though interesting as ingredients of popular mythology, would not be worth mentioning here but for the fact that one or more of them are still repeated".[1] Characteristically it was the Princess of Wales, the most tender-hearted member of the family, who went to keep the Queen company. "Nothing could exceed her tender sympathy and complete understanding of all I feel and suffer."

Then on March 28, 1884, Prince Leopold, the Duke of Albany, died after a fall at Cannes. For his mother, his health and the question whether he was really well enough to marry are recurring topics in this book. He was educated at Oxford described by the Queen as beloved by the Prince but "I think very odious". We should remember that in spite of being always attacked by very serious physical disabilities his interests were scholarly and he developed into an effective and graceful public speaker; he was President of the Royal Society of Literature and Vice-President of the Royal Society of Arts. He was on terms of personal friendship with John Ruskin.

Sympathising with the Queen, Gladstone wrote of the "bright hope and promise laid in the grave of the Duke of Albany" and he added that the "high qualities which adorned the Duke of Albany have not ceased to exist, and cannot be as if they had never been". The Queen appreciated this letter and also Gladstone's speech in the House of Commons when he said that "the father was to a certain extent revived in the son".

In addition, the Queen had to face the worries inevitable for the head of a large family—quarrels between the Duchesses of Connaught and Albany, disputes over precedence originated by the Duchess of Edinburgh, and the difficulty of Princess Louise's marriage.

Possibly the Queen's outburst of grief over Princess Beatrice's marriage is one of the most difficult things for the Twentieth

---

[1] *George I Elector and King* by Ragnhild Hatton, Thames & Hudson, 1978.

Century to share or even to understand. We can certainly appreciate from the earlier volumes of this correspondence that the Queen not only loved the Princess deeply, but admired her greatly. "A dearer, sweeter, more amiable and unselfish child I never found" (April 26, 1876). "She is like a sunbeam in the house and also like a dove—an angel of peace" (May 21, 1878). "My beloved Baby—who is really the apple of my eye and who I pray God may remain with me as long as I live for she is the last I have and I could not live without her" (April 16, 1873). The Queen's sister-in-law (the Duchess of Saxe-Coburg-Gotha) called her "Benjamina". Characteristically the Queen draws a contrast between Princess Beatrice and some of her older children: "Thank God she is not touchy and offended like several of her brothers and sisters are" (October 20, 1873).

The Queen's views on marriage are familiar from their expression in many of the later volumes in this correspondence. "I hate marriages especially of my daughters" (December 30, 1884). But it is not that which marks the deep division between Queen Victoria and the latter half of the Twentieth Century. Rather it is her belief that children should be prepared to abandon marriage so as to be able to comfort their parents in old age.

Cordelia: Sure I shall never marry like my sisters,
             To love my father all.
Lear: But goes thy heart with this?
Cordelia: Ay, good my Lord.
Lear: So young, and so untender?
Cordelia: So young, my Lord, and true.

These beliefs of Cordelia, moving in the light of what was to follow in the play, were appreciated by the Queen and indeed by many people in the Nineteenth Century. They explain why Cheltenham, Bath, Torquay or Budleigh Salterton were peopled by spinsters and sometimes by bachelors who had all abandoned marriage or careers of their own to act as companions to their surviving parent. Did not Tait, the Bishop of London and afterwards Archbishop of Canterbury, make this an almost episcopal injunction? "I believe no blessing will ever come on work however self-denying, which is undertaken to the neglect of those higher duties which belong to *home* life and are imposed by God himself."[1] In the latter half of the Twentieth Century such ideas

[1] *Sister Dora* by Jo Manton, Methuen, 1971.

have been sacrificed to the deity—if God he be—who teaches us that each individual has the right to live his or her own life without giving a backward glance to the home from whence they sprang. To the Victorians such a manner of life would have been as incomprehensible as is theirs to us. And in groping among what is incomprehensible we want to be careful not to think that the Queen's views were out of step with those of her own generation. Phineas Fletcher in *John Halifax, Gentleman* says: "I have said, and I say again, that I believe every true marriage—of which there is probably one in every five thousand of conjugal unions—is brought about by heaven, and heaven only." (We know that the Queen read and enjoyed this book.) In *The Daisy Chain* and *Heartsease* by Charlotte Yonge we have emphasis on the same theme and the feeling that children have a duty to their parents and Mrs. Battiscombe in her admirable book on that writer says: "Filial duty was for Charlotte the Moloch to which everything must be sacrificed; against its claim neither true love nor common sense had any rights."[1]

The letters between Queen Victoria and the German Crown Princess are primarily concerned with events in their two countries or in their immediate families. More often than in previous years the Crown Princess states her disagreement with something which her mother has said to which the Queen replies with all the prowess of her nature. But the Queen's letters are filled with understanding, and deeply affectionate. Their character is not really ruffled by argument—even about the Liberal Government under Mr. Gladstone of which the Crown Princess was clearly a partisan. When she was on a visit to England in the summer of 1881 she went to tea with the Gladstones and the Queen commented: "Was it necessary? He does not deserve it."

In April 1880 had come the totally unexpected news—at least unexpected by the Queen and the Government—of the triumph of Mr. Gladstone at the General Election. Lord Beaconsfield expected to be returned with a majority of about twenty seats but in reality the Liberals had a large majority. (It was 137 seats.) The orator had trounced the statesman. The outpourings of the Queen against her new Prime Minister are well known, notably from the biography of her private secretary, by his son Lord Ponsonby.[2] At the time many people regretted that the Queen should have

---

[1] *Charlotte M Yonge* by Georgina Battiscombe, Constable, 1943.
[2] *Henry Ponsonby* by Arthur Ponsonby, Macmillan, 1942.

succumbed to the antique courtesies of the Lord of Hughenden and that she forgot that the Prince Consort spoke—not incorrectly—"of the laxity of his political conscience".[1]

It is often superficially said that the dislike of Queen Victoria for Gladstone was political; that she was a Conservative and he a Liberal. In her letters to her daughter she says repeatedly that she is no Conservative and this was certainly true. Her last Conservative Prime Minister (Lord Salisbury) said: "I could do very well with two Departments, in fact I have four—the Prime Ministership, the Foreign Office, the Queen and Randolph Churchill." The Queen was no cipher under a Conservative Prime Minister. Over and over again in this exchange of letters the reader will be surprised by views of the Queen which are far removed from the views of upper-class England and from that island mind which was the mark of a Nineteenth Century Conservative. But she was the staunchest of staunch imperialists and she felt—as is clear from almost every page of this book—that she had an especial responsibility for the well-being and safety of the armed forces of the Crown.

There were also personal reasons which separated her from Gladstone. The violence of what he said in the Midlothian Campaign leading up to the Election of 1880 was what she could never forgive. "She considers his whole conduct since '76 to have been one series of violent, passionate invective against and abuse of Lord Beaconsfield." (*Queen Victoria's Letters*, April 8, 1880.) Of course it can be said on the other side that the two men intensely disliked one another, and that Disraeli hit back with no less violence. (He said that Gladstone's conduct was worse than those who committed the Bulgarian atrocities.) But the Queen was undoubtedly right in thinking that Gladstone had introduced a degree of rancour into English politics—perhaps unknown since the Reform Bill and continuing into the present century until 1914. Whether it was something new or not, the Queen intensely disliked it.

There was another point about Gladstone which, with her practical nature, she disliked and indeed could not understand. He was only in politics with half his mind and will. He was longing to retire into a life of contemplation. Mr. J. L. Hammond, who understood the character of Gladstone perhaps better than John

---

[1] Quoted from the Royal Archives in *The Prince Consort* by R. Fulford, Macmillan, 1949.

Morley (his official biographer), says of Mr. Gladstone in 1880: "he was like a man who, although not yet in the *crise de départ* has given provisional orders to his coachman". The year before, Gladstone himself wrote: "A strong man within me wrestles for retirement. But for this I do not know how my poor flesh and blood, or my poor soul and spirit could face the prolongation of cares and burdens so much beyond my strength at any age and at this age so cruelly exclusive of the great work of penitential recollection." Such sentiments the Queen would not have understood or liked. It remained an abiding anxiety for the Queen that he whose mind was incomprehensible to her should be in charge of the government of the country.

Readers would make a serious mistake if they imagined that the Queen's relations with her Prime Minister and his Liberal colleagues were not profoundly different from those which she expressed in private correspondence with her daughter. For one thing she knew that she was writing to a Gladstonian and that a thump for Mr. Gladstone included a flick in the direction of the Crown Princess. In her letters she gives full rein to her feelings of shock at Disraeli's overthrow and of her own indignation that the new Government and its leader, by the violence of their election campaign, had played a major part in the Liberal triumph and the discomfiture of the Conservatives. Above all she felt that the new Government was turning away from those imperial policies in the East, in South Africa, in Egypt and against Russia which had marked the Government of Beaconsfield. In her official correspondence there are of course many examples of her warnings of the consequences of the Government's half-hearted pursuit of those policies which were dear to her heart. Certainly it is true that in the business of Government their relations were bad but in private they were redeemed by consideration and courtesy. For instance, in the very awkward private discussion over Dilke, Gladstone said that it was less difficult than he expected because of the Queen's "beautiful manners".[1]

The Queen's uncle, King William IV, once said to a friend about his Lord Chancellor: "if you will answer for his death I will answer for his damnation". Some writers have believed that the Queen's feelings for Mr. Gladstone were not dissimilar from what her uncle had said. Though the Queen and her Prime Minister differed entirely on the role of Great Britain overseas their differ-

---

[1] See page 130.

ence was always tempered by courtesy. During the five years of his premiership she over and over again expressed anxiety over his health. (Cynics would say that this was merely an expression of her hope that he would be obliged to retire; but for this there seems no evidence.) In the summer of 1880 he was rather seriously ill and spoke to his friends of the sad decline of theological studies at Oxford. This was not conversation which the Queen would have enjoyed. She invited him to Windsor to recuperate. Writing to thank her after the visit he spoke of: "the delightful opportunity for renewing, and once again deepening, his impression of the beauty, majesty and variety which Windsor presents to view in such rich profusion". In 1882 he sent her a present of a candle reflector which, as the Queen noticed, threw an admirable light. In the following year she sent him some letters written by her Saxe-Coburg step-grandmother in German about the English Royal Family in the 1820's and also consulted him about a quotation from Byron for use on the bust of John Brown. He did not attend Princess Beatrice's wedding which gave rise to some foolish chatter. He had had to submit himself to the attentions of a pair of Victorian doctors who had made a careful examination of "the interior symptoms" of his voice and throat. They pronounced silence in the House of Commons and as little speaking as possible in private life. He therefore asked permission to absent himself "from a festive and august occasion when I should be as a statue among living people". At the same time, which was when he resigned from office, the Queen wrote to offer him an earldom as a mark of recognition of his long and distinguished services. He sent the letter to Lord Granville (his closest colleague in the Government) and said that it "moves and almost upsets me". And then he added: "I remain firm in the intention to accept nothing for myself."

The contrast between the two correspondents is absolute. The Crown Princess scarcely ever jests in her letters—possibly she was still somewhat in awe of the Queen. Essentially her mind was political and her letters give us an historical insight into affairs as Prussia, in the hands of an old and rather inactive Emperor, drifted into the clutches of Bismarck. She minded deeply about such things as she did about the treasures of her native land and the buildings of Italy. Hers was a character which had to endure ill-treatment from the Prussian family, indifference from the German people and, it must be added, some thoughtlessness from her mother who was occasionally reluctant to allow her to visit England and even to attend the funeral of her brother. But all disappointments and the feeling of not being wanted were swallowed up in the fatal illness of the Crown Prince which was lying two years ahead of her. Some words of hers which she wrote to a member of the Reichstag have survived: they were written after her husband's death. She said: "Long before I shall rest next to Emperor Frederick in my grave one will hardly know what we wanted, and how much we loved our fatherland for which we wanted to do so much and for which we were permitted to do so little. Yet our tragic fate belongs to German history."

In the Queen's case there was no "tragic fate"—rather the opposite. The Queen had the experience of public affairs and the authority which came naturally to one who had been longer on the throne than any other sovereign of the leading European powers. She had been on the throne for a decade before the Emperor Francis Joseph acceded. No golden jubilee marked the long life of the German Emperor. Even the slow drift to the Left throughout her reign did not embitter her as did the sharper drift to the Right embitter her daughter in Germany. The Queen had very clear ideas of what was right and wrong in public affairs and she wrote consequently on political matters with great confidence but she could instantly break away over some family matter or over something which had caught her attention in England. The poet Cowper said of his own letters: "I write generally in the harum-scarum way." That is to say he wrote naturally and without any too great deliberation about things which were on his mind. So with Queen Victoria. Yet the extraordinary thing to notice is that, although the Queen—in these family letters—was writing hurriedly there are very few "scratchings out" and virtually no spelling mistakes. (I think that I remember only one in the seven years covered by this volume.) The pace at which she wrote is nowhere allowed to influence the convincing force of what she wants to say. But alas! that is not true of her handwriting which remains as difficult as ever to decipher. As an example I give the word "cunning", which if she had ever used it, would have looked something like this "c̈uuuiug", the c dotted to distinguish it from the string of loops in sequence which followed. Rather strangely her daughter never says that there was a word which she could not decipher for it is certain that she knew the kind of word which the Queen would be likely to use and also of course whether it was German or English. The Editor can only read with a rather wan smile the passage where the Queen refers to Lord Goschen and says that his writing was very bad and that his despatches always had to be copied before being submitted to the Queen.

"Few letter-writers have revealed their feelings more openly. Her pen made everything personal and expressive."[1] These words were written by Mr. Raymond Mortimer, who was a true judge of such matters and an unfaltering guide on the Arts and literature. He went on to say how the character of the writer was brought out by "the exclamation marks and the indefatigable underlinings".[1] I bow to his shade and confess that these additions to emphasis will only be found occasionally in this book. For a justification for these omissions I turn to H. W. Fowler, the great master of English prose who said—perhaps rather rudely—"the use of exclamation marks merely shows that the writer does not know his business".[2] Although I may have deviated somewhat from what Mr. Mortimer would have wished I agree entirely with him when he writes that "Queen Victoria's letters seem to me among the most enjoyable in the English language."

As they look back across the years, discriminating men and women will still find satisfaction in reading the most perceptive biography of Queen Victoria, a book which, still popular, celebrated its diamond jubilee in 1980. Lytton Strachey's rather slim volume, with its meagre list of authorities, meagre because the great archive at Windsor was still sealed when the book was written, and with none of the paraphernalia of "scholarship" yet eclipses all that were to follow. At the beginning of 1918, when *Eminent Victorians* was finished, he wrote to his mother to tell her what he planned to do and she, evidently thinking that the most eminent Victorian was to be treated in the same subtle but irreverent way as had Miss Nightingale, Dr. Arnold, Cardinal Manning and General Gordon, wrote: "The Queen has won a place in public affection and a reputation in our history which it would be highly unpopular, and I think not quite fair, to attempt to bring down." Whether Strachey ever wished or attempted to "bring down" Queen Victoria is extremely doubtful. His biographer—a wise and sympathetic writer—points out that when Strachey wrote his life of the Queen "to a very large extent he relinquished

---

[1] *Queen Victoria. Leaves from a Journal* by Raymond Mortimer, André Deutsch, 1961.
[2] *Modern English Usage* by H. W. Fowler, Oxford University Press.

his air of bland superiority" which was certainly noticeable in *Eminent Victorians*.[1]

Rather oddly he wrote first of all the rightly celebrated ending to the book. Here he pictures for the reader the thoughts of former times which passed through the Queen's mind on her death-bed. This passage has been acclaimed, quoted from and adapted and has become one of the most familiar pieces of prose in the English language. T. S. Eliot, not in one of his most agreeable or convincing articles, attacked it severely in *The Times Literary Supplement* in 1926. "We are [Eliot wrote] reading a prose densely packed with images and analyses none of which we actually realise." He went on: "here in eighteen lines are eighteen images or analyses, not one of which is original, not one of which is freshly felt or sincerely evoked". A Cambridge friend of Strachey's, Mr. George Rylands, was in his company when he read the article and as Strachey finished reading it he crumpled up the paper and cried: "It's all true—all true." But was it not really true that *The Times Literary Supplement* was nursing contemporary feeling against Strachey and wrapping it up in language which many will feel was more "highfalutin" than convincing?

Strachey achieved success by working through, and brooding over, the limited authorities which are the foundation of the book. Towards the end of the second year's work he spoke of struggling with Victoria who is proving "a tougher mouthful than even I expected. I must masticate and masticate with a steady persistence." He has given us a superb distillation of all the sources so that we can say as Milton says in "Areopagitica", the book is "the precious life-blood of a master spirit". The result of all this was that he got it right. Nowhere is this more obvious than in the seven years covered by this book. He notices perfectly correctly that as the public watched the Queen weeping for her children and friends their attitude towards her altogether changed. At the same time there was an alteration in the temper of the Queen's mind.

The death of the Prince Consort had, of course, shocked the public but he was never really understood, never really liked by the people of England. So while the Queen hedged herself behind the folds of mourning to display her true feelings and to show to the people the true nature of the Prince whom they had lost, they remained not stirred and not convinced, but rather uninterested.

---

[1] *Lytton Strachey* by Michael Holroyd, Heinemann, 1968.

They became not comforted by tears but consoled by ribaldry. When the news of the Prince's death reached a Norfolk nobleman, he immediately changed into his brightest clothes to show his joy that at least one foreigner was safely out of the way. His antics may have been silly—they were not exclusive to himself. After the Prince's death the Queen and her subjects were travelling along different roads separated by the seclusion of their Ruler and by the mists of melancholy which surrounded her: they were to be re-united during these seven years when the Queen's courage was realised and when she no longer bowed before grief. She addressed to the nation a moving and characteristic letter after the death of Prince Leopold; in this she said: "though much shaken and sorely afflicted by the many sorrows and trials which have fallen upon me during these past years, I will not lose courage, and with the help of Him who has never forsaken me, will strive to labour on for the sake of my children, and for the good of the country I love so well". She did not give way as in the 1860's but feeling the sympathy and support of the public she faced disaster with courage and endurance. When she published her second book on her life in the Highlands she can refer to the sympathy and appreciation "which very rarely falls to the lot of anyone during their lifetime". (See page 160.) Because of the deep feeling which these years developed in the public mind they are supremely important for an understanding of Queen Victoria's eminence among the sovereigns of England. For are they not the foundation of "that long evening, mild, serene, and lighted with a golden glory"?

FAMILIAR NAMES USED IN THIS CORRESPONDENCE

In this list of names, the Queen is Queen Victoria, and the Emperor is William I, German Emperor.

ADA. Duchess of Schleswig-Holstein, daughter of the Queen's half-sister.

ADALBERT. Grandson of Frederick William II and first cousin of the Emperor.

AFFIE. Duke of Edinburgh, the Queen's second son.

ALICE. Grand Duchess of Hesse, the Queen's second daughter.

LITTLE ALICE. Afterwards Princess Alice, Countess of Athlone.

ALICKY or ALIX. The Grand Duchess of Hesse's youngest surviving daughter. Married Emperor Nicholas II.

ALIX. The Princess of Wales.

AMÉLIE. Daughter of the Queen's first cousin—Prince Augustus of Saxe-Coburg. Married the Duke in Bavaria

ARTHUR. The Duke of Connaught, the Queen's third son.

AUGUSTA. Duchess of Mecklenburg-Strelitz. Daughter of first Duke of Cambridge.

AUNT or AUNT ALEXANDRINE. Duchess of Saxe-Coburg-Gotha.

AUNT ELISE. Wife of Frederick William IV of Prussia; daughter of King Maximilian of Bavaria.

BABY or BEATRICE . The Queen's youngest daughter, afterwards Princess Henry of Battenberg.

BERNHARD. Prince Bernhard of Saxe-Meiningen, married Princess Charlotte *q.v.*

BERTIE. The Prince of Wales.

CALMA. Caroline Matilda, Princess of Schleswig-Holstein, sister of Dona *q.v.*

THE CAMBRIDGES. The second Duke of Cambridge, his mother and two sisters.

CHARLES OF PORTUGAL. Afterwards King Carlos I.

CHARLOTTE. Eldest daughter of the Crown Princess.

DONA. Princess Victoria of Schleswig-Holstein, wife of Prince William of Prussia, the future Kaiser.

EDDIE. Eldest son of the Prince of Wales.

EDDIE GLEICHEN. Son of Prince Victor of Hohenlohe-Langenburg and grandson of the Queen's half-sister.

EITEL FRITZ. Second son of Prince William of Prussia.

ELLA. Princess Elizabeth, second daughter of the Grand Duchess of Hesse. Married the Grand Duke Serge.

THE EMPEROR. William I, German Emperor.

THE EMPRESS. Wife of above or, according to context, Eugénie, Empress of the French.

ERNEST OF H. Only son of the last King of Hanover.

ERNEST OF LEININGEN. Eldest son of the Queen's half-brother.

FEODORA. Princess of Hohenlohe-Langenburg, the Queen's half-sister.

FRITZ. The Crown Prince.

FRITZ CARL. Son of Prince Charles and nephew of the Emperor.

FRITZ LEOPOLD. Son of the above.

FRITZ HOLSTEIN. Duke of Schleswig-Holstein and father of Dona *q.v.*

FRITZ WILLIAM. Eldest son of Prince William of Prussia.

UNCLE GEORGE. First cousin of the Queen, the 2nd Duke of Cambridge.

GEORGIE. Second son of the Prince of Wales, afterwards King George V.

HELEN. Princess of Waldeck and Pyrmont, wife of the Duke of Albany.

HELENA. Princess Christian of Schleswig-Holstein, the Queen's third daughter.

HENRY. Second son of the Crown Princess.

HENRY OF THE NETHERLANDS. Brother of King William III.

IRENE. Third daughter of the Grand Duchess of Hesse.

LENCHEN. Princess Helena, *q.v.*

LEOPOLD. Duke of Albany, the Queen's youngest son.

LEOPOLD OF B. Leopold II of the Belgians.

LIKO. Prince Henry of Battenberg.

LILY OF HANOVER. Princess Frederica, daughter of the last King of Hanover.

LORNE. Eldest son of the Duke of Argyll, married Princess Louise, the Queen's fourth daughter.

LOUIS or LOUIS OF H. Grand Duke of Hesse.

ᴜɪs ᴏғ Pᴏʀᴛᴜɢᴀʟ. King Louis I.

ᴜɪsᴇ. See Lᴏʀɴᴇ above. –

ᴜɪsᴄʜᴇɴ. Duchess of Connaught. –

ᴜᴄʏ. Wife of Lord Frederick Cavendish.

Mᴀʀɪᴀɴɴᴇ or Mᴀʀɪᴇᴄʜᴇɴ. Wife of Prince Fritz Carl, mother of the Duchess of Connaught.

Mᴀʀɪᴇ ᴏғ Bᴇʟɢɪᴜᴍ. Wife of King Leopold II.

Mᴀʀɪᴇ. Duchess of Edinburgh or, according to context, Princess Henry of the Netherlands.

Mᴀʀɪᴇ Aʙʙᴀᴛ. Wife of Prince Albert, nephew of the Emperor.

Mᴀʏ. Youngest daughter of the Grand Duchess of Hesse.

Mɪɴɴʏ. Wife of Czar Alexander III.

Mᴏʀᴇᴛᴛᴀ. Princess Victoria, second daughter of the Crown Princess.

Mᴏssʏ. Princess Margaret, youngest daughter of the Crown Princess.

Lᴏʀᴅ Oᴅᴏ. Lord Odo Russell, British Ambassador in Berlin. Later Lord Ampthill.

Oʟɢᴀ ᴏғ Gʀᴇᴇᴄᴇ. Wife of King George I.

Pᴀᴘᴀ. The Prince Consort.

Pᴀᴜʟ. Grand Duke, son of Czar Alexander II.

Pᴇᴅʀᴏ. King Pedro V of Portugal.

Rᴜᴅᴏʟᴘʜ. Crown Prince of Austria. –

Sᴀᴄʜᴀ. Alexander III of Russia. –

Sᴀɴᴅʀᴏ. Prince Alexander of Battenberg. –

Sᴇʀɢᴇ. Grand Duke, son of Alexander II.

Sᴏᴘʜɪᴇ. Princess of Prussia, third daughter of the Crown Princess.

Sᴛᴇᴘʜᴀɴɪᴇ. Daughter of King Leopold II and wife of Crown Prince Rudolph.

Uɴᴄʟᴇ Cʜᴀʀʟᴇs. Prince Charles of Prussia, brother of the Emperor.

Uɴᴄʟᴇ or Uɴᴄʟᴇ E or Uɴᴄʟᴇ Eʀɴᴇsᴛ. Duke of Saxe-Coburg-Gotha, brother of the Prince Consort.

Vɪᴄᴋʏ. See Mᴏʀᴇᴛᴛᴀ.

Vɪᴄᴛᴏʀɪᴀ ᴏғ Hᴇssᴇ. Eldest daughter of the Grand Duchess of Hesse and wife of Prince Louis of Battenberg.

Wᴀʟᴅʏ. Prince Waldemar, third son of the Crown Princess.

Wᴀʟʟʏ. Walburga, Lady Paget.

Sɪʀ Wɪʟʟɪᴀᴍ. Sir William Jenner, the Queen's doctor.

Wɪʟʟɪᴇ or Wɪʟʟɪᴀᴍ. Eldest son of the Crown Princess.

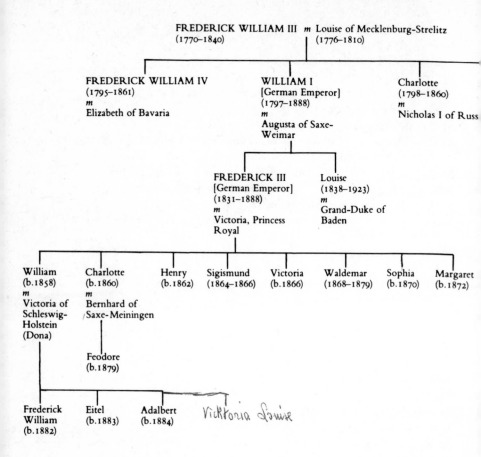

FREDERICK WILLIAM III *m* Louise of Mecklenburg-Strelitz
(1770–1840)   (1776–1810)

FREDERICK WILLIAM IV   WILLIAM I   Charlotte
(1795–1861)   [German Emperor]   (1798–1860)
m   (1797–1888)   *m*
Elizabeth of Bavaria   *m*   Nicholas I of Russ
                              Augusta of Saxe-
                              Weimar

FREDERICK III   Louise
[German Emperor]   (1838–1923)
(1831–1888)   *m*
m   Grand-Duke of
Victoria, Princess   Baden
Royal

William   Charlotte   Henry   Sigismund   Victoria   Waldemar   Sophia   Margaret
(b.1858)   (b.1860)   (b.1862)   (1864–1866)   (b.1866)   (1868–1879)   (b.1870)   (b.1872)
m   *m*
Victoria of   Bernhard of
Schleswig-   Saxe-Meiningen
Holstein
(Dona)

                 Feodore
                 (b.1879)

Frederick   Eitel   Adalbert   Vicktoria Louise
William   (b.1883)   (b.1884)
(b.1882)

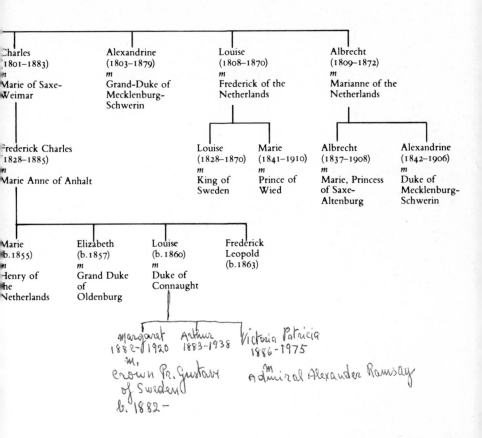

Charles
(1801–1883)
m
Marie of Saxe-
Weimar

Alexandrine
(1803–1879)
m
Grand-Duke of
Mecklenburg-
Schwerin

Louise
(1808–1870)
m
Frederick of the
Netherlands

Albrecht
(1809–1872)
m
Marianne of the
Netherlands

Frederick Charles
(1828–1885)
m
Marie Anne of Anhalt

Louise
(1828–1870)
m
King of
Sweden

Marie
(1841–1910)
m
Prince of
Wied

Albrecht
(1837–1908)
m
Marie, Princess
of Saxe-
Altenburg

Alexandrine
(1842–1906)
m
Duke of
Mecklenburg-
Schwerin

Marie
(b.1855)
m
Henry of
the
Netherlands

Elizabeth
(b.1857)
m
Grand Duke
of
Oldenburg

Louise
(b.1860)
m
Duke of
Connaught

Frederick
Leopold
(b.1863)

Margaret
1882–1920
m.
crown Pr. Gustavr
of Sweden
b. 1882–

Arthur
1883–1938

Victoria Patricia
1886–1975
m
Admiral Alexander Ramsay

THE ROYAL HOUSE OF HOHENZOLLERN

THE BATTENBERG FAMILY

As the family of Battenberg comes frequently into the letters, it may be a convenience to the reader to have a note on their origins and fortunes. The Hesse-Darmstadt family, to which they belonged, reigned over some of the territory east and west of the Rhine, above and below Frankfurt but excluding the City. After a succession of Landgraves—among them the Great Landgravine who was described by Frederick the Great on her tombstone as "femina sexi, vir ingenio"—the family assumed the title of Grand Duke in 1806, becoming Grand Dukes of Hesse and by the Rhine. In the Nineteenth Century marriage was to lift them out of this comparatively uneventful history. In 1841 the daughter of the Grand Duke Louis II married the Cesarevitch (afterwards the Emperor Alexander II). In 1862 the nephew and heir of the Grand Duke married Princess Alice, Queen Victoria's second daughter, and in 1877 became Grand Duke. He was therefore nephew of the Czar and son-in-law of Queen Victoria. His uncle, Prince Alexander, accompanied his sister to Russia, fell in love with one of her circle, Countess von Hauke, and married her in 1851. This was a morganatic marriage which allowed the wife nothing except "the morning gift" on the morning after the consummation of the marriage and which carried no rank or property to the children. The word morganatic derives from the mediaeval Latin—*matrimonium ad morganaticum*, the last word probably being derived from morgengabe, the German for morning gift. At the wedding the husband gave his left hand to the bride.

A few years after the marriage Prince Alexander and his bride were created by the Grand Duke, Prince and Princess of Battenberg—a small town in Hesse-Nassau, on the River Eder. They had a family of 4 sons and 1 daughter, and the family achieved a position among the Princes of Europe which was conspicuous and remarkable. Apart from their own good looks, capacity and charm three reasons may be suggested for their pre-eminence among the morganatic families of Central Europe.

The first was the distinction of Prince Alexander. He had had to leave the Russian Army after his marriage and joined the Austrian Army holding high command in the Franco-Austrian war of 1859. The Emperor of Austria wrote in his own hand to compliment the Grand Duke on "the heroic bravery" of Prince Alexander. He made a triumphant return to Darmstadt driving in an open carriage through cheering crowds.

The second reason was that Princess Alice, Queen Victoria's daughter, accepted the family absolutely. In fact she fostered the ambition of the eldest Battenberg prince to come to England to join the Royal Navy.

The third reason was that the Grand Duchy was lamentably short of male heirs. By the end of 1900, when Princess Alice's only surviving son was reigning, there was no other male prince of the family. Both his uncles, somewhat obscure princes, had made morganatic marriages. The Battenbergs, though not strictly members of the Hessian Royal Family, were recognised as distinguished collateral relations of the Grand Duke. They were not royal, but their good looks and easy manner made them the associates of Royalty, the companions of Kings and Princes. The eldest son married the daughter of the Grand Duke and Princess Alice: the second son, supported by his uncle the Czar, became Prince of Bulgaria, and the third son married Queen Victoria's youngest daughter.

In England the dynastic position of the Battenberg family was of no consequence because marriages with "only the morning gift" were never recognised. But in Prussia it was totally different. Royal families had to flourish in all their pristine purity and simplicity and if their members wished to marry outside royal blood then there was nothing for it except a marriage with "only the morning gift". To us in the Twentieth Century such matters may seem archaic and absurd but to the Hohenzollern family in particular—and even to the Crown Prince—they were intensely important. Those who made such marriages had to feel the full weight of royal disapproval. The German Emperor's brother, Prince Albrecht, made a morganatic marriage after the ending of an unhappy first marriage. The morganatic wife and children naturally attended his funeral and the Crown Princess writing to her mother says that she shook hands with the widow and children and adds: "I am afraid the Empress will dislike our having taken any notice of her, but it was impossible to do otherwise, it would have been very unfeeling and unkind."[1]

---

[1] *Darling Child*, page 64.

THE CORRESPONDENCE

1878

From the Queen

You will probably have seen dear Louischen[1] whom every one likes. Arthur has contrived to see her every day but two. I was a little surprised that they drove down alone together to Frogmore once—and not the least *surveillée*. However it was not often and he is so good. Still it is not what you and I consider quite right, but as it was really only two or three days I said nothing.

From the Queen

It is so frightfully hot that I hardly know how to write. Alice and the truly beautiful children came here to luncheon yesterday. Alicky is too beautiful. Victoria greatly improved in looks; Ella less handsome and engaging than she was.

I am sorry to say that contrary to all expectations, and my wish and advice, Ernest of H.[2] has sent an announcement of his father's death in injudicious terms—though he does not call himself King. However as I was named executrix I shall have to speak very firmly if I am to accept that and it would be very important to know what Fritz could do. An absolute, formal and public renunciation of his rights never could be obtained and would be worthless. A promise to me not to intrigue or interfere would be the best. Then would the private fortune not be returned? And what about Brunswick which we wish to secure to some one of the family. I am sure Ernest means to do nothing whatever; but he is very ill-advised. All the family (all the Cambridges) think so.

From the Queen

Lord Beaconsfield and Mr. Corry spent three nights here and I

---

[1] The future Duchess of Connaught, daughter of Prince Frederick Charles (Fritz Carl) of Prussia, nephew of the Emperor.
[2] Duke of Cumberland and son of the last King of Hanover.

think the former really very well. He never coughed once—walked and drove out and was in the best spirits. I am so glad you have learnt to know and appreciate him. He is unlike other people and unless you know him well you cannot entirely appreciate him.[1] He has a large mind. One other great quality which Lord Beaconsfield possesses—which Mr. Gladstone lacks entirely—and that is a great deal of chivalry and a large, great view of his Sovereign's and country's position.

From the Queen

OSBORNE, JULY 29, 1878

You will be greatly surprised to hear that Lorne and Louise are going to Canada. But for three not five years. It is of course painful to part from her for so long—and so far away—but she can come over each year and there will be an immense field for doing good and for him to distinguish himself. There being so many Scotch there will also be an additional satisfaction. In Canada the effect will be immense and it is carrying out beloved Papa's views, for he wanted our children to be useful in the Colonies. With the exception of Sir C. Dilke, Mr. Anderson and Mr. MacDonald the speeches were most loyal and gratifying. Even that half-crazy Mr. Gladstone spoke well but then he could not avoid it, and the Irish members were very friendly.

From the Queen

OSBORNE, AUGUST 21, 1878

Dear Alice and Louis with their three younger children left us yesterday morning. She was better, but she looks still very weak and delicate and is up to nothing. Louis and the children are very blooming. Alicky the handsomest child I ever saw. They are all dear good children.

From the Queen

BROXMOUTH, DUNBAR, AUGUST 24, 1878

This is a very pretty place and though an ugly house—outside—and without any pretensions, it is a very pretty, com-

---

[1] The Crown Princess saw much of him when he was in Berlin for the Congress.

fortable house inside and the Duchess[1] has made everything so comfortable for us.

What a dreadful thing to be stung so often by a wasp—I thought they never stung more than once.[2]

I wish for the future that, dear child, you would let us know some time beforehand—if you intend to send a prince for an "occasion" because of course I am more nearly related than you are to Arthur.[3] As to dear Willie I shall be delighted to see him in the dear Highlands but must ask him not to bring more than one gentleman and two servants as we can't put up more.

Devonshire is very relaxing.[4] Scarborough or Filey would be better.

From the Queen

BALMORAL CASTLE, SEPTEMBER 9, 1878

Is not this accident on the Thames the most awful wholesale catastrophe ever heard of? It is appalling.[5] Oh the water is an awful place. Sea—river and even a small pond, for the poor Spencer Ponsonby-Fanes have just had their youngest daughter of 18 drowned; poor foolish girl with a sister and a cousin were in a small boat on a little pond on their lawn; it upset—they could not swim and the poor father saw his child drown before his eyes. No one but the brother who had dived for her could swim and she was drowned, the two others being rescued with the greatest difficulty. Is it not too dreadful? The poor mother was absent for the day. What a return for her!

Won't you change the name of the ship Henry is going on? It is so offensive to the French. We never had a Waterloo. Why not call it Kaiser Wilhelm or Der Sieger?[6] By the by I must tell you to ask Fritz why he signs himself to me in his official letters "brother and cousin" only and not "son-in-law", while I sign "affectionate cousin, sister and mother-in-law". He ought to do so.

---

[1] Of Roxburghe.
[2] A wasp got up the Crown Princess's petticoat, and stung her five times.
[3] I cannot explain this passage.
[4] Prince William was at Ilfracombe for sea-bathing.
[5] *The Princess Alice*, a Thames pleasure steamer coming back from Gravesend, had sunk off Woolwich after a collision. Most of her 600 passengers were drowned.
[6] It was no doubt called *Sedan*, but after entreaties from the Crown Princess it was renamed "Prinz Adalbert".

From the Crown Princess

I quite agree with you about the name of Henry's ship. I too entreated that it might be changed so she is now called the "Prince Adalbert" which is by far the nicest, and in recollection of dear old Adalbert who was so devoted to his navy, and a kind relation to us.

From the Queen

The prospect of your becoming a grandmother and I a great-grandmother might no doubt have been advantageously delayed but I am half-pleased at it.[1] But you need never fear my telling the Empress anything concerning your children or families in the way of news. I never do that.

From the Queen

I cannot answer your dear letter properly today but this I will say viz: that I never told Alice you had complained bitterly to me—and that you had never asked me to write—for how could I? I only warned you what I had gathered and I have told you and Herr v. Liebenau (what I am thoroughly certain of) that Alice never wished to catch Willie, for I know she did not. It is a distressing misunderstanding which I trust is now cleared up and which I shall be too happy to aid in smoothing down if required. I think others (unintentionally) have talked and made messes, which is very annoying. Herr v. Liebenau thinks (as I do) Willie should not be pressed to marry too early.[2]

---

[1] The Crown Princess's daughter, Charlotte, was expecting a child.

[2] Most of the letters on this subject have been destroyed. It is known that Prince William had formed an attachment to Princess Alice's second daughter, Ella. No doubt it would have been difficult to arrange because of the dominance of the English connexion, but Queen Victoria always lamented that it did not take place. In his account of his early life, the Kaiser refers to his many visits to Darmstadt when he was a student at Bonn: "Altogether those days were happy beyond description." *My Early Life* by William II, Methuen, 1926. Major von Liebenau was later Master of the Household to the Kaiser.

From the Queen

I am writing to him (Fritz) about Ernest of Hanover. That he *is* and not Ernest of Cumberland—which his children only will be —and his name, after all, you can no more deprive him of than the Orleans and Hessians, Tuscans etc. but Duke of Cumberland he is.[1] His marriage or rather engagement to Thyra was to have (I thought) been a secret for the present. A very plain couple— though very amiable and good which after all is the real thing— they will be.

From the Queen

With respect to your wish to pay me a visit afterwards [i.e. after the Duke of Connaught's wedding] and to remain in England afterwards—I must speak very openly. This year it would be quite impossible for you to stay with me beyond a day after the wedding (that is till the 12th) happy as I always am to see you. But I cannot have you for longer this year.

I am very tired and worn by two years of great anxiety; dear Sir Thomas's death[2] has shaken me very much and I don't feel strong—the anxieties and troubles ahead in India and elsewhere are not likely to lessen my work. Already early in February the wedding takes place which will be an immense exertion and fatigue for me; I have more guests (royalties) than I have ever had excepting at Bertie's marriage where I took no part whatever, and I shall have to appear at large dinners, etc., etc. This will knock me up. But I cannot either lodge you for the first week at B. Palace as Leopold and Marie of Belgium, Prince and Princess Fritz Charles and the Prince and Princess Henry of the Netherlands will be lodged there till the end of the week. After that Arthur and Louischen are to come back straight to me and remain with me quietly and go up to Town from me just as when Affie and Marie come and it is essential there should be no one else on a visit.

I am grieved to disappoint you—but this is the trouble and this year I could not do otherwise.[3]

---

[1] Not meaning to be offensive, the Crown Princess has miscalled him by a slip.
[2] General Sir Thomas Biddulph, Keeper of the Privy Purse.
[3] The wedding was held on March 13, 1879, and in fact the Crown Princess stayed for a few weeks, staying at Buckingham Palace, and then going to Windsor from March 11 to March 15.

From the Queen

"Remember, remember, the 5th of November, gunpowder treason and plot" and Inkerman Day. I fear we shall have to have some of those before these horrible, wicked deceitful Russians are brought to reason and properly humbled.[1]

From the Queen

I know that you will be as wretched as we are about poor dear Alice's sweet children being all ill with this horrible disease! Victoria is safe—but the others very ill and poor dear Ernie got it too! And poor darling Alice so weak! God have mercy on them. And He will.

From the Queen

My heart is very sad and heavy and I hardly can think of anything but the dreadful misfortunes at Darmstadt. Thank God Louis and Ernie (who was at death's door) and the two others are recovering, but that that precious, bright, lovely little flower— sweet little May has been taken is terrible, and we were right in fearing for her. But dear Alice behaves so bravely, Mr. Sahl says "heroically". She submits, with true Christian resignation to God's Will which is the only way to take and bear sorrow. But we must feel very anxious for her afterwards.

From the Queen

Thank God he has mercifully spared (*unberufen*) precious Ernie, that only boy, and since a great alarm again on Wednesday night he seems to be recovering! But the cases have all been of the severest kind and we must be truly grateful to Him who has so mercifully watched over them! Mr. Sahl returned yesterday and gave me many most touching details. Darling Alice's courage and

---

[1] Russian troops had re-occupied territory around Turkey which they had evacuated under the Treaty of Berlin.

resignation under the almost unbearable trial she has had to undergo are quite wonderful but she looks too dreadfully ill and they all tremble for what will follow! She is so weak. And to have to conceal the truth from Ernie, Irene and Alicky (who is quite convalescent) must be fearful.

From the Queen

I quite understand your feelings and agree in them on the Emperor's return. I do hope that all will go smooth. The dear Empress shares these views I know entirely. Only do try and show her confidence and regard for she really is so unhappy, so desponding, so anxious to do her duty and was so devoted a mother to Fritz that peculiarities, which I know exist, should be overlooked and borne with, if possible. She feels very keenly I know and is very alive to affection and attention. I hope and trust the Emperor will be kind and thank Fritz for all his trouble.[1]

From the Queen

But how distressed and alarmed you will all be when you hear of our poor dear Alice being ill with diphtheria since yesterday! It is indeed dreadful! I fear she must have given up all precautions too soon and got it from Ernie or Louis—or else from the house. She has had great trouble with the house which is not well built. However *unberufen* it seems not to be violent or malignant as yet with her.

From the Queen

Alas! It is a severe attack that our poor darling Alice has got—but still the report of Sir William[2] (who I have telegraphed to) is on the whole favourable. But the anxiety is terrible, wearing and to be so far away is agonising.

I fear it was from poor Ernie she got it when she told him of

---

[1] The Emperor had been away recuperating after the attempted assassination in the summer. (See *Darling Child*, page 292.)
[2] The Queen had sent her doctor to Darmstadt—Sir William Jenner.

little May's death. The greatest sympathy is shown. People know how nobly she behaved and stood by me when darling Papa died, and how bravely and devotedly she has watched husband and children and with what Christian resignation she has borne her sad loss—and now to be struck down herself. It is quite dreadful.

Princess Alice died on December 14 as a result of diphtheria. On December 15 the Crown Princess wrote to her mother from Berlin heading the letter "Before going to bed".

"If only I could know how you are. How you have slept, how you feel, and are looking, with this anguish in your heart ... Darling Alice—is she really gone—so good and dear, charming and lovely—so necessary to her husband and her children, so widely beloved, so much admired. I can not realise it—it is too awful, too cruel, too terrible.

"We can not tell the reason for every cloud we see
But each time and season must wisely ordered be"

The letter ran on for 24 pages.

On the following morning—that is of December 16—she added that "I could not conclude last evening and take up my letter this morning". She adds a further fifteen pages.

The calamity of Princess Alice's death and the Crown Princess's anxiety about her mother explain this long letter and the Crown Princess's passionate outbursts of grief.

From the Queen

WINDSOR CASTLE, DECEMBER 16, 1878

I could not write till this evening as I have been overwhelmed with the work of receiving and sending telegrams, settling things, writing and receiving letters.

The grief is great—terrible! My precious child who stood by me and upheld me seventeen years ago on the same day taken, and by such a fearful, awful disease. I was greatly alarmed from the first for the fever was so high—no sleep—the membranes[1] increasing—the knowledge of her great, great weakness! She had darling Papa's nature, and much of his self-sacrificing character and fearless and entire devotion to duty!

From the Queen

WINDSOR CASTLE, DECEMBER 17, 1878

I saw Sir William Jenner this morning. He saw her frequently the last day—and she seemed so pleased to see him, grasped his hand, and was delighted with the letter I sent through him, "Dear handwriting" she said "I am so sorry for all the anxiety this causes dear Mama".

She did not suffer much he thinks that day—and sank from exhaustion very, very much like beloved Papa—and the same day, how wonderful yet how touching—united in their end as in their lives. She had his unselfishness and courage and, I fear, his want of vitality.

The feeling here is quite wonderful. It is as much as in '61. From the highest to the lowest all feel not only for me—but deplore her untimely—and as they said in one of the papers "holy death"—for she gave her life for her children.

Oh! That it can be my own loved child—and that dread for infection which I think very shocking should deter Fritz and others from going there. I do think it very distressing. Poor Louis feels it awfully.

From the Queen

WINDSOR CASTLE, DECEMBER 18, 1878

We had a touching short Service at half past two to which the whole family came. Beethoven's March from the Eroica was played and then the greater part of the Burial Service read and the short fine anthem by Elvey and darling Alice's favourite hymn "Thy Will be Done". In conclusion that fearfully sad "Dead March in Saul" was played.

---

[1] White patches or false membranes on the throat.

From the Crown Princess

Our being forbidden to attend the funeral has jarred greatly on our feelings and made us very unhappy, but the Emperor, instigated by the doctors, would not hear of it. Everybody who knows how great our affliction is—and what is our compassion for Louis and the children—will not attribute to us a want of respect or sympathy or an unbecoming fear of infection of which I myself am totally free—and having myself handled people with diphtheria and seen enough of it in the hospitals during the war.

The Annual Register commented: "The sorrow at this real loss was very true and general in England and in Germany, and we may be pardoned for noting the painful and disgusted feeling with which we read that the Emperor of Germany prevented the Crown Prince and Princess from attending the funeral 'for fear of infection'."

1879

From the Queen

I read over again your long and touching letter of the 15th and 16th and I think there are some points I have not yet answered. You said you wondered if dearest Alice knew she was going and if so what agony of anxiety she would be in. But I don't think she would have been in such anxiety—for she thought she would not live long and had said so to several people—and she had such faith and trust as I knew from those beautiful letters she wrote to me during the illness and after darling little May's death. Those letters are a great treasure to me.

I got an answer from the Emperor about the marriage[1] agreeing to all I wish—but both he and Fritz Carl express a little regret at its being during Lent—which I think very extraordinary for Protestants and add (though our very High Church people have the same idea) our marriage[2] is no amusement but a solemn act and generally a sad one. But then the Emperor adds, which I think still more extraordinary—that as the 10th of March is his mother's birthday which they keep as a day of mourning he hopes the bride won't arrive in England on that day! Now she will not do so but I cannot understand why a birthday of those one has lost here should be a day of mourning? I have always treated it as the reverse. And as they are so very little particular as to mourning (though the dear Empress imagines the very reverse) this seems most strange.

From the Crown Princess

NEUES PALAIS, JANUARY 14, 1879

What sad news is this! Our poor Marie, who was so happy, a widow after having enjoyed her happiness so short a time! It is too melancholy.

---

[1] Of the Duke of Connaught.
[2] The Queen means marriages in England, not the Duke of Connaught's.

Poor Henry was such a good, kind, amiable man, so respected and beloved, and was so devoted to her.[1]

Now she is left alone, a widow after six months in a foreign country. The King, who is not an enviable relation to have, a Queen younger than herself whom she does not know, and her home here, to which she will hardly care to return! It is really very hard and sad! To think that the measles should have carried him off so suddenly. I am sure you will be sorry for her—poor young thing! I suppose she is well provided for as his fortune was immense?

From the Queen

As regards Mr. Barnard's place[2] being "kept up" it certainly will be—unless you swallow up dear Papa's country as Prussia has done so many others—it will certainly be kept up—especially as Affie and Marie will be often there. I have just appointed Mr. Scott, a very good man who has been a good deal in Germany and even lately at Darmstadt. But I shall see Lord Salisbury and speak to him about Mr. Crewe and let you know. He seemed to me rather rough.

I shall burn your letters. I feel equally anxious for the future and understand what you mean; but I think L.[3] will be different now. He seems so seriously disposed. Dear Alice also talked to me a great deal about her dear children and one thing I know she felt most strongly about and that was against early marriages for her girls—or getting them married for marrying's sake. Besides a married daughter is never, as a rule, the same use to her father or mother as an unmarried one—whose only object is their home and its interests. The longer I live the more I think marriages only rarely are a real happiness. The most are convenience—not real happiness—though of course when it is, it is greatly valued but how rarely it lasts.

---

[1] Prince Henry of the Netherlands was Governor of the Grand Duchy of Luxemburg. He died at Luxemburg on January 13 "of an apoplectic seizure supervening on a form of measles. His loss is a loss not only to the province over which he individually ruled but to the whole of Holland who looked to him to revive the faded prestige of the Royal Family". *The Annual Register*, page 174, 1879.
[2] The "place" was the British Counsellor of the Legation at Coburg, which had been held for many years by Mr. C. T. Barnard and who had just retired.
[3] Louis, Princess Alice's husband.

Above: Princess Victoria of Hesse, Miss Jackson, Princess Irene of Hesse, the Grand Duchess of Hesse, Princess Alix of Hesse, the Grand Duke of Hesse, Prince Ernest Louis of Hesse, Princess Elizabeth of Hesse, Baroness Grancy, Princess Marie of Hesse, Major von Harff, Baron von d.Knesebeck, July 1878
Below: Queen Victoria with the Grand Duke of Hesse and his children (left to right) Princess Victoria, Prince Ernest Louis, Princesses Irene, Elizabeth and Alix of Hesse, February 1879.

Above: Prince Waldemar of Prussia with his sisters (left to right) Princesses Sophie, Victoria and Margaret of Prussia, June 1878
Below: Prince Henry of Prussia, January 1883.

From the Crown Princess

About poor Marie and the uncertainty for her future, Arthur will have told you as yet no will has been found, and it is much feared that she will be left with a very, very small provision made for her! Poor Henry was one of the richest princes in Europe, if not the richest.

From the Queen

I wonder who told you where I was going to as I have not talked about it at all and meant to tell you myself. I am not going in search of heat, but of good air, total change of scene and quiet; and nowhere in the North of Italy or South of France could so comfortable a house be found, I hear, as this English gentleman's home, Villa Clara at Baveno.[1]

From the Crown Princess

Our darling Waldie was delighted with his splendid spoons. He is such a dear child. Although rather more spirited than is easy to manage, he is so trustworthy and honest and has such an open, fine, manly disposition. I shall feel it dreadfully when he goes to school, as he is my very own boy. But as he has no brothers alas! to share his studies and his games, it will be necessary (I fear before he is 12) to send him to school.

From the Queen

I am after all not going to travel as the Countess of Kent, as Affie is that;[2] Dowager-Countess would not do; and so (as the Duchess of Lancaster is almost a Royal title) I shall go as Countess of Balmoral which no one can take (Osborne, Claremont and Windsor being all titles and family names) which will sound very pretty.

---

[1] The English gentleman was probably the numismatist, H. W. Henforth (1852-81).
[2] i.e. was Earl of Kent.

From the Crown Princess

MARLBOROUGH HOUSE, MARCH 19, 1879

Many many tender thanks for all your kindness the recollection of which will cheer me—when back at Berlin in a milieu which wants no common strength of mind not to be utterly depressed and become bitter. I fancy I have braved it for 21 years with patience and I hope with courage. But there is nothing to render life attractive there.[1]

From the Queen

WINDSOR CASTLE, MARCH 19, 1879

This is a letter to wish you goodbye. It will I know be a very sad day to you, as you cling so much to your own country and I fear dislike Berlin more and more! It grieves me so to think that you have so many trials and difficulties and that life is so little congenial. It must however be borne with courage and patience!

From the Crown Princess

NEUES PALAIS, MARCH 22, 1879

You will have heard from Bertie that we [the Crown Prince and Princess] both separately paid visits to Frederica of Hanover. Fritz was, I regret to say, disagreeably impressed by her tone and manner and by what she said to him. I was not. I was much captivated by her magnificent appearance and, when the very stern and haughty look she put on (which did not become her ill) melted into a sweet and gentle expression, by her agreeable way of speaking. She of course took up the standpoint that her country and family had simply been plundered and injured and treated with the greatest injustice in an uncalled-for way, and that it is our (i.e. the Emperor and the Government) bounden duty to repair all the mischief they have done and restore what has been lost! Now this is a one-sided view and must lead to illusions. That the King of Hanover chose to be our enemy was his own free will, and the Emperor left no stone unturned to implore him to join us. He would not. If he had his family would still be on the throne, now they are suffering under a reward which the fortunes of war have

---

[1] The Crown Princess had been in England for the wedding of the Duke of Connaught, which took place at Windsor on March 13.

brought upon them. Their money would have been returned them last June had it not been for that unfortunate letter of Ernest which is looked upon here as an insult, and *"une défait"*.[1] You may be certain that we shall both do what we can.

Marianne told me over and over again to thank you for all your kindness. She and her ladies are enthusiastic about England, the marriage—but alas Fritz Carl the very reverse. He cannot get over not having the Garter, not having the Windsor uniform and having been received at Queensborough in plain clothes. It is too ridiculous and nonsensical. In consequence England did not please him at all.

From the Crown Princess

BERLIN, MARCH 24, 1879

One line to say that Waldemar has the diphtheria and Miss Byng also. You can imagine, dear Mama, that I feel anxious.[2]

From the Crown Princess

BERLIN, MARCH 25, 1879

The dear patient is not in an unsatisfactory state though he suffers much, poor dear, from all the accompanying wretched discomfort and pain. His tonsil is as large as a walnut, he can hardly swallow at all or shut his mouth.

What you say about poor Lily of Hanover in your letter Fritz has read; he is no more inclined to judge her harshly. I think he does not understand people's motives at first always quite, and as you know he has his own ideas of the respect and courtesy due to himself which he is always so ready to pay to others.

I think he quite understands now, and I know he is determined to use every means in his power to try and get the money for the Queen and Princesses.[3]

I have not seen Fritz Carl again, but hear from all, that as was universally supposed, he would be rude in England, to resent the

---

[1] The Duke of Cumberland sent a letter to all the Sovereigns of Europe announcing his father's death. He did not assert his succession, but the Queen described the letter as "injudicious". (See letter of July 17, 1878 on page 23.)
[2] Prince Waldemar, the most English of the Crown Princess's sons and perfectly healthy had caught diphtheria. He died on the 27th.
[3] That is the money due from the Hanoverian revenue for Princess Frederica, her mother and sister.

double indignity of having to take his daughter to be married in England, and of not receiving the Garter, the uniform of an English regiment and the Windsor uniform. He thinks that England has no right to have customs or rules of their own and that if English Princes receive the highest Order from here, and the uniform of a regiment there ought to be reciprocity, and if there is not he considers that displeasure ought to be shown in a marked way and all other marks of courtesy, civility and attention should not be taken any notice of as that would be a want of self respect and dignity and national pride. It is no use arguing with him on the subject.

From the Queen

BRITISH EMBASSY, PARIS, MARCH 26, 1879

How terrible this new anxiety is! Are we never to have any more relief from anxiety? This is really too terrible. It makes me so anxious about you—and dear Charlotte and all the others and I am longing for a letter! I feel much for you.

The Empress wrote most kindly about you and Fritz and said, as you do, that Marianne was most grateful, but that she preferred not speaking of F.C. But I must tell you for your and Fritz's information that he said to Colonel McNeill that he hoped never to come to England again!! This beats everything for it is a total want of all breeding. The Garter is quite preposterous. The Windsor uniform had never been given your father-in-law or Prince Charles of Hesse. They told me if he went back in the yacht all would be set right, but no, that is not so. It will be impossible ever to ask him in future if he behaves in this way.

From the Crown Princess

BERLIN, MARCH 27, 1879

With trembling hand I write these few lines. Oh! how great and how bitter this agony is words cannot say! My beloved darling, my sweet Waldie, the dearest and nicest and most promising of my boys is gone. He had such a fine, straightforward, noble, honest, courageous nature, was so much more gifted than his brothers.

From the Crown Princess

Antoinette Hohenzollern is the only relation except the Fritz Carls who have been allowed to visit us. There were so kind! Fritz Carl was terribly affected and the tears rolled down his cheeks.

From the Queen

VILLA CLARA, BAVENO, MARCH 29, 1879

My poor dear darling child, my heart bleeds and aches for you to that extent I cannot describe it. I am so miserable about you. You have, thank God, dear kind Fritz near you who will share all with you and that is a blessing. Could I only do something for you to comfort you? I wish you could come here but you cannot leave Charlotte[1] and if later on you should like one of the cottages at Osborne or Abergeldie I would too gladly offer them. I would wish to do anything for you to help and soothe you at this terrible affliction.

From the Queen

VILLA CLARA, BAVENO, APRIL 6, 1879

You can describe your poor darling's character quite as well as Dickens or George Eliot and I hope you will find time to write a little memoir of the dear young life.

From the Crown Princess

WIESBADEN, APRIL 10, 1879

I was much hurt at Bismarck giving his enormous *soirée* with all the parliamentary people on the evening of our darling child's funeral. I will not say what I think of it.

From the Queen

VILLA CLARA, BAVENO, APRIL 12, 1879

The sad photographs which you sent me kindly and the precious knife which I shall ever value in remembrance of your poor

---

[1] Who was expecting her first child.

darling boy arrived safely yesterday. I will use it and take it always with me and have the date engraved on the blade.[1]

How grieved I am to hear of your sufferings through rheumatism etc. and will speak to Sir William about it. But I cannot be surprised! My wonder is how one lives at all through such terrible trials and shocks as that one and that life is not stopped at once. Mortification and sorrow from ill-usage, ingratitude, and the wickedness and cruelty of others I think does kill far more readily than the deepest sorrow sent by God.

I am very glad Leopold took the Communion with you. It was as it should be.

From the Queen

VILLA CLARA, BAVENO, APRIL 19, 1879

After three wet days running and such rain as I never saw anywhere else—torrents without ceasing—we have had three fine days—yesterday and today quite splendid. On Thursday we went in a steamer up to the very end of the lake into Switzerland where the Swiss Alps rise beautifully in their eternal snow. I recognised those I had seen from the other side in '68! We went as far as Locarno. Anything like the views and colours here I never saw. They are really quite marvellous. Still I cannot admit there is nothing to be compared to Italy.[2] I suppose you mean with the addition of the works of art?

Yesterday we had a splendid day for our visit to Monza (which was very tiring) and the view of the Alps with Mount Rosa quite clear, from the railway between Milan and halfway from here was quite marvellously beautiful in the evening light—then again came the splendid mountains of the Simplon range when the others were no longer visible. The King and Queen met us at the station and took us to the Palace.[3] The turn out was quite peculiar, and the Court enormous but all in "*borghese*" for we went with them in their carriage. It was the first time since '61 I had

---

[1] A Chinese dagger which the Prince always kept by his bedside. A rather strange souvenir, but the Crown Princess thought it might be used as a paper-knife.
[2] "My beloved Italy to which nothing is to be compared, *I* think." Crown Princess, April 14.
[3] The Palace, belonging to the Kings of Italy, close to Milan. It was built towards the end of the Eighteenth Century for the Archduke Ferdinand, Grand Duke of Tuscany.

been to anything of the kind. I felt dreadfully nervous.[1] But he is so good and simple and she is certainly lovely and fascinating. They both spoke most kindly of you and Fritz and she enquired very particularly after you. The Palace is large and thick except the Queen's rooms which are extremely prettily arranged quite in the English style. They came from Rome that morning and returned again at night. She seems to direct everything and he consults her about all.

I am getting on with my Italian and picking up more and more. Baby too especially understands all she hears which I do too.

This is really a charming house.

From the Queen

The debate last night will shock you.[2] To pretend that I would write or telegraph on the policy to be adopted is too monstrous and to think that I am not to be able to condole with losses or rejoice at successes or say a word of encouragement to my poor hard-tried servants in distant parts.

It is all owing to that worthless correspondent of the D. News—Mr. Forbes who in a review insinuated that I had held different language to that of the Government!!!

---

[1] "H.M. started from Baveno in her little everyday bonnet but changed into something more elegant before we arrived. Somewhat to the King's astonishment the Queen kissed him on both cheeks and then Queen Margaret kissed her hand, and our Queen embraced her but this is the proper ceremonial for Queen Regnants." Walburga, Lady Paget: *Embassies of Other Days.*

[2] This was the Prerogative of the Crown Resolution which was supported by a sprinkling of Radical Members of Parliament. The Resolution ran—

"That, to prevent the growing abuse by her Majesty's Ministers of the Prerogative and influence of the Crown, and consequent augmentation of the powers of the Government in enabling them, under cover of the supposed personal interposition of the Sovereign, to withdraw from the cognizance and control of this House matters relating to policy and expenditure properly within the scope of its powers and privileges, it is necessary that the modes and limits of the action of the Prerogative should be more strictly observed."

There were several amendments aimed to disentangle the Queen from direct criticism and to concentrate the attack on the Conservative Government. Lord Hartington who was then leader of the Opposition, said "I have never been more perplexed since I have been in this House" by the Resolution and amendments which they were debating. There was considerable confusion and much burrowing into the history of former times, especially perhaps by Lord Robert Montagu, a thoughtful Conservative who strongly disapproved of Disraeli and

If the Empress speaks to me about Willie's prospects what am I to say—for I know absolutely nothing? Do telegraph something to this effect "she knows nothing" or "she knows".[1]

From the Queen

WINDSOR CASTLE, MAY 17, 1879

I received your telegram. Ready and glad as I am always to help you—in every way—in marriages I feel a great delicacy—especially when there are many difficulties and Willie so very young. I would rather not be mixed up in it being Grandmother of the one and Grand Aunt of the other and not being my *own* family.[2]

---

his recent policy. Gladstone spoke against the Resolution saying that it was a subject which "we have sifted and bolted down to the bran" on former occasions. The Resolution was aimed to show that Beaconsfield had used the Crown to support measures which had not been considered by the Cabinet or the House of Commons.

It may be felt that here the Resolution succeeded. But the implications about the Queen seemed based on journalism rather than on reality. The actual points which emerged seem to have been confined to three. The first was her correspondence with Colonel Wellesley. See Volume 4 of this correspondence (*Darling Child*), page 259. The second was a letter which the Queen wrote to Lady Frere—her husband, Sir Bartle Frere, was Governor of the Cape and was as unpopular with the Opposition as Lord Milner was to become 20 years afterwards. The letter was one of sympathy over the Zulu War and of admiration for the British army in that difficult campaign.

The third point was the telegram which the Queen was said to have sent to Lord Lytton, the Viceroy of India. This was supposed to have been an encouragement to the Viceroy over his policy in Afghanistan and to have cost 1400 rupees. In fact the telegram was sent by the Viceroy to the Queen and described the opening campaign of the Afghan War and how the British troops were faring. The Queen replied to the telegram but not until her answer had been submitted to the Government.

As the Queen said, the trouble arose from an article by Mr. Archibald Forbes, the correspondent of *The Daily News*. He was born in 1838 and died in 1903. He was a remarkable man, and perhaps his most celebrated feat was after the Battle of Ulundi when he rode from Ulundi to Pietermaritzburg—280 miles in 55 hours. The character of the man is revealed in a sketch of him in *Celebrities at Home* (Mr. Archibald Forbes at Maida Vale) by E. H. Yates, 1879. "Under Fire?" he replies to a question of mine. "I cannot tell you how often I have been under fire. A correspondent cannot see anything while hanging in the rear."

[1] Prince William's possible engagement to Princess Augusta Victoria of Schleswig-Holstein. She was the granddaughter of the Queen's half-sister. The Empress was staying with the Queen at Windsor.
[2] Meaning one of her own children.

From the Crown Princess

I saw Sandro Battenberg yesterday. He is so grateful that you are going to receive him, and I am very glad of it. He is really such a very nice, charming, good, young man, so pleasing and amiable, natural, frank and simple, and full of the best intentions. Louis Battenburg is the cleverer of the two but this one is just as "*bien élevé*" and gentlemanlike and also good looking!

I wonder that England has taken his nomination so quietly! He is and must be a Russian vassal though presumably he is not a bit blind to the failings of the Russians. This creation of Bulgaria means a Bulgarisation of Turkey, consequently an indirect taking possession of Turkey by Russia. To prevent this from being complete, there seems to me but one way, which is to increase and strengthen Greece, (a country for which I have neither interest nor sympathy). Turkey will soon have ceased to exist, I fancy, after the new dominion of Bulgaria is once firmly established and I see no counterpoise to Russian influence over Constantinople etc. except English influence in Greece. Russia seems to have gained her point so very much, and the support and patronage she gives to Sandro Battenberg seems to me more like suzerainty. Does it not?[1]

I wish Sandro could marry an Englishwoman and have a few English people about him. Perhaps his visit to England may do a deal of good.

From the Crown Princess

The Emperor is very well and both he and the Empress are infinitely relieved that the Emperor of Russia has given up coming here! It would have put out my father-in-law very much if he had been obliged to receive his guests sitting or lying on the sofa, and the Empress feels how nervous a thing it would be to have the responsibility of the Emperor A's safety at a moment when his subjects are in such a state of general *bouleversement*.

---

[1] Under the Treaty of Berlin, Bulgaria, formerly part of Turkey, was made an independent state and it was handed to Russia until a Prince, suitable to all Parties, could be elected. On April 28, 1879, Prince Alexander of Battenberg was elected as Prince of Bulgaria.

From the Queen

The visit of Sandro and his brother went off extremely well—I liked both brothers so very much; so sensible and clever and so really good. I do not think[1] Sandro a bit Russian or likely to become a Russian vassal though he is personally much attached to the Emperor[2] which is right and just. He seemed so honest and earnest that one must wish him every success. I gave him the GCB which pleased him very much.

From the Queen

Your sore and wounded heart will bleed for the poor, poor Empress—who has lost her all, her only child and the only hope she had left. And in such a horrible way.[3] Good, exemplary, brave but alas! far too daring young man, and to think of his being murdered in such a way—though I am sure it was the affair but of a few seconds—is enough for ever to haunt a mother's heart. You will have seen in the papers the harrowing details but I send some more. I can't tell you the effect it had upon Baby and me when Lady Frere's telegram arrived after dinner at Balmoral. I thought it could not be true and we were quite overwhelmed by it. The sensation all over the country and in London was fearful. I think you will like to hear some details about the poor unhappy Empress. Poor Lord Sydney had to tell her. It seems that by some mistake a letter written by a gentleman to M. Pietri got mixed with the Empress's letters and she opened it, and suspected something though from its vagueness she did not realise what. She gave a scream however and the Doctor Corvisart—(who had heard from Lord Sydney what had occurred and that he was coming) came in; she asked him what the letter meant to which he replied he thought that meant nothing and that if anything very serious had taken place "Lord Sydney arrivera".

In the meantime she got up and Lord Sydney arrived and came up to her rooms with the Duc de Bassano and Doctor Corvisart (a

---

[1] Difficult to decipher.
[2] Of Russia.
[3] The death of the Prince Imperial, see Introduction page 2.

very sensible man) and told her he had come with a telegram with bad news; she threw her arms up and asked "Qu' est ce que c'est— dites moi" and he said he was afraid it was the worst news. Still she would not take it in and again and again he had to repeat the truth. She remained motionless supported by her two gentlemen but never fainted (as the papers said) at all; then threw herself on Lord Sydney and afterwards down on a low chair, and sobbed convulsively without tears. "Mon pauvre fils—seulement 23 ans". She kept repeating. She began to read the telegram and then threw it down saying she would look at it later. She was greatly relieved to think the dear remains had been found—but how! She cried a great deal afterwards when she saw Lord Sydney. She saw Lady Ely today. She could not eat or sleep. The latter I am not surprised at for we could hardly get any sleep that night nor many others and what distresses us terribly is the fact of his having been allowed first to leave Lord Chelmsford with whom he was put in charge and secondly to have been sent with so few men on a reconnaissance. One feels it might have been prevented. He was so much beloved and you know how nice and charming he was. The last time I saw him was here the day before he embarked— and he was in such spirits. He went to London that very evening to his confessor and the next morning at 6 he took the Sacrament with his mother at Chislehurst. She had such a happy letter from him a week ago having recovered his slight indisposition. Only the day before yesterday she had a letter with very good accounts of him and what care they would take of him!! She kept telling the ladies again and said so continually after her dear child left her "Je n'ai plus rien, rien au monde" and then again "Je suis forte, je peut vivre cents ans—et a quoi bon". Oh! the more one thinks of it, the more one realises it, the more fearful it seems.

(22nd)

She had a little sleep last night—but still can take no food. I hope to go and see her tomorrow or Tuesday. The dear Remains may be expected in a month and there will be an immense demonstration. I will let you know all details as I know the interest you take in the poor, dear, unhappy Empress. I think it a great misfortune for I always hoped and thought he would have come back some day as Emperor, and be a very good one with all his love for England.

From the Queen

I left Windsor with Beatrice and Leopold, J. Ely and Sir H. Ponsonby at 5 this afternoon and reached Chislehurst a little past 6, where I was received at the door by Lord Sydney who met me at the station, the Duchesse de Mouchy, Prince Joachim Murat, the Duc de Bassano and several other French gentlemen. M. de Castelbajac, Marquis de Bassano, Duc de Mouchy and Madame Clary all in tears and greatly distressed. The Duchesse de Mouchy, the Duc de Bassano, Prince Joachim took me upstairs to the door of the little antechamber at the dear Empress's room where she stood pale and bowed down with grief—I clasped her in my arms and she sobbed, but quietly, and she then took me into her little boudoir which was very dark all the blinds being down where I had been with her after the Emperor's death and sat an hour with her. She is so uncomplaining, so gentle so resigned not accusing anyone but utterly broken-hearted in her terrible grief. "Pauvre petit, seulement 23 ans" that he has never caused her a moment's sorrow "il était si droit, si loyal", but that she felt it was to be so "Sa destinée l'a entraîné" and most likely it was that he should be spared from great trials in other ways. Yet he was so determined to go that she believes he would have enlisted as a private and have gone all the same if the difficulties which existed at the first about his going had not been got over. That he said his comrades were going and it was too dreadful to have shared their work in peace and not to be able to do so in the dangers of war. He was determined to do something. He was wonderfully courageous— to a fault and that alarmed his poor mother and me too when he went. But then he never was to have been allowed to go and expose himself in this most unnecessary way. She kept saying "c'est affreux, je n'ai rien, rien au monde, je suis si seul". Too heart-rending to hear. She dreads the return of the dear Remains to which every honour will be paid. She keeps asking if he suffered and to which in all sincerity we may say he could not — nor could he with so many wounds. But how he (who was a wonderful horseman and extraordinarily active) could not re-mount or how he was left remains a very painful circumstance! She is very anxious for any relic she can get back. His poor, faithful valet the only person who went with him (which is to be regretted) was at Natal and would have been in utter despair.[1]

---

[1] He went out with the Prince from England.

The poor Empress expects still letters from her dear child will arrive. If his Battery had not gone I believe he would not have thought of it, though he was bent on any opportunity of seeing service. The Empress said everyone must bear their cross and some much more severely than others to which I replied hers was assuredly much heavier than that of others, God knows! She had just rearranged his rooms—and hoped it would please him. Angeli's picture of him, which is very like, is a great comfort to her and hangs in her little room where in a group she has all her souvenirs. She cried very much at times—but could speak of all— only at moments she could not go on. When I begged her not any longer to call me Madame and Majeste but Soeur she burst out crying. She cannot eat. A sort of nervous contraction in her throat prevents her swallowing. She can only take fluids—neat milk and rum but she has some sleep. How willingly I would do anything for her but of what avail is it? Nothing can bring back in this world her precious child.

It is now believed I hear that very likely two "friendly Zulus" led them purposely into this field advising them to unsaddle and rest! They have not been seen again. Uncle George is in great distress about it as he gave such positive directions about it when he went out. The dear Empress feels her only support is in God and in the consciousness that all was for the best! It is a great blessing to see her so resigned and ready to bend to God's Will.

From the Queen

I send you here an account of that heart-rending visit which you can show Fritz but no one else, because it would be a breach of confidence to repeat all she said to me—but you can and should say how resigned she is and how nobly and beautifully she be- haves. When your grief overwhelms you—and I well believe and understand it must do at times—think of this poor bereaved, childless, widowed, exiled Empress, mother, bowed down with grief—but yet able and ready to say "Thy Will Be Done".

From the Queen

WINDSOR CASTLE, JUNE 28, 1879

The questions you ask are in everyone's mouth and there is a terrible feeling in which we all share at the thought that this precious young life should have been sacrificed without being defended and fought for by British officers. I own it is quite dreadful to me! As regards the war itself there is no doubt the right thing has not been done—which is distracting. No head at the head and the want of organisation etc.

I must say we think the newspaper articles you sent me especially one saying he wanted to get away from his Jesuitical mother—quite dreadful! He loved her so much and she is anything but Jesuitical. She hardly ever sees a priest and the one at Chislehurst, Father Goddard (an Englishman) is very inoffensive.

From the Crown Princess

NEUES PALAIS, JUNE 30, 1879

What you say about the Zulu war is most interesting to me. Is not a little reform indicated in certain military arrangements? Is the outpost duty sufficiently studied? English soldiers have a better chance of being more efficient and more masters of their work than any others because they serve so much longer. Would it not seem as if the system of drill were a little superannuated in some of its details and, as if many a practical hint for what is most modern and has proved most practical, might be taken from the German "*reglement*" which of course would not do to copy because it is based on the conscription and three year service etc. It is those perpetual "petty manoeuvres in peace time" which seem to me so good. Do you not think dear Papa would have said so? I wonder what General Walker or Sir Howard Elphinstone say on the subject? We have some Englishmen serving in the German army who are thought so highly of, one who is Molkte's right hand is General Wright. I am sorry they do not go back and make themselves and their knowledge and experience useful to their country and to our British Army!

I fancy the English cavalry ride faster and better than they do here and that the English artillery look superior as to men, horses, harness etc. Whether as to guns I do not know. But the German infantry seem to me quicker, better drilled, more easily and rapidly moved about here and there. I should fancy the English rifle practice must beat the German as the Englishmen are such excellent shots. I am afraid I am boring you with all this, but one is perpetually thinking of what the reason is and of what is at fault when anything goes wrong, and how it could be remedied and improved.

Today we have had the painful task of looking over all beloved Waldie's wardrobe. What pain it was to look into his little suits of clothes for the last time. It is very foolish to be so much upset by such exterior things and to be attached to such objects but so it is, and as Queen Constance says in King John "Grief stuffs out his clothes and puts on his pretty ways . . . Shall I never see my gentle Arthur more . . .".[1] This is not all in one passage I know. I remember when I was a child how that used to make me cry!

I have the Daily Telegraph always so I read all the news.

From the Crown Princess

NEUES PALAIS, JULY 5, 1879

Bonapartism as a principle is not worth much, each Empire has brought some bad and some great good to France. The person of the Prince Imperial will be a greater loss to his country than the disappearance of the Party could be—amongst which there are so many unscrupulous and worthless men.

I also think it is not fair to put the whole blame of the Franco-German war on the Emperor. Fritz and my mother-in-law maintain that the Empress had said "c'est ma guerre"—when it broke out.

Bismarck (who in my eyes is the most mischievous and dangerous person alive) did however not fan the flame—until of course there was no option left—and then of course he tried to animate his nation against the enemy. But we were not ready, if you remember and will look at my letters at that time; so little so—that we expected the French to have crossed the frontiers and won several battles before we could have appeared with all our forces on the Rhine. This was Fritz's firm opinion and it was quite true.

I prefer saying nothing about German affairs and our Government now. I think the policy so disgraceful and think the Germans—I do not know what for submitting to it all, and being so blind and so short-sighted as not to see the ruin and mischief which is being worked. I never remember things in so bad a state

[1] King John, Act III, scene iv. A version from memory.

as they are now. I never saw such reckless, absurd, bad management and such bad principles.[1]

From the Queen

We went to the Agricultural Show which would have been very fine on account of its arrangements and immense extent, but which was to a great extent spoilt by the awful state of mud— which was so deep even in the ring that the poor beasts and horses (such splendid ones) slid about as if they walked on paper, and could not remain standing or they would have sunk so deeply in that they could not have dragged their legs out again. We had to drive on boards and a brick bottom to get in at all.

From the Crown Princess

NEUES PALAIS, JULY 10, 1879

I send you a little line I received from Willie, which is the latest we have heard about his affairs. Bismarck and Schleinitz[2] are drawing up memoirs for the Emperor before seeing which he will not give us a decided answer. Willie is quite wild about Victoria!

She is a most charming girl. Her figure is much prettier than her face, but her voice and walk and manner have something very sympathetic and agreeable and graceful which Calma is not though her head is decidedly the prettier of the two. Willie does not admire her.

From the Queen

WINDSOR CASTLE, JULY 16, 1879

I cannot write as I wished and intended but I feel like a poor hunted hare. At Osborne where we go D.V. on Saturday I trust to collect my confused ideas. All I have gone through, the terrible harrowing scenes I have witnessed—all have shaken me dreadfully.

---

[1] Bismarck's opportunism which encouraged him to swing away from the Liberals after their defeat in 1878, and to support a motley group of Conservatives and Catholics.
[2] Alexander Schleinitz, Prussian Foreign Minister.

Above: The Hereditary
Prince and Princess of Saxe-
Meiningen, March 1879
Below: Prince William of
Prussia and Princess Victoria
of Schleswig-Holstein, June
1880.

Prss. Charlotte of Prussia

Willie and Dona

Above: (left to right) Princesses Alexandra, Victoria Melita and Marie and Prince Alfred of Edinburgh at a picnic, August 1881
Below: (left to right) The Grand Duke of Hesse, Princess Beatrice, Queen Victoria, Princess Alix and Prince Ernest Louis of Hesse, the Duchess of Connaught with her daughter, Princess Margaret, and the dogs, Spot, Gay Girl and Wat. Balmoral, October 21, 1882.

From the Queen

I feel much for you and understand the longing for sympathy in one's children and friends. It is terribly trying. But I think Willie does not mean to be unfeeling and, that as time goes on—especially when he marries—perhaps he may become better in that respect if the wife is kind and amiable. Never fear to write to me all your troubles for I understand them and feel warmly, truly for you. I do feel dreadfully tired with what I have to do—and depressed by it and by the impossibility of doing anything I should like—drawing, reading—playing. We have had so many visitors too! Constant interruptions.

From the Queen

I received your dear letter of the 20th yesterday and am greatly grieved at the "row" there has been.[1] It is to me inconceivable and incomprehensible—especially the part about the mourning which is really not kind. But no one can force you not to wear mourning in your own house or when there are no functions—and then you can wear white or grey, and that I would insist on doing! Countess Blücher always wore her very deep mourning and no one ever objected to it.

But I do advise not to speak about it to others, complaining except to me—for as you have got permission, the least said the soonest mended. Unfortunately such things leave a very painful impression behind which can't be got over and I am truly grieved at it for your and Fritz's sake.

From the Queen

I write a hurried line just an hour before starting for Balmoral. I trust I may get some rest which I am greatly in need of there. But anxiety, worry and work have pressed hard on me. The arrival of all the officers (I shall see the Generals at Balmoral) has been

---

[1] This letter has not survived; the row no doubt concerned the reluctance of the Crown Prince and Princess to take a part in the social life of Berlin after Prince Waldemar's death.

almost too much. And the knowledge that Carey is what I felt sure he was—a miserable creature who fled for his life and who now saves himself by lies which is coming out clearly by his now showing sorrow. A disgrace which fills me with grief unspeakable as it does the Army![1] I gave the Victoria Cross on Sunday to Lord William Beresford who is quite a hero.[2] Better don't speak to Lenchen about Captain Carey as she from the first!!! took his part! But you and Fritz shall know what I know.

From the Queen

We have Lord Chelmsford here and most interesting it is to hear him. He is a singularly pleasing, intelligent person who has been very unjustly attacked. He was so generous to others that he preferred suffering himself to blaming them. He is very thin and looks very worn—but is in good spirits and very grateful for my confidence and he it is, who has crushed Cetewayo (pronounced Ketchwayo) by the victory of Ulundi and he would have carried it out and finished it as surely as Sir G. Wolseley who had the bad taste to be very offensive to Lord Chelmsford when he came out. He came here on the 2nd and I asked him to stay on to see Arthur who with Louischen arrives today. I go to meet them at Ballater and they will be received here by all our people. A somewhat tasteless arch—with an enormous crown—which I am rather unhappy about has been designed by poor Beaton[3] and we have English, Scotch and Prussian flags.

From the Crown Princess

SEPTEMBER 11, 1879

You so kindly say—to you so long an absence from all your

---

[1] Captain Carey's case has been long discussed. Perhaps he hardly deserved what the Queen says. A good account of him will be found in *The Washing of the Spears* by Donald Morris (1966).
[2] Lord William Beresford (1847-1900). He was, perhaps, at times inclined to confuse the fighting against the Zulus with a boar-hunt, but he was a man of enormous courage and resource. At the battle of Ulundi, just after the Prince was killed, he rescued a huge, wounded sergeant, by putting him on the back of his horse. He told the Queen that he would not accept the V.C. unless it was also given to a non-commissioned officer who had kept the Zulus at bay while he was rescuing the sergeant.
[3] Clerk of the Works at Balmoral.

associations would be very painful. No doubt leaving Charlotte and her little menage, my two little graves, a few, very few, very kind friends and a few institutions in which I take an interest are painful, but for the rest there are no associations for me at Berlin which I could regret. The social and political atmosphere is terrible—vitiated and painful. The life has no charms, only great fatigues and anxieties. Liberty, independence exist not and we have simply to obey, and have every sort of galling interference in our own home. The spirit of espionage, malevolence, and jealousy and malice is rampant and there are many wicked people whose harmful influence cripple and hinder one at every step one takes. Home life, as in dear England, is not known. It might be possible to have it if one could be independent.

Of course all this need not be, but habit, tradition and the current at present in power are so strong that one is powerless to fight against it. All this has worn away gradually a deal of my courage and a deal of my strength, and I feel it a blessed release to escape a little. Our poor home I cannot think of without an agony. In every room I seem to see my darling boy in life, in illness and in death.[1]

From the Queen

BALMORAL, SEPTEMBER 12, 1879

We have had since the 9th the visit of Sir E. Wood who commanded the flying column in Zululand and has rendered invaluable services there and gone through dangers and hardships of all kinds; and Colonel Buller—a wonderful man from the brave and gallant things he did, and the way in which he saved life and did special services. He commanded a body of Irregular Horse and seems to have had a charmed life. Both are real heroes and so modest. The former received the KCG and the latter the Victoria Cross both from me here, and will be made my A.D.C. They think and hope the work is done.

From the Queen

BALMORAL, SEPTEMBER 17, 1879

I can give you no further details respecting Kabul—but my troops have met with no resistance as yet. The force is large the Generals good and the neighbouring tribes friendly. You say you

---

[1] The Princess was on her way to Italy where she spent nearly a year.

are sorry this Afghan war was necessary. Of course everyone is—at any war but if we had not asserted our position when the Russians had asserted theirs we should have given up the position to them. I regret we sent away the troops so soon and did not take more as Lord Napier wished. You I know take much of your Indian knowledge from Mr. Grant Duff—a most violent man and I can't resist sending you this extract from his speech as a specimen of good taste and patriotism at the present moment![1] Certainly the Liberal (most illiberal in every way and devoted to Russia) press and opposition have shown an absence of all patriotism most painful to witness—and often paralysing the Government. Sir E. Wood, one of our most distinguished [soldiers] if not the most of the present day, and in Zululand only 41, is old Lord Hatherley's nephew, belongs to a very Radical family and he told me that he was shocked and grieved beyond measure at the want of patriotism of the so-called (for they are not) Liberal Party.

Those beautiful lines you quote I know so well and love so much. The verse

> And he who first met the Highlands' swelling blue
> Will love each peak which shows a kindred hue,
> Hail in each crag a friend's familiar face,
> And clasp the mountain in his mind's embrace.[2]

There is a lovely hymn which darling Alice loved so much and which we had sung on the 18th of December at our Memorial Service.

> "My God, my Father, while I stray,
> Far from my home, on life's rough way,
> O teach me from my heart to say,
> Thy Will be done.
>
> If Thou has called me to resign
> What most I prize, it ne'er was mine;
> I only yield Thee what is Thine;
> Thy Will be done".[3]

---

[1] The extract has not survived. But it was almost certainly the speech to his constituents at Elgin on September 11 when speaking of Lord Salisbury he said, "The blood that has been shed has been as really shed by him as if he had slain with his own hand the unhappy men who had been massacred."
[2] Byron: "The Island", ii, xii.
[3] The Queen was evidently quoting from memory.

From the Crown Princess

The extract you send me of Mr. Grant Duff's speech is very strong language, but it is evidently picked out of his speech by opponents who wish to do him harm. I have not read his speeches. I believe he is a violent man but certainly not to speak to. On the contrary, most laborious and fair and a very learned and scientific man who studies everything he lays hold of with profoundness and energy. Of course his judgement is liable to errors as everybody's is. I believe I have heard that he and Lord Salisbury hate each other; of course I never had a chance of verifying this but the very attack contained in the paragraph you sent me most likely arises from this personal enmity. I have not an idea of what Mr. Grant Duff thinks of the present state of things. He is so interesting and cultivated a man and like many Scotchmen, combines much shrewdness with the learning of a German professor. Education and botany and geography, literature Spanish and Italian are the subjects I can really enjoy hearing him talk about.

You say you wish I had brought my little girls. If you knew what a fight we had with the Emperor and Empress to let me have them at Pegli for the winter. The Emperor said it was not good for the education of Prussian Princesses to leave Berlin etc., etc. I could not help laughing though I felt more hurt and galled than I can say. I think being the mama of four daughters I might know more about what is necessary for girls than the dear Emperor who understands nothing about education. Certainly I have been spared nothing that was painful or hurtful or wounding by my parents-in-law lately but I had rather not return to the subject and I bear them no malice or grudge.

From the Crown Princess

We left dear, beautiful, enchanting Venice on the 10th and went to Monza on a private visit to the King and Queen. They were most kind to us, and both desire me to send many messages to you. They were so pleased to see you in the spring. Also the Duchess of Genoa wishes to be respectfully remembered to you. We stayed the night at Monza. The Duke of Aosta was there too with his three little boys so with the little sons of the King's there were four little boys playing and romping about. What a pang it gave me to see them in their sailor's dresses.

From the Queen

I am afraid I am as bad a sightseer as Willie, not from want of interest but that it fatigues me most dreadfully and finally bores me too. One or two fine things at a time is all I like or am able for.

From the Queen

Since I wrote I have seen the young friend of the dear Prince Imperial—Lieut. Bigge of the Artillery who distinguished himself at Kamhala and he is staying on with her (the Empress). He is a charming person—of the very highest character, clever, amiable and agreeable as well as good looking.

From the Crown Princess

Willie left for Berlin two days ago. His delight was great. Luckily for him he thinks nothing so nice as Potsdam and Berlin. He sees nothing to admire or to interest him in other countries and this I regret a little as it is always well not to be narrow minded, and really to admire all over the world what is really worth observing.

From the Crown Princess

There are some very fine villas. The one of the Marchese Pallavicini here and the one of the Duchess of Galliera at Voltri (close by) and the one of the Marchesa Spinola. They would be quite charming in March, April and May too—too hot later, and before rather too cold as there are no means of warming them.

I have taken off my crepe and I cannot describe to you how painful it is to me. I hate myself for taking it off, and yet I feel I ought to begin. It is only an outward thing but how one clings to it when one wears it for such a reason. Of course I wear all black and shall do so for some months longer. I tell you this little detail as you are always so kind about these things and have the same feeling as I have about the mourning one wears for those one loves best! It all seems a sacred thing to me.

From the Queen

All you say about Charlotte I quite enter into. Is it not the one thing I have always been so anxious and distressed about? It is what has done dear Bertie so much harm—and is a most unfortunate tendency in the upper classes! That visiting is (at least in England) the worst thing I know and such a bore. The gentlemen go out shooting and the ladies spend the whole day idling and gossiping together. Alix never hardly goes now—she hates it so. And Marie dislikes it very much indeed.

Willie's want of interest or taste—and mere love of Potsdam is quite tiresome and provoking—but I think young people have such an *esprit de contradiction* that it very likely will get better if no notice is taken of that.

From the Queen

As regards the dear Empress E. I can give you one instance of total misapprehension and of how her name was made use of. It was repeatedly said she belonged to the clerical and ultramontane party which I always denied as I seldom saw anyone less priest-ridden than she was and is. Well this was utterly untrue and she herself said to the English person whom I saw that she could not understand how that could have been said. She never goes to Mass but on Sunday (excepting on very exceptional occasions). The English R. Catholics have been hardly civil to her!! So much for that.

From the Crown Princess

I always maintained that the Empress Eugénie was not a fanatical ultramontane because I remember that when her confessor asked her "when the Emperor was going to the Crimea" she refused to answer and said she would not be asked such questions. Do you not recollect Lord Clarendon told it me when we were at

Paris 1855? Of course I am laughed at in Germany when I say so and even Fritz will not believe me.

From the Crown Princess

Alas dear Fritz is gone! He went off I may say like a shot at 12 hours notice. The Emperor wished him to return now and kindly said in his letter that as Fritz was still in mourning he would not expect him to be present at the carnival. He means that he may return to us after the 18th of January which is a delightful prospect and more than we had ventured to hope for. Of course I am very sad and disappointed at our not being together at Christmas which we had of course taken for granted.

From the Crown Princess

I deeply regret that some enthusiastic artists and professors and architects in Oxford make such a to do about the restoration of St. Mark's at Venice. It seemed to me most unnecessary and rather absurd and has given great offence in Italy. There are so many competent people who would do anything to protect all their grand works of art from destruction that private letters to anyone like Minghetti, Morelli and Boni would have been quite sufficient. Hints might have been given, questions asked, fears and hopes expressed and then enlightened, cultivated and intelligent men who would have been only too happy to give this subject all their attention and in their turn given information on the real state of the matter; whereas the publicity of the meeting, and discussion at Oxford could hardly be otherwise than offensive to the Italians and seem to me a slight want of tact which is a thing to be avoided in international, as in personal, intercourse if you wish to remain on a good footing. I am sure dear Papa would have seen this.[1]

---

[1] Substantial demolition of part of the Doge's Palace had been completed under Signor Boni, followed by "restoration". St. Mark's was threatened with the same treatment and the agitation at Oxford sprang largely from Ruskin's teaching. At this time he wrote: "At this very hour the Committee of Venetian builders are meeting to plot the total destruction, and re-erection according to their own notions, and for their own emolument, of the entire west front of St. Mark's—that which Barbarossa knelt under, and before which Dandolo took his vow."

We are not faultless either in England with our national monuments. Poor Temple Bar and Northumberland House are a witness to this, and part of Westminster Abbey I thought not half dusted and cleaned. The pictures at Hampton Court are not cared for as they should be. Dozens are misnamed—the good and the bad are muddled together many in dark rooms where one cannot see them properly and the best would be so much better seen, enjoyed, known and cared for if they were in the National Gallery (as your property) where I know they would ever remain! Instead of comparatively hidden as they now are and in areas which are never warmed in the winter time. To begin with the Mantegnas.

How I wish dear Mama you would order an inquiry on the subject to have Sir Frederick Leighton and Mr. Burton and Mr. Scharf consulted. I am sure that it would be a great boon to Art.

Forgive my returning again to this subject which I already was bold enough to mention the spring before last and this February when I had the happiness of being with you! You have one of the best picture connoisseurs and art historians in the house in the person of Mr. Bell.

The Hampton Court Gallery wants fresh varnish and fresh frames for some pictures, then a great weeding out of the very valuable and beautiful pictures from the trash and the right names and dates put on the pictures because there are some awful blunders in the names and it only misleads the public, besides being a disgrace in our day where learning and science have done so much for gaining an accurate knowledge of art and artists of bygone days.

Our Christmas presents, dearest Mama, consist of the book of our darling whom we miss so bitterly this Christmas. Then a water-colour done by a celebrated German artist whom I know well and who happened to be staying here when we arrived. I asked this particular view for you as it is a favourite spot of ours and the civil people of Pegli have called it Victoria Rock—"Scoglia Vittoria" after your eldest daughter. I hope you will like it.

From the Crown Princess

PEGLI, DECEMBER 22, 1879

Today we lunched at the Duchess of Galliera's and I saw the poor Duke and Duchess Montpensier. I was pleased to see them again poor things! The poor Duchess is looking so thin and worn and aged and she has a look of patient suffering about her that goes to one's heart. He has adopted the Banting system and has grown quite slim, has a white beard and white hair which changes him very much. Their son Antoine was with them, he is a slender delicate boy, and his face reminds me much of dear Queen Marie-Amelie. The Duchess of Galliera is a most agreeable and clever old lady with a charming home.[1]

---

[1] Both she and her husband were extremely wealthy. He gave £800,000 towards the enlargement of the harbour at Genoa. The Duchess built two hospitals outside Paris and one outside Genoa. Their son was "inclined to communistic ideas" and would only accept a part of his parents' fortune. She left a large legacy to the Crown Princess. See *The Letters of Harriet, Countess Granville*, Longman, 1894.

1880

From the Crown Princess

PEGALI, JANUARY 1, 1880

The Montpensiers were here yesterday, and much upset by a telegram they had just received from Spain, by which they concluded that the King and Queen's life had been attempted in some sort of way, but they only know of their escape from danger and nothing else.[1] Really Sovereigns nowadays will have to insure their lives in some new office to be founded for the purpose, and seem to be as safe as an Irish landlord.

From the Queen

OSBORNE, JANUARY 2, 1880

This awful accident on the Tay Bridge—so fearful in every way—(and I fear 100 lives lost)—gave us all a terrible shock as only six months ago we travelled over it! What a mercy we got over safe. I fear it was not securely built but "cheaply" which is monstrous.[2]

From the Crown Princess

PEGLI, JANUARY 13, 1880

I hear that Willie's knee is nearly all right again. As for his affairs,[3] they are very difficult to manage, the Emperor is much

---

[1] The King of Spain, when driving in the streets of Madrid on December 30, was fired at by Otero Gonzales, a waiter of weak intellect. The Duchess of Montpensier was aunt to the King of Spain.
[2] On the night of December 28, 1879, a hurricane destroyed 400 yards of the Tay Bridge as the Edinburgh to Dundee express was crossing. The train and part of the Bridge were blown into the water. The Court of Enquiry in April held that the Bridge "was badly designed, badly constructed and badly maintained". It was built with wrought-iron, lattice girders throughout.
[3] His desire to marry Princess Victoria of Schleswig-Holstein.

prejudiced, and Prince Bismarck (whom one cannot trust) is always away. I trust Fritz's presence will do good. It is much to be desired that some sort of a conclusion and decision should be come to.

From the Crown Princess

PEGLI, JANUARY 18, 1880

I cannot tell you how deeply I feel dear Fritz Holstein's death. For so many years he has been such a kind, true friend. We agreed so completely on so many serious subjects and I had a feeling of admiration and veneration for his virtues, his noble and excellent character, the patience and dignity with which he bore all his misfortunes. They were of no common kind, and the position into which the cruel and unjust persecutions of his enemies had driven him was one most galling to a man so honest, so conscientious and so patriotic.[1] How many battles I have fought for him, and how indignant I have always felt when his name and fair fame were so shamefully attacked for the sake of political convenience.

That he should have left this world—before his dear child's fate is decided is doubly sad. It pre-occupied him very much. If we ever do have the happiness of possessing his dear daughter in our family, there is nothing I would not do to be a comfort and a help to her. I know how good she is, how much her father's favourite, what pains he had taken with her education. I suppose now all transactions about Willie's affairs will have to be carried on with Christian.

From the Crown Princess

PEGLI, JANUARY 20, 1880

Although in great misery, as I have just had two wisdom teeth drawn without chloroform—I will not delay thanking you for your very dear and kind letter.

The indignities that were heaped on poor Fritz's[2] head were

---

[1] Much of Germany and Austria favoured his claim as reigning Duke of Schleswig-Holstein. Prussia and Bismarck were determined to thwart this and, after the war between Prussia and Austria of 1866, they were successful.
[2] Schleswig-Holstein.

really so cruel, but of course the Emperor was simply led and dictated to by "the Great Man" and his entourage in all that.

From the Crown Princess

PEGLI, JANUARY 26, 1880

My old wedding day yesterday I spent without Fritz as he was kept at Berlin by Prince Bismarck's return which had been delayed; this important personage is quite above studying anybody's convenience except his own, and we all have to dance attendance whenever it pleases him. This time however Fritz is most anxious to see him about Willie's prospects, and it is better that Fritz should speak his mind, not send a letter or another person to Prince Bismarck.

From the Crown Princess

PEGLI, JANUARY 29, 1880

Yes indeed, may dearest Fritz and the dear children be spared to me, for their affection and my care for them are my only happiness in this difficult and trying position in which I am placed. Life often appears very hard to me at Berlin "et je me sens bien las".

Everything seems to go so wrong and all the bad people uppermost and the good ones so powerless and hidden away. To be friends with the present regime is impossible, and yet to be in opposition is a thing as impossible. I always feel like a fly struggling in a very tangled web, and feelings of weariness and depression, often of disgust and hopelessness take possession of me. And yet I know how necessary it is always to encourage and support Fritz whose naturally good and sweet temper has been much ruffled by cares and difficulties and disappointments of all kinds, and needs smoothing and humouring at times, etc.

He has left Berlin and will be here on Saturday morning. He has telegraphed me that the Emperor and Bismarck no longer oppose Willie's wishes, and the Emperor is willing to give his consent. But this is all I know at present.

From the Crown Princess

Willie will most likely go to Gotha on the 13th to see Victoria, as Ada[1] has a house there! Uncle Ernest is coming abroad then, I believe. He has a house at Nice as you know! (of some of the inmates, the less said the better). He will pass by here and see us I hear.

From the Crown Princess

What you say about Willie's prospects is quite true. Of course so much has been done by Bismarck (persistently and systematically) to ruin poor Fritz Holstein's character in the eyes of Germany that a great feeling of animosity has been raised against him and this no doubt will be remembered when the news of his daughter's engagement to Willie is announced, but this will wear off I am sure when Victoria becomes known—for she is so sweet and sensible a girl that she must win all hearts and we shall be there to protect her and I hope will be able to do so.

A brilliant *"parti"* in the eyes of the world it certainly is not, and that will wound the inordinate parvenu pride and vanity of the Berlin people who since 1871 think themselves the only great people in the world; it is often very grotesque and funny, but it can also be very insulting to the feelings of foreigners. On the other hand they dislike everything foreign so much, that I fancy they will be better pleased with a Princess, bred and born and educated in Germany—and more spite, ill-will, backbiting and criticism of the unkindest sort, she never can have to endure than I have gone through for 22 years. Besides all the other Queens and Princesses of the Prussian family have with three exceptions (Queen Elise, Princess Albrecht of the Netherlands and myself) all been from the small reigning German families i.e. Brunswick (three times), Darmstadt, Weimar, Strelitz, and Altenburg. The Great Elector Frederick William married a princess of Schleswig-Holstein-Beck. Queen Louise lived in the fourth storey of a hotel at Frankfurt when Frederick William III made her acquaintance, and was so poor that she had to borrow a gown to be presented in. There

---

[1] The Duchess of Schleswig-Holstein, mother of Victoria.

was an old family law in Prussia that forbid marriages with princesses of reigning houses of other foreign countries for fear of political intrigues and political obligations. Queen Louise was the only Queen to whom they were kind. Poor Aunt Elise was never forgiven for having been a Catholic and having Austrian sympathies and my mama-in-law has reaped much ingratitude. In Prussia they are very loyal to their King and Emperor and the Princes of the family, but the wives are not included and the kind, warm sympathetic loyalty met with in England does not exist abroad, i.e. certainly not at Berlin.

From the Queen

OSBORNE, FEBRUARY 18, 1880

What has not happened since I last wrote! That frightful accident[1] to poor dear Louise who is going on quite well—thank God. And then the awful monstrous new attempt on the poor Emperor of Russia's life.[2] In his own house! It is too, too awful. What a merciful escape—and poor dear Marie, what a state she must be in about both parents. Poor Affie, it is terrible for him. They ought all to go away at once and he abdicate.

To return to dear Louise, it seems the horses pulled—and turned the corner too sharply—the sledge went over a heap of snow and upset and the horses ran away and dragged the sledge (a covered one) 400 yards! Poor dear Louise fell on her head and got a severe blow, cut her ear and strained the muscles and sinews of her neck which gave her much pain. The reports however have continued favourable and steadily improving. Lorne was also hurt but slightly and Eva Langham much bruised.

I did not mean that the rank of Victoria of H. was any objection for I do think that marriages with smaller Houses often makes it easier. I meant that on account of the poor family being *mal vue*, as they were in a painful and difficult position, that it would not be liked. You know people often dislike those they have ill-used.

But I perceive in my stupidity I have not wished you joy of Willie's engagement which took place on the 13th. Uncle and

---

[1] Princess Louise was sleighing near Ottawa.
[2] About 7 in the evening on February 5 as the Czar, with the Duchess of Edinburgh, was going in to dinner there was an explosion below the dining-room. Two butlers, eight footmen and ten soldiers were said to have been killed.

Aunt A.[1] telegraphed it "Happy event just taken place in our presence". I am sure I wish them all happiness.

From the Crown Princess

Willie has written most touching letters (in his own funny style) about his great happiness. He engaged himself to dear Victoria on the 14th, and had to leave again on the next day not to attract attention as it is all to be kept secret. We received the letters yesterday, and the news caused us great emotion as you can imagine, but we also feel very thankful and much relieved.

From the Crown Princess

Fritz makes me laugh with his dismal forebodings but he is convinced that some day or other the Russian attempt will be copied at Berlin, and that these horrors only excite imitation.

Of course the science of destruction has been carried to a great perfection, dynamite, nitro-glycerine, torpedoes, etc., are horrible engines of death which have been thought charmingly useful in time of war, and when accessible to wicked people—or even to excited maniacs—may deal most frightful damage, still I am inclined to think that in spite of all this, human life is become more sacred than it was. Formerly Emperors of Russia who were in anyone's way—were throttled, poisoned, and assassinated in one way or another. "*Le despotism tempéré par l'assassinat*" as Voltaire called the Russian form of government whereas now—assassins are no longer to be found amongst the officers of the Imperial guard and nobility, etc., but are confined to a band of reckless, lawless men who are for the moment dreadfully dangerous. How far spread this conspiracy is of course most difficult to guess. What connection with the "internationals" and communists of other countries the nihilists have is not known, but in Russia there is so little honesty, truth and justice that it will be very difficult to find out the real criminals and any amount of innocent people may be suspected and even punished. It is a horrible thought.

About Willie, I will only add that I do think it will be a very

---

[1] Uncle Ernest and Aunt Alexandrine—perhaps rather curious spectators.

unpopular match at Berlin, because the poor Holsteins are *mal vus* and there is a widespread—though very false idea—that they are not equal in rank but I am sure these prejudices will wear off very quickly.

From the Queen

I will at once write to you about my going abroad. It was really not certain till quite lately that I was going and I only do so to be *The Hesse family.* present at the Confirmation of those dear, motherless grandchildren, as it will be a help to them and to Louis, and also to visit my own darling Child's grave. I would much rather have remained quite quiet this year, and gone D.V. next year but this happening I felt it a duty, as they have no mother. I shall only be away about three weeks—maybe a little more going on to Baden before Easter and then only for two days to Darmstadt and back for a few days to Baden. I never, dear Child, expected you to come as I knew you were to stay away anyhow till April and think it would be of little use, for you know I have not a single spare room in the House, which is so very small that I cannot even give anyone a room to dress in so we should not enjoy each other.[1] Therefore much as I should like to see my dear little [great] grandchild I think it would be better not to ask Fritz to bring Charlotte, Bernhard and Baby there. Whatever dear Fritz likes to do I shall be most happy, of course, to see him—but as I said before I haven't a room to offer him which I hope he will understand!

I dread the visit to Darmstadt more than I can say but I am to go to the Schloss, as I dread her house—where she received me, so lovingly, though I shall of course go to see it.

I shall burn what you say about Charlotte. Married children are very often a great trial at first but one gets accustomed to their follies as time goes on and many things right themselves. Still it is very wrong of young people not to listen and take advice for they have no experience. Parents have much to go through—much to bear.

---

[1] The Queen was staying at the Villa Hohenlohe at Baden-Baden.

From the Queen

On Tuesday 9th the Empress of Austria came and stopped for luncheon and was most amiable. She is a little aged, but still very handsome and graceful and distinguished looking and the figure beautiful, only her dress was so tight she could hardly move or sit down.

Poor little Stephanie's engagement took everyone by surprise including the Empress and Leopold of B.[1] The poor thing has been completely shut up—never seen anyone—never been to a dance or a play etc. and suddenly the C. Prince of Austria is brought, speaks to her and she is engaged and brought out!! It is a most wonderful arrangement but you like children's engagements and so you won't be so astonished.

From the Crown Princess

Dear Uncle Ernest was here yesterday, he came from Nice to pay me a visit, and I thought him looking very well and flourishing—though extremely stout.

I decidedly think with you that dear little Stephanie's marriage is very sudden, and taking such a great leap all of a sudden, is of course very trying to a young girl's mental and moral development! Though I was engaged at 14—and there are many other examples of the same kind, yet in principle I am strongly against it and think it far better to be a little older, but what I always pleaded is that there are cases where peculiar circumstances make it advisable and desirable—and unavoidable. I have heard no details yet. I suppose the Crown Prince (who has been rather wild and flighty) was urged to marry and chose Stephanie young as she was. It will be a great trial to the poor dear child to be grown up on such short notice and engaged to a young man she does not know, and had never seen. The newspapers at Berlin have got hold of Willie's marriage—and it becomes very awkward, one does really not know what to say as everyone asks. I wish the Emperor would not insist on keeping it secret from the Prussian family—anyway it will only offend them and make it disagree-

---

[1] The daughter of King Leopold II was engaged to the Crown Prince Rudolph of Austria.

able for Willie and Dona. One might tell one's friends and acquaintances without publishing it in any way officially.

I can not tell you, dear Mama, how painful the thought is to me of not seeing you when you go to Germany and of not being present at the Confirmation of Alice's beloved girls! I feel it very much indeed. I hope you will tell those dear children so when you see them.

From the Queen

I write now to say that I have twice seen Ada's dear girls and think both dear and amiable as well as pretty.[1] Calma is the prettiest but Victoria has a sweet, winning smile. She is unlike Ada, but like in manner. She looks thoroughly amiable but rather delicate I should say. Calma's teeth spoil her a little. Victoria has beautiful teeth. I much regret the delay about the announcement of the engagement. I shall write to Willie now.

I must tell you of another marriage which will very likely surprise you. When you told me last year that Uncle Ernest maintained Frederica of Hanover was married to Herr von Pawel I told you it was totally false; and so it was and is; but not the attachment though I was not aware of it. I knew last summer and she confided this long attachment to me and asked me to help her and to give my sanction to it. Of course we should have wished a better marriage in a worldly point of view for one so handsome and distinguished but as she can never give her heart to another, and as he is equally devoted to her and was so devoted to her poor father—and as she is 32 and old enough to know her own mind I felt it right and kind towards this noble-hearted girl who has suffered so much to consent to it, and I shall therefore tomorrow give my consent in Council to this marriage. She is a British Princess and my subject and wishes to live in England quite as a *particulière* and I shall give her a small apartment. He will be naturalised. He is hated by Windhorst[2] and all of Ernest of H.'s unwise councillors and he and the Queen are perfectly furious at it. The Cambridges except Augusta Strelitz are furious too but

---

[1] The Holstein sisters were staying at Cumberland Lodge with their uncle Prince Christian and Princess Helena.
[2] Ludwig Windhorst. A leading Roman Catholic in the Reichstag who denounced the annexation of Hanover by the Prussians.

that will blow over as she can hurt no one, poor thing. The ceremony will take place in the private Chapel here as soon as I return from Germany.

Did you never get a little pamphlet about Mr. Gladstone which I sent you? I thought it would amuse you as it is so clever.[1]

From the Crown Princess

Of course I was not very much astonished at the news you gave me about Frederica of Hanover. I knew she had an attachment for this gentleman. She is so charming and distinguished a creature that one feels sorry she should not take a more prominent place in the world, and make a marriage more in accordance with the usual notions of rank etc. Though I doubt not she will be far happier as the wife of a man she really loves, and in beloved England where homes are best and happiest.

But do tell me about the gentleman. I thought the father (old Pawel) so odious and he made himself such a bad name at Coburg and was so little liked and respected, I do trust the son is worthy of Frederica's devotion and that her noble heart has not misplaced its confidence and affection! I do not know whether it be true but it is said that Ernest of Cumberland would never give his consent.

The announcement to the family at Berlin has gone off very well; the only one who wouldn't congratulate was Uncle Charles.

From the Queen

I have seen Ada's dear girls twice since I last wrote and think them dear and amiable. Victoria has a very winning sweet manner which reminds me, as does her laugh, of poor Ada. I think she is well calculated to be an element of peace in ruffled waters. I have told her so and I should think she could not be otherwise than gentle. They have both charming manners in society and are beginning to be less alarmed I hope.

Neither Leopold B. or the Emperor of Austria knew anything of the Archduke Rudolf's plans. It seems Stephanie was entirely his own choice. It is a great thing that the Emperor and Empress

---

[1] Possibly *New Gleanings from Gladstone* published by Blackwood.

have at length allowed the marriage or rather the engagement to be announced, and I hope Willie will travel and see the world a little before he marries, which I trust will be next year. Those very long engagements are very trying and not very good and poor Victoria will be 22 in October.

23rd

I just hear Willie comes over tomorrow!! I will try and manage to see him for a moment.

From the Queen

WINDSOR CASTLE, MARCH 24, 1880

I received your dear letter of the 21st this morning and will hasten to answer your questions. First Herr von Pawel is totally unlike his odious father—and is very agreeable and gentlemanlike and was truly devoted to Lily's poor father and is so to her. The unkindness she meets with from her family is dreadful—and (excepting Augusta Strelitz) the Cambridge family are very unkind. Leopold has been her great help throughout. Second as regards Leopold himself he is not engaged to Miss Maynard who is a very nice girl, and pretty.

I think altogether the Government will do well in the elections. I shall be glad to be away.

From the Crown Princess

PEGLI, MARCH 26, 1880

I am so delighted that you think Victoria so gentle, and amiable, and sweet. She always struck me as such. Her smile and her manner and expression must disarm—even the bristly, thorny people of Berlin with their sharp tongues and their cutting sarcasm about everybody and everything.

My wishes are exactly the same as yours about Willie. I much wish he should see a bit of the world before marrying, though all the time he was here, it was the same as in Belgium or Holland and in London, he did not care to look at anything, took no interest whatever in works of art, did not in the least admire beautiful scenery—and would not look at a guide book or any other book which could give him information about places to be seen! In this way you will admit that travelling is not of much use, it is decidedly not his turn.

I hope you will have a prosperous journey. My thoughts will be much with you at Darmstadt. It will be very very trying for you, but in the increased sorrow which the return of the bitter anniversary of tomorrow brings me I can feel for you all the more. That dear place without darling Alice is too sad. Fritz will be so glad to see you and be present at the Confirmation instead of me.

From the Crown Princess

PEGLI, MARCH 27, 1880

Congratulations on William's engagement come in now on all sides; it is often a sore trial to speak of joy, happiness and festivities and receive congratulations, when one has an aching void at heart! But such is life, while some are looking eagerly forward others feel that they must ever be casting longing looks backwards to the time that was, and there is a melancholy, jealous feeling of consolation in the feeling that we remember, when all others forget the loved ones that once brightened our home with their dear presence. But I am very very grateful for Willie's happiness—and sure dear Victoria will be a blessing to everyone because she is so gentle and good.

From the Queen

VILLA HOHENLOHE, BADEN BADEN, MARCH 29, 1880

I was very glad to get a glimpse of Willie on Wednesday. His complexion was rather in a distressing state.

From the Crown Princess

PALAZZO CAFFARELLI,[1] ROME

Rome is so much altered since I was here last—it is terribly stripped of its charm and its poetry but how much remains to marvel at and admire. The King and Queen asked so much after you.

---

[1] The German Embassy.

From the Queen

I ought to have written earlier—but I have so much to do—and much worry and annoyance at the result (quite unexpected by the reckless Liberals themselves) of the elections. I think it a great calamity—only the party is so split up, so divided, and the majorities by which the so-called Liberals have come in, constantly so small—and the majorities for the Conservative members—in the City and other important places—so overwhelming that I hardly know how they will form a Government, certainly not a lasting one, and I think Lord Beaconsfield, with a very powerful Opposition, will have it in his power to control them and prevent mischief.[1] But Mr. Gladstone's mad, unpatriotic ravings and the sad want of patriotism of the Opposition have done this harm which is very grievous to me; it is a serious sorrow and trouble—it is that strange, ungrateful love of change which I do believe is the chief if not sole cause of this extraordinary result. People ignorant and unreasoning think a change of Government will give them a good harvest and restore commerce which suffered from speculators in '73 and '74 and had nothing to do with the Government.

The dear girls looked so well and answered beautifully.[2] Ella is lovely—beyond all expression and so sweet and gentle. I could not but think with regret of what might have been. But I will say no more of all that painful past. That is over.[3]

From the Crown Princess

I can imagine that the possible change of ministry must be a great source of anxiety to you. Many in Germany are of course much disturbed, and fancy the peace of Europe will be compromised and that the Liberal Party has a particular leaning towards France etc. The desire for office and the desire for change are evils, but I fancy even the Liberals must have learned a great deal in a

---

[1] 349 Liberals were elected, and 243 Conservatives.
[2] Princess Victoria and Elizabeth (Ella) daughters of Princess Alice, who were confirmed at Darmstadt.
[3] The possible marriage of Princess Elizabeth and the future Kaiser.

few years and, if Mr. Gladstone does not take office, surely they will be moderate.

Your description of the day at Darmstadt moved me much. Yes dear Ella is sweet and lovely; still I cannot help hoping and thinking that all is best as it is, and that of both young people especially.

From the Crown Princess

LA CAVA, HOTEL DE LONDRA, SUNDAY APRIL 18, 1880

Naples I found so changed and spoilt! All the cachet and originality is gone, it was so gay, so picturesque and beautiful now there are quais and modern housing, and save for the background of Mount Vesuvius and the view and beautiful Capri it might be any other town—Geneva or Nice. I was so disappointed. I went to see Lady Holland and found her much aged but most kind and civil. She lives in an old palace with small terraces and a hill of beautiful gardens. I went over the school (i.e. institution) of Augusta's friend Madame Schwabe in which I take great interest. You were so kind once as to assist me for the bazaar we got up at Berlin in favour of this institution for poor children.

Would you be inclined to give Fritz and me an object for our birthdays which I saw at Rome and which would give us the very greatest pleasure? It is a picture. I do not know whether it is still to be had but I know the price was not outrageous. Would you telegraph to me whether you would do such a thing? Then I might leave directions at Rome for someone to see about it as I am afraid it will be gone.

You are always so very generous to us that I am almost ashamed of asking, but so early in the year I thought that you might not have settled birthday gifts yet, and that you might not mind fixing on this for us which would be the thing of all others to delight us, I fancy the picture is by Tintoretto (it is not much damaged). I shall only be three days at Rome therefore your telegram would have just time to reach me.

From the Crown Princess

NAPLES, HOTEL BRISTOL, APRIL 22, 1880

On this my beloved little Mossy's birthday I send you a few lines before leaving for Rome. Our little darling will miss us today. She is such a love, such a little sunbeam, so good and so gifted, she will be a charming little person one day, but sometimes I fear not a very happy one, for she is so sensitive and her little heart so tender and warm and loving, so clinging that she is sure to suffer a good deal through life—as those must whose feelings *1* are deep and keen, and who have much love to bestow. *Oh yes!*

You are by this time no doubt deeply engaged in business and politics. Lord Beaconsfield will no doubt be glad of rest and liberty and quiet after all his arduous duties which at his age must be doubly trying. It was marvellous that at his age, and with his delicate health, he should have been able to stand all the work, responsibility and anxiety so long! His excellent temper and nerves have contributed to this I am sure.

From the Crown Princess

PALAZZO CAFFARELLI, ROME, APRIL 25, 1880

Wally Paget's artistic endeavours (i.e. the painting) are not so very happy—your picture is rather distressing, and also certain cupids painted on glass etc., but she has taken the greatest pains with the Embassy!

From the Queen

WINDSOR CASTLE, APRIL 27, 1880

These are very trying, worrying, painful days. It is a terrible change. Dear, kind, wise Lord Beaconsfield so dignified and worthy is "overwhelmed" as he says to leave me, for whom he had really the most wonderful devotion and attachment and I don't think he was at all pleased to be relieved. He was so anxious to see things settled and England more and more raised and strengthened—and the result was so totally unexpected on both sides, the ingratitude of the country so great that he feels the disappointment much. Mr. Gladstone, too, as Prime Minister seems hardly possible to believe. I had felt so sure he could not return and it is a bitter trial for there is no more disagreeable Minister to have to deal with. It is a weak Cabinet. Lords Hartington and Granville said they had no chance without him, and he says (I understand) he would have supported them if they had formed without him. His terrible, restless violence has caused this lamentable change which I fear will upset much good—and take away all confidence. I dread extreme measures—reductions etc. having been proposed. But first I thought the Government very moderate but I hear today that some violent men are to be taken in but not without my getting assurances on the subject.

The Duchess of Bedford is to be Mistress of the Robes. She is a very old acquaintance of mine. We knew each other as children and girls. The Duke of Westminster is to be Master of the Horse.

Our wedding went off well and was very pretty—the private Chapel being decorated with garlands of flowers, green and white, azaleas and palms and primroses near the altar. No one was in uniform. Lily[1] looked beautiful in her bridal dress—every inch a Queen she looked; her dress was my gift made at Paris with the Irish lace trimming and the veil the same. I led her in and gave her away. Her own mother refusing to give her her blessing and her sister and brother casting her off. She looks on me as her mother, and on Beatrice and Leopold as her sister and brother. They went off to Claremont till today. The bridesmaids were charmingly dressed—all in white with wreaths of lilies of the valley and white veils.

Did you see Wally's paintings!!!?

From the Crown Princess

FLORENCE, MAY 1, 1880

All Europe [is] looking with the greatest interest towards England and the changes there. Much of the alarm felt on the Continent is needless I am sure. Mr. Gladstone in office will prove, I trust, more prudent than out of office; still I can imagine how anxious you must feel before you know how it will all work with all these "growing questions" on hand, for decidedly the Eastern question will come up again. All Turkey seems to be in a state of unrest Bulgaria and Roumania troubled with great difficulties, Austria finding Bosnia impossible to hold without double the money and double the army. Russia always on the lookout for the right moment to seize what she wants—and Prince Bismarck at this moment (I think foolishly) convinced that the Gladstone Cabinet are enemies to Germany and friends of France which makes him inclined to lean again towards Russia; he has no interest in interfering with any design of Russia's on Constantinople —his only aim and interest is not to be isolated in case of France making war upon Germany! If he finds he can not make

---

[1] Princess Frederica of Hanover.

sure of England's and Austria's support (moral support only at present) of course he would turn to Russia, and if he is to obtain Russian alliance he can only do so by letting the Russians do what they like in the East. That is as clear as the sun at mid-day.

I own I think with horror of such a combination! Nothing is morally so bad for Germany as an intimate friendship with despotic and military Russia; it must likewise engender a dislike to England. The seeds which were sown in 1854 and have ripened into bitter fruit; the Russians have spared no pains to this effect! If only a war with France can be warded off for the next twenty years or even the next ten years jealousies, hatred and vengeance will go to sleep and then the war will not come at all.

You will think me very ridiculous and very absurd and perhaps be angry and disgusted with me—but an idea which I heard ventilated once, and which I could not agree with then, comes up again in my mind. If Turkey must disappear (which of course I do not know) better than that the Russians should be at Constantinople as the Austrians cannot, why should not a new state be organised, and Affie and Marie be there? It does sound very wild I own, and formerly I thought it preposterous. But now I ask myself what is to become of the East if the present state of things cannot and will not last and the Turkish Government cannot be kept on its legs. This is merely a thought of mine—this fantastic idea has never been mentioned again for some years past I believe and has of course no more importance than just being one of the many combinations that are suggested for and by the critical and uncertain state of things.

Surely England never can stand by to see the Russians at Constantinople? Laugh at my ideas as much as you like, dearest Mama, but do not be angry with me. I have not so much as hinted at this chance thought to Fritz or anyone at home; most likely many another solution can be found but it is just one way provided the poor Turks are past helping and past caring. If it is displeasing that I said this please dismiss it from your mind. You know you told me I might say what I thought.

You ask about Wally Paget's paintings. Oh dear! Since my unfortunate sincerity with Sir Coutts Lindsay[1]—I have become

---

[1] There is no knowing what the remark was. Sir Coutts Lindsay was no doubt a better painter than poor Wally—but not much. His most distinguished service to Art was founding the Grosvenor Gallery in 1877. (See *Bibliothca Lindesiana* by Nicholas Barker, Quaritch, 1977.)

very hypocritical to be on the safe side (at least to people's faces). So I do not say "Oh! dear how very awful". (I merely thought it). Wally is however, happily for her, convinced she is a great artist and has irreproachable taste so she has no misgivings and they must make her miserable if she had them.

From the Queen

I am very tired and have much to do. Tomorrow is another Council. I send you here a list of the Government. All these Radicals are a great trial—but they may not prove dangerous when in office. Still it alarms people. The first Council was a great trial. To take people I cannot trust and whose object was to drive the late Government, which had done so well, out merely to put themselves in, and who will have to pursue much the same policy or there will (be) war and every sort of disaster—is dreadful—is a dreadful trial. To me "the people's William" is a most disagreeable person—half crazy, and so excited—(though he has been respectful and proper in his manner and professes devotion) to have to deal with. I insisted on receiving assurances on the subject of the principles and languages of Mr. Chamberlain and especially Sir C. Dilke. The last named has made confessions of sins, and promises not to repeat them. He is only an Under Secretary.

The great principle of the Conservative Party is to be for the Throne and Country and of the Liberals "the Party". This is just the difference which now for long I have experienced.

I also send you dear Lord Beaconsfield's letter to me so beautifully and touchingly expressed.[1]

I also send you a very pretty article on Lily's marriage. As we know no morganatic marriage in England I shall announce it just as I did Ernest of Hanover's and Louise's.

From the Queen

How you made me laugh about Wally's artistic efforts!! The

---

[1] Part of this letter is quoted in *Disraeli* by Robert Blake: "His separation from Your Majesty is almost overwhelming. His relations with Your Majesty were his chief, he might almost say his only, happiness and interest in this world."

adventure with Sir C. Lindsay we often laugh at though it was fearful for you!

Eddy and Georgie have returned safe and well and unspoilt.[1] Eddy is immensely grown and as tall as his father and so like Alix's family but better looking than her brothers and uncles. Georgie is not a bit grown and is nearly a head and a half shorter than his brother. Dona and Calma lunched here yesterday and leave tonight. I am very sorry that we did not see more of them as Beatrice especially wished much to do, but Lenchen made great difficulties about their coming. I only wish you to know, as we should so much have liked to see more of Dona.

From the Queen

Mr. G. has already blundered fearfully—and the difficulties appal Lord Granville and others. What do you say to Mr. G.'s undignified apology? It is too bad but the fault was, Lord G. says, not the letter but what went before it.[2]

From the Crown Princess

How the usual frigidness and bitterness of the people here pains me when one comes back; and a little cordiality and kindness would make up so much for the sullenness and stiffness and perpetual "official" life here. Of course I keep that to myself but things and people grate horribly on my feelings, one is so isolated.

I am shocked at the state of politics here. Bismarck plays the very D with everyone, and everyone takes it as a matter of course. Their apathy and servility and want of independence and dignity is grievous and shows how the German character has deteriorated through the inordinate vanity this man has instilled into people blinding them to better and higher feelings and aspirations. It

---

[1] From the voyage on the *Bacchante* to the West Indies.

[2] The Emperor of Austria was reported, wrongly, to have expressed the hope that Beaconsfield would win the General Election. Speaking in the Midlothian Campaign Gladstone said "there is not a spot upon the whole map where you can lay your finger and say, 'There Austria did good'". Afterwards, when it was clear that the Emperor had expressed no such wish, Mr. Gladstone wrote a somewhat grovelling apology. "This is the letter of an English gentleman" was the Emperor's comment.

saddens us both very much. A more unwholesome and unsatisfactory state of things cannot be imagined. Where is public opinion? Where is an honest and energetic opposition to counterbalance a power so unlimited and so much abused. Despotism is rampant and the public seem utterly blind and to have lost all political instinct (if they ever had much).

But I will not bore you with these things. Luckily you live in a less vitiated atmosphere and much does one envy other countries. A huge and perfect army and a statesman whom none can trust or believe—but everyone fears—do not in my opinion constitute the beatitude but everyone here seems to think the present state of Imperial and Prussian Germany the envy, dread and admiration of the world. They feel so very big, and their talk is so very tall that it is very trying to others who had dreamed of a better future, of a free and pacific Germany with a wise and enlightened government. Dreams of this kind will not come true, I fear.

From the Queen

BALMORAL CASTLE, JUNE 10, 1880

You say I am not to say I have but a few active years left, I shall try and be active to the last—but I feel a difference this year in walking etc. It may get better and stronger again.

From the Crown Princess

NEUES PALAIS, JUNE 18, 1880

The Russian Ambassador[1] here is a tremendous intriguant and gets round Prince Bismarck (to a certain extent). Prince B. has no particular interest in the present question therefore he is very impartial. Of course if he thought that he could once and for ever make sure of the Russians as his allies by letting them take Constantinople he would do so in a minute. But he does not trust them, and therefore prefers being friends with Austria. This is sensible enough for him. As matters now stand he would rejoice if things could be settled in a way advantageous to England and Austria.

I am not Russophobe one bit, and think such a feeling silly and unjust, but the tendency of Russia is to spread and expand. It is so curiously constituted that the realm does not break up—there

---

[1] Count Satorov (1835-1918).

may be murder and violence at St. Petersburg but the whole fabric of the Russian Empire is almost too corrupt for a revolution. If things ever mend there i.e. if more morality and honesty is ever to take root it will be by degrees and not by revolution, which would shake the foundations of the Empire from one end to the other.

But they will continue to overflow and try to spread all over the Eastern world. They do not bring culture, reforms and civilisation with them—but they are very clever at conquering; that the rest of Europe and especially England should restrain this tendency, is only in the interest of the world.

From the Crown Princess

All you say about the Emperor of Russia is too true! You know how difficult it is to know the truth in family matters—and how many stories and lies are afloat always. The impression of St. Petersburg—and of most Russians abroad also diplomatists and foreigners who have visited the Court, is that the Empress suffered cruelly from her husband's infidelity and that she never uttered a murmur, complaint or reproach—nor ever mentioned the subject to a living soul, but died of a broken heart.[1] Affie and Marie are convinced that she never knew the existence of this lady or of the children but that the Emperor was most tender and kind to her to the last.

Russians have told me the lady is impertinent to the Emperor before others and shows him a want of respect, which is very shocking, that she is ugly, vulgar and very greedy and *effrontée* that the children live at the Winter Palace etc. But one hears such very contradictory accounts that they leave one the option of believing the best and mildest versions which one had so much rather believe out of affection for the Emperor, who is so kind and amiable a man, and for the dignity and peace of the family. The conduct of the Grand Dukes Nicholas and Constantine[2] is universally

---

[1] The Czar, Alexander II, married in 1841 the Princess Marie of Hesse (1824-80). He had a large family by the Empress but his habits were irregular. In the 1860's, he formed a permanent connexion with Princess Dolgorouka whom he was to marry morganatically after the Empress's death.

[2] Brothers of the Emperor: they allowed no criticism of him even within the family.

condemned, but one hears much good now of the Emperor's sons especially of the two younger ones—and the married ones till now make excellent and devoted husbands.

From the Crown Princess

I am so glad you liked the little picture we sent you and are even copying it in water colours. This amused me so much. What courage you have, and how active you are.

From the Queen

My darling children left me the day before yesterday evening and we miss them terribly. Two sweeter dearer girls I never saw! Victoria is extremely dear and knows so much. Ella is sweet, sensible and also very intelligent and most lovely—indeed I rarely saw a more lovely girl and so loving and affectionate and with such charming manners. How happy our darling Alice would be if she saw them.

With regard to what you say about the Emperor of Russia (which letter I have burned). I told you already what I know but since then I have heard more from a perfectly reliable source for it comes from Darmstadt (which please don't mention). It is that (which you also told me) the immorality in the highest circles is "unfathomable" that the feeling towards the Emperor is disloyal and that his conduct leads to this. That it is so open and that that woman and her children lived in the Winter Palace and in the Palace at Zarsko! That the Emperor took every spare moment to go to her—even during the funeral ceremonies. Is it not too horrible? How can his children endure this? The same person says that the Cesarevitch is universally respected on account of his very exemplary domestic life. May it remain so! Up to a certain time the present Emperor was very well conducted and the Emperor Nicholas much more so still. You say the youngest child was born at Livadia—that was last winter. But one was born there before! And one the very night the poor Grand Duchess Marie died. Is it not too disgusting? If I had been the Empress I would have refused to comply with such a request which is an insult—and would have left Russia. If such terrible things have to be done they ought to be hidden away out of sight—and the object be a person who

(Left to right) The Prince of Wales, Duke of Edinburgh, Duke of Connaught and Duke of Albany, Abergeldie, September 21, 1881.

The Emperor William I with Crown Prince Frederick William, Prince William and his son, Prince William, June 1882.

could not pretend to appear. I own *cela me révolte* and I think no wife should submit to such an insult.

From the Queen

The Grand Duke Alexis has arrived—and gone to Glasgow for the launch of an extraordinary yacht of the Popoff shape, and he is coming to lunch here on Friday.[1]

Today the Duc d'Aumale came and was very agreeable as usual. He is as shocked as we and ever so many of the supporters of the present Government are at the dreadful way in which things are—oh far worse than I even thought. Mr. Gladstone seems to me very infirm of purpose—weak, irresolute and ready to give way to extreme opinions. There is no support in the Government. I feel it is a reed—where I used to have a rock to lean on.

From the Queen

FROGMORE GARDEN, JULY 12, 1880

I shall certainly take my Carlsbad when I go to Osborne. I took it for seven years and did not, last year, and I always thought that I got that bad, feverish, bilious derangement in November in consequence of leaving it off.

From the Crown Princess

NEUES PALAIS, JULY 17, 1880

Willie is very busy with his military duties and full of zeal (almost too much and too exclusively so for my taste) though I am sure it is a right thing but here it has the effect on people for narrowing their minds and their interests and imparting harshness to their character. So much of it and nothing else is a pity but for the present it must be so.

---

[1] "The shape of the Livadia is quite unlike any vessel that ever went to sea." Her design was settled after a careful system of trials, conducted by Dr. Tydeman, of the Royal Dockyard, Amsterdam, in conjunction with Admiral Popoff. The hull of the vessel was rather in the shape of a turbot, "The apartments for the Emperor were comparable to palaces on land." Her tonnage was 11,600 tons, with 3 screw propellers. *The Illustrated London News*, July 1880.

The Grand Duke Alexis, son of the Emperor of Russia, was an Admiral in the Imperial Navy.

From the Queen

I just find I was too late for the messenger, on account of the ebb tide, which is most provoking so that this must go by post.

You seem to imagine that matters only go badly with the Irish Bill and that otherwise good measures are brought forward. You are totally mistaken if you think that. Not one measure which has been proposed has given satisfaction and no one more dissatisfied than the so-called Liberals themselves. Everything is going as badly as can be and I feel thoroughly disgusted and humiliated. We are already gone down very low!

No one is more liberal at heart than I am, but we are in a miserable condition thanks to the "People's William". You must have misunderstood me about Turkey. I admit and agree in the truth of the necessity of being prepared for what may come (which the Government are not, and do not see the necessity of being well prepared against Russia). But here no one wishes to drive the Sultan away but to keep him where he is. But the injudicious conduct of this Government (just as in '46 Lord Palmerston did with Queen Isabella's marriage) has *brusquéd* the question and it may lead to most serious complications.

I don't know Mr. G. Duff—and certainly would not speak to him about the East and especially not about India as you must remember the monstrous language he held about the latter. He was purposely put into an office quite removed from India for that reason. Lord Lytton was not to blame about this deficit[1]— probably Sir J. Strachey—but Lord Ripon even says otherwise the revenue is not in an unsatisfactory state. You ask me if Mr. Goschen's despatches are not very interesting. I have seen hardly any and only two or three letters (all is done by cipher telegram almost) and they did not strike me as particularly so. He does not write particularly well (that is a special gift) and his handwriting is quite unreadable and has always to be copied first.[2]

---

[1] It was found earlier in the year that the cost of the Afghan War had been underestimated by £12,000,000. Sir John Strachey was held responsible for this blunder.

[2] George Joachim Goschen (1831-1907) declined the Viceroyalty of India in this year, but agreed to go as ambassador to the Sultan in an effort to force the Turks to carry out the provisions of the Treaty of Berlin.

From the Queen

OSBORNE, JULY 31, 1880

I am sorry to see you so vexed about Charlotte. As regards the baby I think you are hardly a fair judge. Hardly anyone I know has such a *culte* for little babies as you have, and young people are generally not so much wrapped up in them. I know dear Grandmama went into such ecstasies over them, so that I felt the reverse.

I think there is so much contradiction in young people that they often show just the contrary. As regards the great love of amusement, that is quite another thing and much to be regretted and then I blame her husband very much. If he allows it, what can you say?

It was most interesting to see the poor stained and tattered colours of the 1st Battalion of the 24th which had been saved by those two poor young lieutenants who lost their lives in consequence. They were recovered afterwards and the top with the Royal Crest was found elsewhere. I laid a wreath of immortelle on the top of it as a mark of respect and admiration for these two brave men who gave their lives to save them.[1]

From the Crown Princess

NEUES PALAIS, AUGUST 5, 1880

Willie is chauvinistic and ultra-Prussian to a degree and with a violence which is often very painful to me; I avoid all discussions—always turn off the subject and remain silent. How often one's feelings get rubbed the wrong way I cannot say; for bigotry and narrow-mindedness are things so very distasteful and yet one must be tolerant even to that. Prussian princes have a certain *genre* and it runs in the blood, but with my own children I often feel like a hen that has hatched ducklings and it often gives me great pain as one is so wrapped up in them. However life is full of difficulties, intricacies, and contradictions and trials and they do not grow less as time goes on; and one must make the best of them.

---

[1] The Colours were lost at *Isandhlwana*. The two young lieutenants were Teignmouth Melvill and Nevill Coghill.

From the Crown Princess

I am quite ashamed to feel as upset as I do today—but we have a tame pussy, that belonged to Waldie, and of which we are all excessively fond! A quarter of a hour ago a stupid jäger goes into the garden and seeing the dear little thing sitting on the road shoots her, then hangs her against a tree and cuts off her nose. I am very silly perhaps but I cannot help crying! She has been our constant companion for three years. We took her when a little kitten. This morning as usual she was lying on my bed and purring and rubbing her head against my cheek. She always shared my tea of a morning, and this morning she was particularly affectionate. To think of her being so cruelly used when we took care of her for so long. She used to know Waldie's step so well that she always ran to meet him.

It seems the keeper gets a little money for shooting cats so he thought he had a good chance. Poor little animal. I was so attached to her and loved to feel her sitting on my lap or my shoulder—or on my pillow and with her pretty purring sound! I am foolishly fond of cats you know. The girlies are in great distress. I shall not take another pet certainly. People are so brutal here with poor dogs and especially cats. They think nothing of ill-using and killing them and I cannot bear it. The children are comforting themselves by burying her in Waldie's garden by the side of his favourite dachshund who was driven over—if you remember. He was so dreadfully unhappy about it.

From the Crown Princess

The man[1] was neither punished nor reproved. Count Eulenburg only laughed, and Willie (who does not understand a sentiment for pets) thought it was laudable zeal in pursuance of his duty on the part of the keeper, as cats might harm pheasants, so I get very little sympathy.

Today we give a large dinner to the Anthropological Society—also to Professor Nordenskyold. It interests me very much to see all these gentlemen.

---

[1] The jäger.

From the Queen

And now let me say how horrified and how distressed I am about your cat! It is monstrous—and the man ought to be hung on the tree. I could cry with you as I adore my pets. When they belonged to a loved and lost object it must be quite a grief! We always put a collar with V.R. on our pet cats and that preserves them. Our keeper once shot a pet one of Beatrice's. Keepers are very stupid but none would dream of mutilating an animal here! I think it right and only due to the affection of dumb animals, who (the very intelligent and highly developed ones) I believe to have souls, to mourn for them truly and deeply.

From the Crown Princess

NEUES PALAIS, AUGUST 14, 1880

Today Henry is eighteen—therefore "of age", according to the Prussian family statute. One is always glad when this age is safely reached, and thankful they have been spared.

But these days are not without their bitterness to me now. Much as dear Henry is loved I do not feel very proud of him. But he is very affectionate and amiable and makes friends wherever he goes.

From the Crown Princess

NEUES PALAIS, AUGUST 17, 1880

I am afraid that my speaking so openly about the children has produced a wrong impression upon you, and that you fancy I am ungrateful. Really this is not so—but as you take an interest in all of them, I thought I could give my opinion freely on their characters. Who should love them if not I, who bear with their peculiarities, and who always trembles for fear of any danger to the two sons I have left out of my four. But not every mother has had to combat with so many difficulties as I had in the education of these two, and not every mother has worked so hard at it and bestowed so much trouble and care upon it and had to bear with so much for their sakes; so I have a little ambition for them considering they are dear Papa's and your grandsons and I would wish to see them a little different from, and superior to, the many princes that come under my eye here.

Thank God they are steady till now and for that one cannot be thankful enough. But one's children are like plants on which a gardener bestows alike all care and trouble, and not all develop and grow so satisfactorily in every way as he wishes; one would be blind not to be able to distinguish between the nobler natures and the less gifted ones. Dear Papa and Uncle Ernest were brothers and yet how different. There is the same difference between our two dear eldest and our darling Waldie (though in other ways). That I shall ever miss and ever mourn does not mean that I repine uselessly, or shut my eyes to the blessings and benefits that remain. This is all I meant.

From the Queen

OSBORNE, AUGUST 21, 1880

I quite understand what you mean about your other boys and the dear one taken; I only tremble when I hear too great lamentation over the deficiencies of those left.

From the Queen

BALMORAL CASTLE, SEPTEMBER 14, 1880

You ask me if the Government are watchful of Russia etc. etc? I answer simply no! "Merry Pebble's" sole object is to upset everything his predecessor did and therefore it is hard work to keep them up to the mark but I never cease pointing out the dangers—and I think Lord Hartington and Lord Granville do see them. Mr G. is not what he was—he is *très baissé* and really a little crazy. He has not recovered his illness yet and I doubt (and fervently hope) he won't be able to go through another session.

I am very proud of Sir F. Roberts' wonderful march[1] and brilliant victory. No one knows what our brave troops have to go through in our constant Indian and Colonial warfare. It is fearful; very different to Europe.

From the Crown Princess

NEUES PALAIS, SEPTEMBER 17, 1880

I am so sorry not to have been able to write sooner, but I could

---

[1] To Kandahar.

— 88 —

not, never having one single moment of peace, rest or quiet in this mad sort of life we are leading. You say I have had a long holiday and no doubt I have, and had I not I should perhaps not be here to write to you! But you have of course no idea that since the 27th of May we have not had one meal, or one evening to ourselves and have been entertaining and receiving incessantly and during the absence of the Emperor and Empress have done all they do, so that I am dead tired, and do not know how I shall get through the winter at Berlin at all with this terrible climate, suffocating rooms, impossibility to go out so often, and late hours. You know that one man's food is another man's poison, and what the Emperor and Empress can do with perfect impunity, even at their age, half kills me. Emily Russell can stand it no better than I can. She spends days in bed with racking headaches after these interminable dinners and *soirées* and yet she is a thorough "cosmopolitan" and likes Society and going out so much and is always so civil and amiable to everyone.

If you had seen the Emperor riding for four hours today, and not tired afterwards and as fresh as a daisy evening or morning you would come to the same conclusion as I have, that his age must have been put down wrong in the Gotha Almanac and that he can only be 60 instead of 84.

From the Queen

BALMORAL CASTLE, SEPTEMBER 28, 1880

The state of the Eastern question is terrible all brought on by Mr. Gladstone's muddling; and in confidence I may say I think (and many others are struck by it) poor Lord Granville no longer up to his work, which has fallen upon him and which seems to break him down. He is *baissé* and this is terrible—at this moment. Mr. Gladstone also greatly altered but only bent on enmity to Turkey and friendship for Russia!!! You can imagine my anxiety, worry and distress—to have to work with people whom you entirely disagree with and who seem to have disturbed everything. That conference in Berlin disturbed the treaty.[1] It is weary, weary anxious work. Tell Lord Odo to frighten the Government as much as he can.

---

[1] The Conference of Berlin was re-opened earlier in this year to discuss the questions of Greece and Montenegro.

From the Queen

Yesterday we drove over to Invercauld—so sadly altered now. The pretty garden all spoiled and neglected, and the house a sort of grand affair which I think far less comfortable than the old unpretending one we all knew and liked so well.[1]

From the Queen

You say I am worried! God knows I am—and disgusted. I have warned and tried to do all I can but in vain and I now feel disheartened and disgusted. The mad passion of one half-crazy enthusiast is ruining all the good of 6 years peaceful, wise government and I often wish I could retire quietly and let people work out their own policy and reap its fruits.

Respecting Charlotte I am sorry she should go on in this way after all is settled and Willie contented, and you have got what you so ardently wished. It seems very foolish and wrong. Much I cannot however say on this subject (though I like and love Dona and think her well-suited for her position) as there was much two years ago which was very painful to me.

You mention Lord Odo for a possible successor to Lord G(ranville). No one can think more highly of Lord Odo than I do—but he has a good deal that is foreign in him.[2]

From the Crown Princess

On the whole things have gone off well at Cologne.[3] The public were most nice and civil and amiable. The grand cathedral looked more enormous and imposing than ever, but it is not so rich and beautified inside as the Italian or even the French cathedrals and not, by half, so interesting as our English churches

---

[1] The Farquharsons of Invercauld were old friends of the Royal Family, but at this time the head of the family was a friend of the Prince of Wales, a London "fashionable" and one of the founders of the Bachelors' Club. Such a neighbour in the Highlands was regrettable to the Queen.
[2] Meaning that he was brought up abroad. (See *Lord William Russell and his Wife* by Georgiana Blakiston, John Murray, 1972.)
[3] The completion of the Cathedral.

of the same date because there are so few tombs, monuments and epitaphs, and no one of great interest is buried there. I said to everyone how proud and grateful I was that you and dear Papa in former years had contributed so largely towards the funds for the restoration of the building.

The Te Deum was a very meagre affair. I never saw so poor a ceremony or so little show in a Catholic church but the clergy, with few exceptions, kept quite aloof as was natural.

The two days were dreadfully fatiguing. We stood for four hours at a stretch, and one was ready to drop and chilled to the bone.

From the Crown Princess

WIESBADEN, OCTOBER 26, 1880

You ask why Victoria is to have three ladies. All the Prussian princesses have three ladies when they marry. I had, Marie Abbat has. It is only since the year '69 that I am without an *oberhofmeisterin*. I was only two years without filling the place of second lady in waiting. It would not do for Victoria to begin with less (as the land lies). In the abstract I think so many quite useless, and a very great *gêne* but during the Emperor and Empress's lifetime nothing can be changed.

From the Crown Princess

WIESBADEN, OCTOBER 29, 1880

I am growing very unsightly, have lost almost all my hair, and what remains has turned very grey—my face is full of lines and wrinkles especially round the eyes and mouth.

From the Crown Princess

WIESBADEN, NOVEMBER 12, 1880

Fritz wishes me to tell you that on Monday we had a letter from General Schweinitz enclosing one from St. Petersburg from our Military Attache General Werder, the intimate friend of the Emperor Alexander, saying the Emperor was married to Princess Dolgorouka on the 26th of July in presence of General Count Alderberg and General Ryleev. He has given the name of Yourievski to his wife and children. It is not to be made known till the 2nd or 3rd of December. The Emperor Alexander has desired a letter to be written to my father-in-law informing him of the fact. The Emperor (my father-in-law) wrote this to Fritz two days ago.

We know from another source that after the marriage ceremony the Emperor sent for Minny and the Cesarewitch and presented his wife to them and asked them to be kind to her. The unbecoming haste with which the Emperor had the marriage rite performed, while the mourning for the poor Empress was yet so fresh, I think can be accounted for, and to a certain extent be justified by his desire to do his duty as a man of honour by a lady and her and his children whom he had placed in so painful a position. He feels his health breaking and his life very uncertain in the condition Russia now is in, and most likely wishes to legalise the liaison he had formed, before a sudden death might prevent him from making this reparation. What one must feel bitterly is the want of respect to the poor Empress's memory. General Schweinitz says that anything is better however than the former state of things which was a crying "scandal".

From the Queen

WINDSOR CASTLE, DECEMBER 8, 1880

Sir F. and Lady Roberts also are here tonight. He is a great man, and so small in appearance but a very keen, eagle eye. It is so interesting to hear about his wonderful march and he is so modest. He was so ill the day of the great battle that they had to give him champagne—which one of his A.D.C.s found—every half hour. He managed to get through it but was dreadfully exhausted afterwards. On the march he had to be carried some days. His wife is a very nice person and must have been very pretty. She is an excellent soldier's wife and devoted to him and proud of him.

I have written confidentially to the Empress of Austria that she would be exposed to very great danger if she came over to hunt in Ireland where the hounds are even in danger of being shot or poisoned and several popular landlords have been stopped from hunting. You seem not to know what a frightful state Ireland is in, or won't you believe it as a so-called Liberal (in fact my illiberal Government is in.) Everyone on both sides say bad as it has often been, it never was so bad as it is now. The law is completely set at defiance and no one gets any rents, and the harvest has been excellent. Very strong measures will have to be taken for such a state of savage, cruel lawlessness must be put an end to or God knows how far it may spread!

From the Queen

I write again on a subject which interests you more even than politics viz; *Art*. Good Mr. Redgrave has retired on account of failing health and especially eyesight.[1] Knowing the interest you take in these things I thought before I decided I would send you a list of applications and ask your opinion. You once were anxious about Mr. Robinson getting the National Gallery. Mr. Poynter is a very good artist. Mr. Horsely also. Poor dear Mr. Corbould is I fear hardly fit.

From the Crown Princess

WIESBADEN, DECEMBER 10, 1880

The disturbance about the Jews is going on just the same, and people are so violent and excited. It is most painful and disagreeable in a town where the Jews do all for the public, and at Berlin are so generous and charitable. I own one is shocked and disgusted at this movement.

From the Crown Princess

WIESBADEN, DECEMBER 11, 1880

I am sure you were most wise in writing to the Empress of Austria, as really it does seem a queer and risky thing to go to Ireland just now when it is in such a state of ferment.

You say you suppose I do not believe it is a terrible state! Of course I do—it is too evident. One knows it has often been so before, Fenians etc., have been great difficulties to deal with, and yet they subsided and I trust this will also. I must really protest, dear Mama, against being called "so-called" liberal. I hope I am a staunch and a true one from deep conviction. My idea of a liberal is simply a commonsense view of things, and a wish to be fair, and tolerant and charitable, and to improve at all times that which wants improving; in fact to try and raise each branch of existence into something as good as it can be made, not to change and destroy things because they are old and traditional nor to preserve what is no longer useful merely because it is old.

---

[1] Keeper of the Queen's pictures (1857-80).

No one can have a greater horror and dread of Communism than I have and I think many measures of Prince Bismarck such as "universal suffrage" "manhood suffrage" utterly foolish, most dangerous and quite destructive of all good government. There are a great many doctrines of modern liberalism I do not and cannot agree with; and were I a man I should feel it impossible to join any party that held them. I hold the British Constitution to be the best and most useful and blessed form of government in the world and yet I feel that the world goes on, things change from day to day, new wants spring up that must be met, many a time-honoured thing becomes senseless and superfluous that was once indispensable. Wild liberals and violent conservatives are alike distasteful to me as their ideas lead to the same mischief. These are my very terrible opinions and always have been—and I suppose always will be as I see more to justify and confirm them every day.

May I just ask one question. I heard sometime in a roundabout way—that good old Mr. Redgrave was going to retire or had retired. If you have not yet bestowed the appointment of surveyor of your pictures, I earnestly plead for old Mr. J. Robinson, who is without a doubt the first authority and connoisseur in England.

From the Queen

WINDSOR CASTLE, DECEMBER 15, 1880

I have again a stupid headache and can't write as I would wish in detail about the dreadful and very alarming state of affairs in Ireland which you are not at all aware of. It is worse than it ever was before, all the Whigs and reasonable and real Liberals are most terribly alarmed—and the Government does nothing and is divided, weak and vacillating to a degree that is arousing the indignation of England. I will tell Sir Henry Ponsonby (himself a great Liberal partisan) to write to you about it.

From the Crown Princess

WIESBADEN, DECEMBER 25, 1880

Yesterday we had a very tiresome stiff ceremonial evening party, and today the same tiresome dinner. Never to see any member of one's family out of uniform is such a bore, and makes everything so stiff.

1881

From the Crown Princess

We spent yesterday evening with the Emperor and Empress. It is the last time we have Willie unmarried, in the same house, in his own rooms with us. He thinks me absurdly sentimental to observe this, and says it is all the same to him in what place or house or room he lives.

From the Queen

OSBORNE, JANUARY 6, 1881

My letter sent yesterday was so long and my time so unpleasantly taken up by disagreement respecting my speech, about which I was very disgracefully treated, that I could not thank you for your dear, and affectionate letter.[1]

From the Queen

OSBORNE, JANUARY 22, 1881

I so greatly admire dear Fritz's speech about the poor, ill-treated Jews.[2] Mr. Scott wrote from Coburg that Uncle Ernest was equally indignant and said the feeling was not general in other parts of Germany.

From the Crown Princess

BERLIN, FEBRUARY 27, 1881

All has gone off very well till now. Dear Dona looked charming, and everyone was taken with her sweetness and grace! Her

---

[1] This refers to a storm over the right of the Queen to alter the speech in her name made at the opening of Parliament. A full account of the trouble will be found in vol. i of A. G. Gardiner's *Life of Sir William Harcourt*, Appendix I.
[2] The anti-Jewish riots were in the large towns of Prussia and were thought to be fomented by "Socialist agitators" but the outbreaks were not limited and the most rancorous antipathy towards the Jews was shown by the students of the University of Berlin.

face wore a look of innocent happiness which did one good to see. Her *toilette* was very becoming—a light blue and gold brocade—with pink and white China asters. Her pearls and your beautiful pendant round her neck. The weather was fine and everyone in a good humour. The crowd cheered and seemed pleased and the decorations were really very pretty indeed.

I was quite exhausted yesterday evening or I would have written directly. I had a diadem on, which pressed my head a great deal and did not take it off for six hours and a half. The reception in the Schloss also went off very well and even Prince Bismarck appeared. Today will be very trying and I wish it were over.

My parents-in-law are wonderful and never tired—standing, heat, *toilettes*, talking—nothing seems to knock them up.

I thought so much of you, dearest Mama, and of the days when I arrived here. It is made far easier to Victoria than it was to me and I hope she will never suffer from home sickness as I do to this day.

From the Crown Princess

BERLIN, FEBRUARY 28, 1881

All went off very well last night; it was exhausting, suffocating and interminable as all the Berlin state weddings are. I had my diadem on for seven and a half hours. The standing was such that my legs feel as if they were going to come off.

Sweet Dona looked quite lovely—so sweet and self-possessed not shy and yet so modest and gentle. She wore a radiant smile on her face and her wedding dress became her so well. Even the stiff crown suited her. She was most graceful and dignified during the *Fackeltanz* and everyone sung her praises and seemed charmed.

Of the service I will say nothing. It consists in a harangue which the young couple listened to standing, and which is so cold and so funereal that one has not the impression of attending a wedding! Service it cannot be called. The assembly was most brilliant. I am sure you would have been touched at the dear young bride's appearance and demeanour. May he make her happy and be as good a husband as she deserves.[1]

---

[1] The marriage was celebrated in the Schloss at Berlin with "great pomp" as was noticed in England. In spite of exhaustion the Crown Princess entertained her brother, the Prince of Wales, and fifty-three royal relations for dinner on March 1. The number was counted by the Prince of Wales. (See *King Edward VII* by Sir Philip Magnus.)

From the Queen

You think dear Dona so pretty. We[1] do not; nor do others. But sweet, gentle, graceful and ladylike. But how you with your brilliant eyes and small mouth and beautiful shoulders can say the jewels will suit her better than you shocks me very much.

From the Queen

WINDSOR CASTLE, MARCH 16, 1881

I share your horror, condemnation and sorrow at the death (unparalleled) of the poor, kind Emperor Alexander. A sense of horror thrills me through and through! Where such a criminal succeeds the effect is dreadful. The details are too terrible. No punishment is bad enough for the murderers who planned it; hanging is too good. That he, the mildest and best sovereign Russia had, should be the victim of such fiends is too grievous. Poor darling Marie on whom her poor father doted, it is too much almost to bear. But she is very courageous.[2]

From the Queen

WINDSOR CASTLE, MARCH 30, 1881

Everything has gone off well D.V. at Petersburg—but poor Sacha has been and is kept a complete prisoner.[3] What an existence. What a country. By this time dear Fritz is safe back. He will tell you much about everything. The state of affairs is simply dreadful from what Sir J. Cowell and Bertie write. Is it not shocking that that woman, who has just been taken up, should be a lady nearly related to a friend of Marie's? She, Lord Dufferin writes, has been at the head of the nihilists for ten or twelve years and was mixed up with everything.[4]

Have you ever seen that monstrous paper published here called

---

[1] Meaning herself and the family still at home—Princess Beatrice and Prince Leopold. "She becomes prettier every day and turns everyone's head"—Crown Princess, March 5.
[2] The Emperor was assassinated on the streets of St. Petersburg on March 13.
[3] The Emperor Alexander III.
[4] Possibly Jesse Helfmann, who was reprieved from hanging because she was pregnant, but more probably Vera Figner, a spirited lady who lived to be 90 and objected to being called "Comrade" by the Bolsheviks.

"Freiheit". It is to be prosecuted for it openly preaches assassination and the language is beyond anything I ever saw.[1] In every country I think there is now a determination not to allow such abuse of asylum to be permitted.

The Germans have been very unjust about the Transvaal. Their Government was so dreadful that we were driven to annex it—and I think it is very unfortunate to have made the peace.[2] But I think we must not look at it as settled at all yet. The Boers are very treacherous.

From the Crown Princess

BERLIN, APRIL 6, 1881

Poor Lord Beaconsfield is very weak still I fear, though the papers say he is better. It is such a pity he has homeopathic doctors—they can do no good.

We were so much struck with Sandro Battenberg when he was here.[3] He is grown so handsome and seemed so nice and sensible, manly and yet modest. I am sure you would have been pleased with him.

From the Queen

OSBORNE, APRIL 13, 1881

I never answered you about the little bust of me when a child. I have desired that someone who understands should go and look at

---

[1] This was the day on which Johann Most, the German editor of *Freiheit*, was prosecuted. The article described the assassination of the Emperor as a heroic deed which should be more frequently performed against other tyrants. Herr Most was sentenced to 16 months' imprisonment, with hard labour.

[2] The Transvaal had been annexed in 1877. In December 1879 the Boers took up arms and in the following year had a decisive victory at Majuba Hill. The Pretoria Convention recognised the independence of Transvaal in the spring of 1881 and was agreed to by Mr. Gladstone's government.

[3] Alexander Battenberg, the Prince of Bulgaria. He and the Crown Princess's second daughter, Princess Victoria, became warmly attached to one another—an attachment which caused the greatest indignation among the Prussian Royal Family. The Crown Princess strongly favoured the marriage, and it was hoped that when the Crown Prince became Emperor he would consent to the marriage. This was not possible.

Prince Alexander married an opera-singer and died in 1893. The Princess married, in 1890, Prince Adolph of Schaumberg-Lippe who died in 1916. She subsequently married M. Zoubkoff, and provided some material for the popular press by riding pillion on his motor-bicycle. She died in 1929.

Above: The Duke of Connaught, Cairo, September 1882
Below: The Duke and Duchess of Connaught with Princess Margaret and Prince Arthur, October 1883.

Prns. Charlotte

Above: The Hereditary Princess of Saxe-Meiningen and her daughter, Princess Feodore, September 1879
Below: Prince William of Prussia and his son, Prince William, June 1883.

this bust. I hardly think Grandmama ever gave Sir J. Conroy a bust of me.

From the Crown Princess

BERLIN, APRIL 18, 1881

The Grand Duke Constantine is in a terrible mess I fear, popular opinion so excited against him that his safety is doubtful. He has I fear made himself an awful reputation but it is ridiculous to accuse him of conspiracy in the Emperor's assassination. I do pity his unfortunate wife.[1] All the brothers and sisters in the Russian family are too deplorable, only three marriages Michael's, the Emperor's and Vladimir's seem to go on straight. Marie's two youngest brothers are so much to be pitied and are so nice and well brought up and so unhappy and lonely now poor things.[2] We continue to hear a great deal about Russia daily, and what one does hear is too melancholy.

From the Queen

OSBORNE, APRIL 20, 1881

A heavy cloud has fallen over this Empire; a great statesman who in six years raised its name again and placed it where it ought to be, has passed away at the very time when Kandahar is given up—a wretched peace in Africa—and disorder is rampant in Ireland—while murder is openly preached in every country. To me the blow is terrible and I was quite ill yesterday and am still feeling poorly and shaken. Dear Lord Beaconsfield was the truest, kindest friend and wisest counsellor and he too is gone! I feel much crushed by it.

From the Queen

OSBORNE, APRIL 23, 1881

Many thanks for your dear letter of sympathy on this dreadful loss of the 20th. All parties combine in mourning now one of the greatest, wisest and most dispassionate statesmen this country ever

---

[1] The Grand Duke was the second son of the Emperor Nicholas I and he married Princess Alexandra of Saxe-Altenburg.
[2] The Grand Dukes Serge and Paul.

possessed—and whose sóle objects were the good and the great-
ness of this Empire as well as that of his sovereign whom he
served—as none have—more devotedly from his great personal
affection for me. You say his loyalty ought not to be put foremost
of his merits as I am blessed by loyalty in general. Yes, as a general
term, this may be true but I know too well for discussion what a
difference there was in his loyalty. My good, my comfort were
his first objects—not the party's or his own.

And now with the Liberal Party alas! The creed is party and self
first and country and sovereign last. I feel this most sadly, and
more and more each succeeding Liberal or I fear Radical Government. They have to be told and taught what they owe to me—
and I suffer much from this. It is the one thing which is so totally
different. You would see this at once if you were here.

Few people understand me so well as dear Lord Beaconsfield,
or what gentle, true tenderness there was in his nature combined
with such great firmness and courage, and how he struggled with
a feeble frame and bad health with his indomitable will and self
control. He bore his indignities so meekly. I think the sudden
change of complete inactivity, when he left office, did him harm.
He was a year older than he thought—therefore past 76. His
devoted friend Lord Rowton who is broken-hearted and nursed
him for last week, day and night, gets nothing, which is what he
wished, as he served him from love—but all his papers and complete power over them. Hughenden goes to his nephew when he
is 26. The brother who was not worthy of him has a good place
which he gave him.

I agree with you in thinking the executions in Russia will have
no effect but they were absolutely necessary—only they should
have been strictly private. Public executions are horrid.

From the Queen

BUCKINGHAM PALACE, MAY 4, 1881

On Saturday we drove over to Hughenden, a long drive, and I
went to his grave; the church is very pretty and so is the position
but the small dark vault—which they left open for me to see—and
you go down into a tunnel is dreary and disagreeable though very
dry.

The honoured remains were covered with flowers. We then
drove to the house where all was just as when I visited him three
years and a half ago—very sad; it is not a cheerful house though

the garden and grounds and the hilly ground all round it is very pretty. He loved it dearly.

From the Crown Princess

A curious marriage has taken place. Young Paul of Mecklenburg married his cousin Marie Windisch-Grätz the day before yesterday. No one knew that the ceremony was to take place on that day; the bride's sister who was at Schwerin only heard it half-an-hour beforehand and could not appear. There was a *mariage civile* and then a Protestant wedding—and the bridegroom left immediately after the ceremony and will not return until he has found a Catholic priest who will perform the Roman Catholic rite. They have been looking for a priest for a whole year and more and could not find one. The Pope refused his consent to the marriage unless the usual promises were given—for the children to be brought up in the Roman religion. This was of course not given. The father Windisch-Grätz has also refused his consent. If Paul fails to find a priest they must content themselves with the civil and Protestant marriage.

Is it not a curious predicament to be placed in?

I have been the last two evenings to hear Wagner's celebrated trilogy and have already [illegible] "Rheingold" and "Valkyrie". It's impossible to imagine anything more dull and tiresome and heavy—and fatiguing to listen to—though there are lovely snatches of melody in the orchestral part—the whole is one long recitation from beginning to end. I own I could hardly stand it—in spite of its being undoubtedly poetical and original as a work of art. We have had the really immense pleasure of seeing Rossi act a few times! It is magnificent. He has but one rival in this and that is Salvini. How I wish you could see or hear him! You know I am not a play-going individual and rarely set my foot into the theatre but this is so splendid that my enthusiasm is very great. True genius is so rare and so heaven-born a thing that it makes a powerful impression when one comes across it.

From the Queen

The marriage you told me of is very curious—but surely a Protestant and Civil marriage is enough though not amongst R.

Caths: you know the same happened with Princess Battenberg and finally she became a Protestant.

Wagner's trilogy must have been rather overpowering and so noisy. Rossi I have always heard was very fine but I should not have been worthy as I don't understand Italian well enough to follow a play. I understand common things but not high flown ones.

I have not read the book you mention.[1] I have so little time to read, that I am ages getting through books. Kingsley's life I am reading which would interest you very much. It is so full of my sort of interest and his letters are charming.[2] But I will order the book you mention.

From the Queen

WINDSOR CASTLE, MAY 14, 1881

You ask me about the Bishop of Aberdeen.[3] He has no right whatever to be called Bishop of Aberdeen for episcopacy in Scotland is different as you say. But he is a Bishop and like the colonial ones can confirm etc. He has the *"Heilige Weihre"*[4] (such nonsense) but he must not be called Bishop of Aberdeen. Bishop Suther is the uncle by marriage of Lord Erroll who is however a very strong Presbyterian.

Lenchen won't let me come to Cumberland Lodge as it is painting so I can't see your embroidery alas yet!

From the Crown Princess

NEUES PALAIS, MAY 14, 1881

The Emperor of Russia's new proclamation[5] does not please me at all, and only means I fear that he intends to go on in the old

---

[1] "Nicholas I, Alexander II and Alexander III"—The Crown Princess, May 8.
[2] *Charles Kingsley: his Letters and Memories of his life by his Wife*, 1877.
[3] Thomas George Suther, 1814–83. Rector of St. George's, Edinburgh, 1837–55. Defeated by one vote by Christopher Wordsworth for Bishopric of St. Andrews. Bishop of Aberdeen, 1857–83.
[4] Consecration. These comments of the Queen would not be acceptable to many churchmen, and may remind them of the learned Dr. Routh who said at a dinner for his 95th birthday, "The Church is in great peril from a Kirk-going Queen." *Dr. Routh* by R. D. Middleton, Oxford Press, 1938.
[5] On May 10 when he appealed for the loyalty of the people to help him to overcome "the vile rebellion which disgraces the Russian people".

style, which, considering what it has brought Russia to, is very sad.

Poor Sandro's proclamation I thought seemed courageous and sensible.

The details which are mentioned now about poor Sultan Abdul Aziz's murder—we heard at the time from Aristarchi Bey and others who never doubted it for a moment, and Ignatiev seems to know all about it. It is a mystery to me that Sir Henry Layard and Sir Henry Elliot should give no credit to the story. What does Mr. Goschen say I wonder?[1]

We had a most interesting evening yesterday. I wish you had been there! Rossi came over here and repeated a Canto of Dante by heart in the most magnificent and impressive way which really moved one deeply.

What a gift—such a memory, such a voice and such a grand power of feeling and rendering the intention of so great a poet. I own I enjoyed it immensely and so did even those who had not read Dante in Italian.

From the Crown Princess

NEUES PALAIS, MAY 17, 1881

I cannot tell you what is going to come of the Mecklenburg marriage beyond that the husband is at Wiesbaden and the wife has remained at Schwerin and they are not to meet until they find a Roman Catholic priest who will marry them over again. What they will do should they fail to find such a priest (of which I am almost certain) I do not know. It reminds me of a story "*I promessi sposi*" (by Manzoni) exactly.

I cannot help being rather shocked at the French being at Tunis. There is so much room for them in Africa to extend their rule (if it must be) near their own possessions that I regret their going to the very place which is so important to the Italians and where they have more interests to take care of than the French and more right to be the first in influence.

The Emperor has no objections to my going to England with the children whatever, so I may now accept the Duchess of Bedford's kind offer of Norris Castle.[2]

---

[1] See *Darling Child*, page 213.
[2] A Nash building on the Isle of Wight.

From the Queen

Leopold comes here today and I wish to tell you that he is going to be made a Peer tomorrow which has long been his wish. But under conditions viz; that he is always to be called Prince Leopold in my house, at Court, in the Court Circular and never generally without that name being prefixed to the title to which he willingly agrees. I always say no one can be a Prince but anyone can be a Duke. He is to have the fine old Scottish title of Duke of Albany and the others the Earl of Claremont and Arklow.

And now I must tell you something which I fear will be a disappointment to you and I am much distressed to have to cause it. It is namely about your proposal to visit Balmoral. I had hoped to have been able to arrange all to meet your wishes and indeed was even contemplating making all arrangements for it when, a few days ago, Affie came to see me and was very low and distressed at the alarming accounts from Russia and also at the depressed state of dear Marie who feels all this most terribly. He has implored me to let her come to Balmoral this autumn with him and I feel that under existing circumstances and taking all into consideration I cannot refuse Affie's request. I feel that I am now the only parent dear Marie has and that I am doubly bound to do all in my power for her. It would be quite impossible for me to receive you also at Balmoral and much distressed as I am to cause you any disappointment I feel quite sure that you will see the great difficulty that I am placed in and that you will quite understand my reasons.

From the Queen

As time goes on the love and affection of a mother and her appreciation of one's sorrows, trials and difficulties becomes a greater comfort. My trials are so great and many—the loss of devoted friends and valued advisers is so keenly felt—that I can only foresee that my declining years will be very trying ones.

From the Queen

Mrs. Gladstone told me you had been to tea with her and Mr. G. Was that necessary? He does not deserve it. I shall be delighted to take tea with you at Norris but I never dine out, not with anyone, neither with Bertie or Affie or Lenchen etc. It tires me so much to go out at night.

From the Queen

Mrs. Drummond the dear Dean's great friend and one of his executors came here yesterday and brought me some of the dear Dean's hair, part of which I send you here. It had to be disinfected.[1]

From the Queen

I wish to tell you which I forgot that you should always direct to Louise abroad "Lady Sundridge"[2] as she is particularly anxious to keep her incognita.

I am glad to say that I have at last succeeded in getting a good successor to our beloved Dean[3]—though one really at all like him it will be impossible to find. This is Mr. Bradley, Head of Balliol College, Oxford—Canon of Worcester and formerly a very successful Master of Marlborough School—the "bosom friend" of dear Dean Stanley and whose views are just like his. It was not quite easy to get it done—but our good old Dean[4] carried it for me.

I am sitting out under the trees and it has come on to pour so

---

[1] The collection of a lock of hair as a souvenir of the dead was by no means unusual in the Nineteenth Century. When King Victor Emmanuel died the Queen asked Lady Paget to get some of the King's hair for her. The Queen, who had known him in earlier times, was surprised to find that the red hair which she remembered had been dyed black. *Embassies of Other Days* by Walburga, Lady Paget.
[2] A subsidiary title of the Dukes of Argyll.
[3] of Westminster.
[4] of Windsor

violently, so that I don't know how to get into the house even.

I had to have the Clarence brought to where I was sitting under the large umbrella—as I could not get away for the frightful rain and hail. It will do such awful harm to the crops!

I wanted also to say I had read (yesterday) that pamphlet about Monaco which Mr. Gladstone sent me—and wanted to know if you wish me to do or say anything about it. It is too horrid and ought to be put down.[1]

From the Crown Princess

NORRIS CASTLE, AUGUST 25, 1881

I arrived here late yesterday evening after a most interesting and enjoyable day. In the morning (in London) I went out to do a little shopping, and then paid Lady Charlotte Schreiber a visit to see all her fine things and also the work she has from the Turkish Compassionate Fund. We hurried through lunch and started off with a Special which stopped at Arundel so that I had an opportunity of seeing the Castle for the first time. How very fine it is. What a splendid situation and what a view from the windows. There is a something about it which reminds me of beloved Windsor (in miniature). The present Duke is having much built and done up—and in a most judicious way very simple but of the best style and taste. I was so interested in seeing the rooms where you and dear Papa lived. I am very glad indeed to have seen it. My curiosity was not appeased until we stopped at Chichester and went to see the Cathedral which though small and with but few monuments is very fine. The Dean led us about and gave us tea in his house. The view from the gardens of the Bishop's Palace is quite lovely.

It is quite sad and lonely here without you, and the children are so full of dear Grandmama and all her kindness that it does my heart good, "and" says Sophie "she is so nice to kiss you cannot think".

---

[1] The gambling.

From the Queen

We have had the most deplorable weather. The first day it rained without ceasing, we visited the Royal Infirmary only finished two years ago which is magnificent. Such comfort—such convenience. I believe there are five to six hundred beds. Anyone is taken in without recommendation—free—the worst cases being preferred. There are 130 nurses under a nice Sister Superintendent—a Miss Pringle—a great friend of Miss Nightingale's.

Yesterday morning the excitement everywhere was tremendous and the first thing in the morning the sun shone, then it clouded over but we thought the wind would keep off much rain at any rate. I walked in the garden and saw the countless thousands who covered Arthur's Seat and all the surrounding crags like an ant hill. At 2 there was a slight sprinkling of rain but still it cleared and even the light made an attempt to come through. But alas! just as we started—in an open carriage Marie and Beatrice with me—Uncle George (with his Staff) Affie and Arthur in full uniform and my gentlemen, and it began to pour and went on without a moment's interruption all the evening—only getting worse to the end—in which these really splendid men—40,000 in number marched past with great energy and perseverance but it was most distressing and provoking as it would have been so splendid otherwise. Still it all passed off well and without any casualties but everyone was wet through and through and the poor men must have suffered enormously. Marie, Baby and I in spite of the waterproofs and umbrellas got partly wet through especially when we sat. I had a large dinner in the evening of those connected with the Volunteer Review and Archers and Guards.

From the Crown Princess

In the evening I went to the play just for half-an-hour Moliere's old piece *Les Fourberies de Scapin* and just the very beginning of "Oedipus", but I was obliged to leave very soon to get to the electric exhibition which is only to be seen to advantage at night. The crowd was immense. I saw the Duchess of Manchester walking about there, also Lord Salisbury and his three sons. Our German Commissionaire took us about and of course one got rather pushed and squashed and trod upon. They have marvellous telephones and phonographs and many different specimens of lighting up by electricity. I am sure it is a most useful exhibition and at any rate very interesting.[1]

From the Crown Princess

[The Crown Princess is describing a ceremony which had taken place at Kiel.]

To me much was very painful at Kiel. For all speeches and toasts in which of course the greatest enthusiasm for the Emperor, Germany and Prussia was expressed no one mentioned poor Fritz's name. I own it jarred on my feelings. I am glad that Victoria escaped having to come. She was however always mentioned and there is no doubt that all parties in the Duchies sincerely rejoice in the marriage and are very kindly disposed towards Willie and Fritz and also I believe myself.

From the Queen

BALMORAL CASTLE, OCTOBER 25, 1881

I shall be very pleased that the old pictures at Buckingham Palace and Windsor should be photographed by this man Braun. Would you say that he should communicate with Sir Henry Ponsonby? I have also given directions that the Inspector of Police, Winkler, should remain.

You are rather severe on Charlotte. I don't consider myself "uneducated" and yet I could not live in churches, the frescos and galleries as you do.

From the Crown Princess

NEUES PALAIS, OCTOBER 27, 1881

Today the elections take place here and the people are more excited than I have ever seen them. Usually they are utterly indifferent. Alas! had they not been so we should not have an all-powerful Bismarck who is undermining everything. If he suc-

---

[1] The important international Electrical Exhibition in the Palais de l'Industrie. When the Crown Princess built Friedrichshof some ten years later it had beautiful electric light fittings.

ceeds in carrying out his plans Germany will one day be the prey of communism. I am much alarmed I assure you. The quiet, safe-going liberal party here in Germany are the only safeguard for the future but they are also the only ones who oppose in principle Prince B.'s mad schemes and therefore communists, ultramon-tanes and conservatives club together and go with him against the liberals. Who will gain the day I do know. Parliamentarism is only a shadow. The Press is weak and the government machinery is tremendously powerful and well-organised and in the hands of one man who does exactly what he pleases and who is bent on accumulating all the means in his power of carrying out his will. The Crown is simply a name, in reality nothing at all.

From the Crown Princess

NEUES PALAIS, NOVEMBER 5, 1881

I am very glad the German elections have returned so many liberals, and I hope it will show Prince Bismarck that the Germans are not all delighted with his government though I do not think he cares one bit. I wonder why he does not say straight out "as long as I live both the Constitution and the Crown are sus-pended" because that is the exact state of the matter.

No doubt he is quite patriotic and sincere, and thinks it for the good of Germany. He thinks a great central power is necessary, and that one will must decide, and the state be everything and do everything like one vast set of machinery—say the "Inflexible" for instance where the captain alone works everything by elec-tricity and directs the ship etc. So Prince Bismarck wishes, with the pressure of his little finger, to direct the whole and thinks it doubly necessary for safety's sake in case of being attacked by France or Russia.

I do not like this state of things but most Prussians and conser-vatives do, and our two sons think it perfection and every other country miserably governed.

From the Queen

BALMORAL CASTLE, NOVEMBER 8, 1881

I quite agree in what you say about that dreadful man—it is deplorable. No wonder you dislike Conservatives; but you would not if you lived here. Here they are the only security.

From the Crown Princess

As for a nurse I do not know and have not been consulted on the subject. William does not wish me to have anything to do with it, and has charged Lenchen with the arrangements! You can imagine that I am much hurt at this. Pray do not say anything to Lenchen about it as she is most kind and of course cannot help it if Willie wishes to consult her instead of me. Under these circumstances I do not mean to give the layette as I had intended. Dona seems very well and very happy and will go to Potsdam from the Marmor Palais on the 1st of December. I am sure she will be an excellent and devoted Mama as she is a wife. She is much beloved already. I only tell you this about their arrangements quite in confidence and I should not like it mentioned.

We had rather a fright the day before yesterday in the evening. The Emperor had taken too much ice at dinner the day before, and was a little disordered, and in consequence afterwards was taken with a fainting fit but it did not last long and he was all right afterwards and is quite well again now and able to do all as usual.

From the Queen

BALMORAL CASTLE, NOVEMBER 15, 1881

I can't tell you how shocked and grieved I am at Willie's behaviour—which I had heard of from Lenchen. I strongly advised her to refuse to have anything to do with it, nurse etc. as I do think it very wrong that she, your younger sister should be asked to do what you ought to have been consulted in. My sons did not [do] a thing about doctor, nurse or permanent nurse without consulting me; also dear Alice and Lenchen the first time.

From the Crown Princess

BERLIN, NOVEMBER 21, 1881

You will be glad to hear that for the last few days Willie has been much kinder and nicer and more respectful in his manner to me; I think because his Papa spoke to Victoria on the subject! But we have not spoken of any of Victoria's arrangements. Perhaps that will come!

From the Queen

Leopold wished to announce his engagement himself to you. Having failed several times, and fearing that his health would again deter the young princess from accepting him it was impossible to mention anything beforehand. I insisted that she should know everything about his health and that she should know what she undertook. And so she did and took some time to think over it before she decided. He saw her first in the summer and liked her very much. He thinks her very nice looking and she has the very highest character.[1]

From the Queen

WINDSOR CASTLE, NOVEMBER 23, 1881

Leopold seems very happy. To me his marrying at all is a grief, and a shock which I can't get over. But I am much pleased at his choice, for I have heard such very high and excellent character of her, and she seems to possess much character. I know you thought her plain but Leopold does not think so and nor do others who have seen her.

From the Queen

WINDSOR CASTLE, NOVEMBER 26, 1881

You say you can't be enthusiastic about Leopold's bride! I never can be about any marriage and can naturally be less about Leopold's than about any other for I think his marrying such a risk and experiment. But everyone (from different sides) spoke most highly of Helen Waldeck and her charming character, excellent education, solid, sterling qualities! Victoria and Ella like her very much.

From the Queen

WINDSOR CASTLE, NOVEMBER 29, 1881

As you expressed surprise at the whole affair and naturally do not know how it came to pass, I will tell you exactly what

---

[1] Princess Helen of Waldeck and Pyrmont (1861–1922).

happened. I had not given Princess Waldeck and her daughters a thought though I had frequently heard of them and there was no question of any particular person—as I told you—though Leopold was always very anxious to find a nice wife. But when Prince William of Würtemburg came to Osborne I asked him after his mother-in-law who I had seen in England in '60 and he said she was at Soden. It then suddenly struck me that Leopold being at Wolfsgarten and so close to Frankfurt and Soden might go and look at Princess Hélène having heard so much praise of Princess William and of the young Queen of the Netherlands. So I wrote to tell him and he went there but did not see them the first time; but went a second time to enquire in my name after the Princess Waldeck, and to express my regret at having missed seeing her daughter Princess William. He then wrote to me at Balmoral how much struck he was by Hélène (or rather Helen as she is generally called) and when he came back almost directly after repeated this and asked me to try and find out whether he might go and see more of her. This I did as well as everything about her character and told them also (what they wished to know) what Leopold's health was through a very safe, discreet person. This led to an agreement that they were to meet at Frankfurt and that both parties should be left free to judge if they liked one another and suited. They next took a few days to consider and then both taking a decided fancy to one another, which has since increased more and more, Leopold proposed and was accepted by her. It was entirely my own idea.

From the Crown Princess

BERLIN, DECEMBER 17, 1881

I don't know why Herbert Bismarck has been sent to London? Perhaps to see a little of the world, perhaps to make him forget Princess Caroletta—perhaps to be a spy on poor Münster who by some here is considered "too English" in his sympathies and feelings; perhaps Prince Bismarck wants his son's opinion on English affairs, or is it only for change of air, I do not know, but I do not envy the people at the Embassy. Lately Herbert has a little calmed down and toned down. Still the young tiger has much of the temper of the old one, and has done a vast deal of harm by exciting his father against people and by persecuting harmless individuals. It is extraordinary how much influence the sons have on their father.

From the Crown Princess

I wish you could see my room dearest Mama; I have made it as pretty as I can. It is not near so full of furniture, pictures and knick-knacks as those of my relations; and perhaps you wouldn't like the colour of the walls that are only distempered a soft sage green to show off my few good pictures (mostly old ones) and the curtains are only plain green merino.

I have matting on the floor and a few old oriental rugs on it. I love my room very much if it were not a passage for everyone— and had another look-out except the hideous dirty walls of the houses, and the unbearable noise didn't try my head so. I should never like to move out of it. If you had once sat in it and looked at all the things I should like it so much better still. I am sure you would admire the bits of old furniture I have picked up in Italy and here in Germany also at Paris. They give a look of comfort and soberness to the room which a smart, new thing never has. I have struck out as much of the ugly street as possible—by panes of old stained glass. I have some flowers. I dislike a crowded room and want plenty of room to move about.

1882

From the Crown Princess

Have you read the Emperor's Proclamation to his ministers? It reminds me of Charles X—and is a lamentable thing. People fancy Fritz has had something to do with it, whereas he first read it in the newspapers and was horrified at anything so useless and ill-advised being written. No one has any idea of how obstinate our dear Emperor is when he has an idea of this kind in his head. Altogether the present state of things in politics and at Court is as disagreeable for us as possible, and we honestly wish ourselves far away which you will understand.[1]

From the Crown Princess

Never have I seen matters worse. But in one respect there is comfort, the nation has waked up a little, and now perceives how its rights and liberties are being tampered with, and how mad the half-socialistic, half-absolutist and protectionist plans are Prince B. tries to carry, and by hook or by crook shielding himself behind the aged Emperor for whom there is such universal love and veneration.

As for Fritz's position—it gets more unbearable from day to day; his name is always dragged into the newspapers! In the public at large they do not know what to make of him—the liberals are staggered in their faith in him because it is spread on purpose that he is quite satisfied with Bismarck's nonsense—on the other hand the powerful party round the Emperor do everything they can to do us harm—both to Fritz and me and have made this Eulenburg[2]

---

[1] The Royal Rescript was signed by the Emperor, as King of Prussia, and countersigned by Bismarck. The part of the Rescript which caused comment was a passage to the effect that Government officials, by virtue of the Discipline Law, could be removed from their post "if they did not hold aloof, even at election, from all agitation against the Government".
[2] Count Eulenburg, a member of the Crown Prince's Court, was prevented by the Emperor from accepting the Embassy at The Hague.

affair in which they have had their fingers and they have triumphed in every way to our detriment. Sometimes I am so discouraged that I am weary of my existence altogether! The dear Emperor has gone over to Bismarck completely because he now wants peace with France; and the peace which he is now making is as inopportune as the war he made on the Catholics was unjust and unfair. However it is very trying to be able to speak no more to the Emperor on a subject we used always almost to agree on. Willie and Henry are quite devoted to the Bismarck policy and think it sublime so there we are—alone and sad. People say "Oh the Crown Prince would approve of everything that the Government do were it not for his English wife. It is she that wanted to get rid of Eulenburg" etc. I will not weary you with more; but I am quite worn out and if you hear I have the typhoid or am off my head pray do not be astonished.

From the Queen

WINDSOR CASTLE, FEBRUARY 27, 1882

As I may have no time to write tomorrow, I write these few lines to thank you for your dear letter of 25th and to answer Fritz's message.[1]

I have taken no part whatever in the matter beyond expressing much sympathy for the unfortunate Countess Noër in her affliction, who in addition to her great sorrow has most unexpectedly found her children's inheritance threatened and who cannot be expected not to take their part as you or any other widowed mother would do? My position prevents my taking any part in this unfortunate affair.

From the Queen

WINDSOR CASTLE, MARCH 6, 1882

I asked Lenchen to write to you for me as I literally spent the whole of Friday and likewise of Saturday merely in opening

---

[1] The letter has not survived. Prince Christian's uncle, Prince Frederick of Schleswig-Holstein, was created Prince of Noër by the Emperor of Austria. His son married Carmelite Eisenblat, a Venezuelan lady, and was then created Count of Noër by the German Emperor. He died in 1881 and, as his marriage was morganatic, the inheritance reverted presumably to the royal branch of the family.

telegrams of which 138 were received on the former day and 68 on the latter; and letters. Anything like the enthusiasm, loyalty, sympathy and affection shown me is not to be described. It is worth being shot at to see how much one is loved.[1]

I was not and am not the least alarmed. I never saw anything, but heard the report which I thought was an explosion of steam! And I only realised it when I saw the man (whose face I never saw) violently hustled and people running in all directions. Dear Beatrice, who showed great courage and calmness and never moved or said a word, saw it all. The wretched man is strange and wicked but not mad. He had fourteen bullets on him, and the act was clearly premeditated but not in any way political. The accounts in the papers are correct, only not that the carriage stopped. We drove straight to the Castle. I have been driving about since as usual and through the town and the people seem so pleased to see me. This morning I received an address from the Eton boys in the Quadrangle which was extremely well read by two of them, and I read a short answer. Nearly 900 came up and I saw the Maharajah's two boys. The oldest is such a nice, handsome boy.[2]

From the Queen

WINDSOR CASTLE, MARCH 7, 1882

R. Maclean is well born and has most respectable relations but has always been utterly worthless.[3]

From the Crown Princess

BERLIN, MARCH 25, 1882

Do you think, dear Mama, you could say a word about the Monte Carlo business to Lord Lyons? The gentleman to whom the villa belongs in which you are living is a member of the

---

[1] The Queen had been fired at as she was getting into her carriage at Windsor Station when she was returning from London.
[2] Dhuleep Singh.
[3] Variously called Roderick or Frederick. He was tried at Reading Assizes on April 19, and found not guilty of attempting to assassinate the Queen as being insane.

committee.[1] The Hereditary Prince of Monaco—who is so far better than the Duchess of Hamilton and her daughter made him out to be—hates the gambling, and they say he would stop it directly if he were the reigning Prince. If Lord Lyons could only drop a word to M. de Freycinet to the intent that you took an interest in the question (if such a thing be possible) it might cause the French Government to look a little closer into the affair.

The closing of Baden-Baden, Wiesbaden and Homburg has been such a success (so much more ground has been bought and built upon since the horrid gaming tables have disappeared.) Were they still there you never could have stayed at the Villa Hohenlohe so infested was the whole neighbourhood with the worst society. Neither Uncle Ernest, Bertie, Christian nor Alfred share my views I know but that one cannot help. One must have spent some time at the Riviera to have a notion of the harm Monte Carlo does.

From the Queen

CHALET DES ROSIERS, MENTONE, APRIL 11, 1882

To me the idea of poor Leopold's marrying in a fortnight and a half—still a complete invalid—not able to walk yet—is terrible. It is a sad exhibition and I fear everyone must be shocked at it and blame me! I pity her but she seems only to think of him with love and affection.[2]

From the Queen

WINDSOR CASTLE, APRIL 19, 1882

This day week we were at lovely Mentone which we miss sadly—the bright sunshine and the sea, mountains, vegetation and lightness of the air and the brightness and gaiety of everything. Still it is at least a month more forward here than usual. The lilacs are out in blossom and chestnuts blooming away, all the thorns in leaf; many oaks out even—and the primroses still out. I sent a wreath of them to place on the grave of my dear and even more

---

[1] At Mentone. The Prince of Monaco had granted a concession for gambling at Monte Carlo for 50 years from 1861. The concession passed into the hands of a joint-stock company of which presumably the owner of the villa was a member. In her letter of March 29 the Queen says that she spoke of it to Lord Lyons but he was "afraid that actual meddling with it will not do".
[2] He was staying at the hotel at Mentone, and slipped on some orange peel.

missed and regretted friend Lord Beaconsfield today—the first anniversary of his death. I sent them to him in his dear lifetime as they were his favourite flowers.

Oh! were he only here now to try and put order into the frightful misrule of the present people which is really appalling. Murder upon murder in Ireland and no one getting any rents. As an instance I send you this deplorable account from Lord Kenmare (my Lord Chamberlain) once a rich man, a Liberal and Roman Catholic and a most popular, kind-hearted man who lived so much there at beautiful Killarney and who was so kind to his people. Pray show it to Fritz for I think you are under the happy illusion that the state is not as frightful as it is. Open rebellion would be far better.

From the Queen

WINDSOR CASTLE, APRIL 29, 1882

[The Queen is describing Prince Leopold's wedding.[1]]

Truly glad would I have been to have seen you here, dearest child, as you may well believe—but I could not have lodged you, and every single corner was full; not a mouse could have been put in. And then as I naturally wished to give the Waldecks the *pas*—above all other princes and princesses (the King and Queen of the Netherlands excepted) I felt it might not do, as I knew how very particular they are at Berlin about these things.

She answered so plainly and distinctly much louder than he did—that it was heard all through the Chapel. The King of the Netherlands is as quiet and unobtrusive as possible; a totally altered man and all owing to her. She[2] is charming, so amiable, kind, friendly and cheerful. She would be very pretty were it not for her complexion which has suffered very much from the damp climate and is very red. The little sister of Helen is a darling and such a handsome child.

---

[1] He married Princess Helen of Waldeck-Pyrmont on April 27 in St. George's Chapel at Windsor. The bride's elder sister had lately married the King of the Netherlands on whom—in spite of earlier criticism by the Queen—the Garter was conferred. The youngest sister, Elizabeth, was 7.
[2] Queen Emma of the Netherlands.

From the Queen

Oh! but I can think of nothing but this unexampled horror of what has just happened in Ireland, which fills everyone's mind and one can think of nothing, nothing else. Horrible, awful beyond belief! The daring, the atrocity of it all no words can describe! And this coming on top of that fatal Act of Release! Surrender to rebels! And Mr Gladstone's eyes are not yet opened. It is too dreadful.[1]

Poor, poor Lucy—she behaves so beautifully and bravely. She was able to see his poor face—which was unaltered and peaceful when the remains arrived yesterday.

From the Crown Princess

We are much upset by the news that the whole of the splendid International Hygienic Exhibition at Berlin, which was to be opened next week in great state, is burned to the ground. I fear the loss and disappointment will be very great.

The wind was so tremendous yesterday that it is no wonder the fire could not be kept under. Fritz was busy writing his speech for the opening. The Emperor takes great interest in the undertaking, I had set great hopes on the lectures to be held for the people!

From the Queen

I saw Mr Gladstone yesterday; greatly shaken—and seemingly despondent and as if his energy was gone; very pale. I of course spoke of the necessity of strengthening measures—but also how fatal I thought the step of letting the suspects out was, before a stringent measure had been passed. He defended himself but, when I said I knew Mr Burke (one of the victims) had been of the same opinion and greatly deprecated it, it seemed to shake him and he said the catastrophe had certainly followed very rapidly.

---

[1] The Chief Secretary, Lord Frederick Cavendish, and the Under-Secretary, Mr. Burke, were stabbed to death while walking in Phoenix Park. Lord Frederick had married Lucy Lyttelton. On May 2, four days before the murder, Parnell, Dillon and O'Kelly were released from Kilmainham Gaol.

People however begin to feel that the many and many other poor people who were murdered were comparatively unavenged till a Lord and a relation were killed.[1] There is much truth in this alas!—at the same time the alarm of course is caused by the daringness of the act—killing a member of the Government and as it were under the windows of the Lord Lieutenant.

From the Crown Princess

NEUES PALAIS, JUNE 6, 1882

I do not know whether you have ever heard of a scheme of a railway through the Euphrates valley to the Persian Gulf from Aleppo etc. Could this be realised it would more than compensate for what we must lose in Egypt; and would completely baffle Russian progress in the East. Of course this scheme could only be carried out unofficially and without the help of government but it would be a grand thing worthy of England.

The Russians could have no more influence over the Shah of Persia—and the Black Sea would not become a Russian lake, and we should not be balked in all we did by having to work with a French ally—as we now have at Cairo. Lord Stratford de Redcliffe liked the scheme. Might I send you a pamphlet on the subject? Should there be a chance of carrying it out by a private company the less it is discussed in public or talked of the better.[2]

From the Queen

BALMORAL CASTLE, JUNE 9, 1882

Don't you think a little too much fuss is made about this great grandchild of the Emperor? Only our own children and Bertie's eldest son were christened *en grande tenue* in uniform and *grandes toilettes.* All my other grandchildren in England were christened in the morning at Windsor and Buckingham Palace and Bertie's girls at Marlborough House, no uniform mere morning dress. And I think too much fuss is unnecessary.

---

[1] Lady Frederick Cavendish was Mrs. Gladstone's niece.
[2] The germ of the Baghdad Railway which was built and largely financed by the German Government at the beginning of the Twentieth Century.

From the Crown Princess

I send you a very ugly but amusing photo of the Emperor, Fritz, Willie and Baby, four generations together on one picture. I cannot write on politics today but I am anxious to do so soon. I am much distressed at England allowing the wind to be taken out of her sails by Germany—in Turkey and in Egypt; it was so unnecessary and if the Germans instead of the English make the Euphrates valley railway—it will be as sad and bad a mistake as allowing the French to take part in the Egyptian affairs. I wonder neither Lord Derby nor Lord Granville saw that. We English have an interest in the East and not the French and Germans.

From the Queen

BALMORAL CASTLE, JUNE 13, 1882

I can understand your anxiety and annoyance about Egypt. Dear Lord Beaconsfield foresaw it, as he did all pertaining to the honour, and power and dignity of Great Britain, and had he been at the head of affairs all, that was wise and right, would have been done. But since this most unsuccessful and unlucky government came in all this has been let go and I know from my own Ambassadors and Ministers abroad we are neither trusted or respected or minded. You may imagine what my feelings of bitter anguish and indignation are, the more so as I warn constantly—but it is of no use whatsoever. Lord Granville would I think do what is right had he strength of character—but he is very weak and much aged, and Mr Gladstone don't care for foreign affairs or the power of England beyond Europe at all. Lord Derby you must remember is totally incapable for foreign affairs. Do nothing—keep out of everything—and shut yourself up. That is his cotton-spinning creed. And he takes no part.

From the Crown Princess

NEUES PALAIS, JUNE 17, 1882

We are much disappointed that Willie and Dona call the baby William instead of Fritz after the two grandfathers; we thought they might have done that.

From the Queen

How absurd of Willie and Dona to call the child William. As they have not told me, when I write to Dona to thank her for her letter and some of the child's hair I shall say "Of course you will call him Fritz after his two Grandpapas", and shall see what they answer.

From the Queen

You will rejoice at the success of the bombardment which was inevitable though one regrets the loss of life of innocent people deeply. But the wickedness of Arabi—as well as his insolence had to be put down and it is well that at last we should show that we are in earnest. It is curious and interesting as being the first time that our Ironclads and new ships have been tested.[1]

From the Queen

We are entirely engrossed with Egypt and the preparations for the expedition to be sent out. Alas! my darling Arthur is going and it quite upsets me. The doctors pronounced him fit to go and so he is right to go—but it is a new and terrible anxiety in my old age and one which I feel very deeply. You have gone through that and therefore can feel for me and Louischen. In a fortnight they go.

From the Crown Princess

I always forget to mention the sale of the Duke of Hamilton's works of art which I think such a pity; but the best and most valuable part of his possessions is going to be sold soon; it is his

---

[1] The bombardment of Alexandria took place on July 11 from battleships under the command of Sir Beauchamp Seymour. The forts returned the fire, and several ships were hit, but none disabled. The leader of the Egyptian nationalists was Arabi Pasha and it was clear that there could be no settlement while he was at large. The Gladstone Cabinet decided to send in an army which destroyed the power of Arabi at Tel-el-Kebir in September.

library—he has some books that are quite unique—amongst or rather before all others—a manuscript copy of Dante all illustrated in 88 pages by Sandro Botticelli. This extraordinary treasure ought not to leave England. The Berlin Museum would like to buy the whole collection for £88,000 if the parliament will vote the money.[1] I must say I think it a shame that England should be spoiled of such a treasure and I do not understand the British Museum and the Bodleian Library at Oxford not making an arrangement with the Duke of Hamilton, and his not having the right patriotism to offer his treasures to our own national collections before foreigners treat with him for them. The French missals and miniatures of the fifteenth and sixteenth centuries are said to be exquisite. Perhaps Mr Robinson knows them and could tell you, if he were caused to get accurate information on the subject. I know there ought to be no delay as the sale will be before long. I could not help drawing your attention to this. It will be the same soon with the Duke of Marlborough's pictures and library, it is said though I do not know for certain. If our great English families are obliged to sell their unique collections at least I think, if possible, the nation ought to secure them. Mr Gladstone as a lover of art and learning, would I am sure—even from a financial point of view—think money well invested that is spent on increasing the art collections of the nation. The day will come when these things can no longer be had and all is readily snapped up by the new collections of America and the Continent.

From the Queen

OSBORNE, JULY 31, 1882

Mr Robinson has been constantly looking out for pictures and things at the Sale and I have bought a very fine original full-length portrait of Edward VI by one of Holbein's best pupils. The National Gallery have bought several very fine things. I have also got another small drawing after Raphael of St George and the Dragon which had Charles I's mark on it. Other things I wished to have went too high.

---

[1] The Hamilton sale was held in June and July and included the famous collections formed by William Beckford, great-grandfather of the then Duke of Hamilton. The sale was held at Christie's and realised over £400,000.

From the Crown Princess

Many many thanks for your dear letter of the 9th. You know how pleased I always am to receive one, but I should be quite distressed if you tired your eyes, tired yourself or took up your time by writing to me when you have so much else to think of. We are also very thankful for the details from the newspapers. What a good thing that Turkey has given in, and declared Arabi a rebel. This will surely make everything much easier. I am so glad that correspondent of the Daily Telegraph has been dismissed, it was really too bad to calumniate our poor men. It was taken up with such glee by the German press—so glad to pick any holes they can find in us and all our doings.

From the Queen

OSBORNE, AUGUST 15, 1882

I yesterday received Ceteywayo (Ketchwayo) and the interview went off very well. He is a very fine-looking man, who has a pleasant, intelligent countenance and dignified bearing and seems very intelligent. The three chiefs who came with him and who all commanded squadrons at Isandhlwana, Kambula and Ulundi are not good-looking though all tall; and of course the hideous European frock-coats, boots and trousers spoiled their appearance terribly. They all wore that peculiar ring round their heads which denotes their being married. They don't bow—but saluted in Zulu fashion using a word which I can't remember and raising up their right arm above their head. Nothing political passed.

From the Crown Princess

BAVENO, AUGUST 18, 1882

The day before yesterday we went to a place called Macugnaga at the foot of the Monte Rosa. The scenery is too glorious—and the air lovely as pure and not as cold as in the Engadine, and the Val d'Anzasca is far finer than the Engadine valley; the vegetation is so beautiful. We were up at 6,000 feet. We spent the night in a primitive hotel there and came back yesterday evening. We went most of the way on foot, on mules, and carried in chairs. We left the house in the morning at 5 o'clock.

From the Queen

I send you here two more copies of letters of dear Arthur to me. They were all before the great victory of Tel-el-Kebir—followed so rapidly as it was by the occupation of Cairo, and the capture of Arabi is most satisfactory. May we only not be foolish afterwards.

But oh! the dreadful blow that has fallen upon us since.[1] The dear, excellent Dean after only a very short illness. The loss is quite irreparable, overwhelming! I don't know what I shall do. He was of such enormous use—in every possible way, smoothed all difficulties, was so devoted, so sympathetic—loved all of you and your children so much. He did everything on all sad and happy occasions to make me comfortable. In short no more serious blow almost could have happened and gloomy Windsor will be quite unbearable. The last of that group of dear old devoted friends gone—Sir C. Phipps began it—then General Grey and Countess Blücher, Sir James,[2] dear Augusta,[3] Lady Car,[4] Sir Thomas Biddulph and now the Dean; for the little Dean[5] though publicly a far greater loss—was not one of our own Household and knew us much later though he was so valued but the two both gone and also Canon Pearson seems far far too much. I feel quite crushed by it.

From the Crown Princess

We are much pleased to see Rudolf and Stephanie. She has grown up into such a tall, handsome creature, with a splendid figure, loads of fair hair, a complexion like milk and roses, lips like coral and such an· intelligent expression. She is very lively and wonderfully well-informed and wise for her age reminding me of her poor dear Aunt Charlotte. She seems as gay and happy as one can be and so much in love with Rudolf. She strikes everyone very much and her beauty is set off by magnificent *toilettes*.

---

[1] Death of the Dean of Windsor (Gerald Valerian Wellesley) who had been Dean since 1864.
[2] Clark—the Queen's doctor.
[3] Lady Augusta Stanley.
[4] Lady Caroline Barrington.
[5] Of Westminster.

From the Queen

Yesterday evening we heard of the triumphal entry of the Khedive into Cairo which must have been most striking—streets lined with British troops. As to what will be done or rather how it is to be done for I think even Mr Gladstone (who has no strong sense of the dignity and power of England abroad) and most of the other Ministers feel that we must (short of annexation) have a firm stronghold over Egypt. A large force will have to be left there.

How charming Olga of Greece is, so handsome and so dear and charming. She has none of the brusquerie of the rest of the Russian family even including our dear, excellent Marie.

From the Crown Princess

May I refer once more to the sale of the Duke of Hamilton's library—and that precious illustration of Dante by Botticelli? I heard yesterday that it was again offered to the German (Berlin) Museum authorities in a lump; and the auction which was to have taken place in October or November will not come off I suppose! I cannot reconcile myself to the idea of this unique treasure leaving England for good—without even an attempt to secure it, how it will be regretted in later years. I fear there is a great hurry about it and that they are communicating by telegraph so I hope no time will be lost—in case it is to be bought for the British Museum. They boast here of having the finest collections of England over here in a few years! I own I should be very sorry.

From the Queen

Dear Arthur in a letter to Louischen received yesterday says he hopes no fuss will be made with him; though his Brigade was harder worked and endured more privations they had less fighting (which was no one but the enemy's fault who fled on two occasions when they came out) than the others. I know other near relations, who shall be nameless, who would have blown their own trumpets instead.[1]

From the Crown Princess

I am very glad to hear about the Botticelli manuscript and the other lovely and valuable Italian manuscripts. There is only a very limited number of these beautiful and interesting things in the world. New museums spring up every day, consequently new bidders in the market, and in America any money is given for treasures of that kind, which seem to me to be best placed in the British Museum. That is why I ventured to speak.[2]

From the Crown Princess

NEUES PALAIS, OCTOBER 17, 1882

We have had a disagreeable accident. My bed caught fire and was burnt a good deal—it might have been very bad as the fire had caught the hangings on the walls and this old house is like tinder! Luckily the servants managed to put it out with much '*dégat*' to my things. We spent the night on two sofas in different rooms. I am very busy for tomorrow we are going to give a ball—and to light the courtyard with electric light.

From the Crown Princess

NEUES PALAIS, OCTOBER 26, 1882

I hear to my great distress that the Hamilton library with the Botticelli manuscript and the seven other unique Italian missals have been bought from the Duke of Hamilton by the German government. Therefore these art treasures, which have for some

---

[1] Probably the Duke of Connaught's father-in-law, Fritz Carl, was one.
[2] The Queen wrote on October 10: "I also enclose you what Mr Gladstone says about the Dante. Please return it. So you will see it is not overlooked."

Mr. Gladstone was a well-known admirer of Dante: "I never look at Dante unless I can have a great continuous draught of him." But evidently nothing could be done, and it was announced at the end of October that the Prussian Government had secured the greatest part of the Hamilton collection of manuscripts.

years been in England, are now lost to the British nation which I cannot but regret bitterly.

When I first wrote from Meran there was still time for the British Museum to buy them; now it is too late. I can only hope now that the British Museum did not really want them or care for them because it would be too grievous that another government should have taken a treasure out of our country which we wanted at home. I think the Duke of Hamilton (if I am not wronging him) has been most unpatriotic in offering these treasures to a foreign government without knowing whether the British nation wished to possess them or not.[1]

From the Queen

BALMORAL CASTLE, OCTOBER 27, 1882

Colonel Ewart who commanded the Household Cavalry and who is a very admirable officer and such a modest, nice person, came here yesterday and stays till tomorrow and I gave his health and that of the officers and men of the Household Brigade. He has much that is interesting to tell. The discomforts and sufferings—short as the whole campaign was—are sad to hear and I am shocked and grieved to say that the medical arrangements were very defective. The rapid movement of course was in part the cause of this—but there was neglect on board some of the ships, which is quite disgraceful.

Netley is very full and I shall go there as soon as I can. They are very comfortable and most kindly nursed and looked after there. But I grieve to say—every three or four days someone dies; chiefly from dysentery and fever.

From the Queen

WINDSOR CASTLE, NOVEMBER 18, 1882

I think much of today—so unclouded and bright—so full of emotions. It was a great pleasure to have you there with me,[2] and I am sure this proud day for my heart will never be forgotten.

---

[1] The thirteenth Duke, 1845-95. He was a great, red-faced boxing Duke described by *Truth* as "unweighted by any sense of responsibility and beset by all the deadly sins".

[2] The Crown Princess was in England for the return of the troops from Egypt, who were reviewed by the Queen in St. James's Park.

One almost grieved that like everything in this world it should be past.

My heart was in my mouth as my darling Arthur rode past at the head of the brave men he led into action—and looking so like darling, beloved Papa. It was almost overpowering.

From the Queen

Everything went off admirably yesterday. The day was very fine and bright though very cold. The sight was very gay and pretty with all the different uniforms the Indians, the bands and the Guards. I gave away 330 medals pinning on a good many on the officers and men and giving the others into their hands. My speech I got through without hesitation but it was a very nervous thing.[1]

From the Queen

As regards the print collection begun by my dear grandfather who even in times of the greatest difficulty political and financial did all he could to have this precious collection. Then dear Papa and Uncle Ernest took the greatest pains to add to and improve it—and finally dear Papa took especial care that it should be so tied up that should Ernest wish to sell the various collections he could not do so. Knowing this you may well imagine my horror and indignation when Bertie showed me (being suspicious) Affie's letter. Though I expect we know all the details and also that there is no security whatever that the money would not be used for the very worst purposes the principal agnatics have refused consent and so it cannot be touched.

Uncle E. should make some necessary reductions and then it would all right itself.

As regards his memoirs I think it monstrous to insinuate what he does and if he does anything to throw a wrong light on beloved Papa I shall be obliged to publish letters he will not like. It would be well he should know this.

---

[1] The Queen was conferring medals on officers and men for the campaign in Egypt.

From the Queen

I am to have Sir C. Dilke in the Cabinet—a bitter pill—but as he has expressed regret for his faults and will (as I have insisted) express this publicly and, as he will not be brought in personal contact with me, I cannot avoid it.[1] Mr Dodson (a respectable elderly man who looks like a shopkeeper) will become Chancellor of the Duchy of Lancaster and Sir C. Dilke succeed him as President of the Local Board. They come tomorrow to a Council.

From the Queen

The end of a year is always rather tragic and the older one grows the fewer new ones one can expect to see, the more serious it becomes. But one can only trust and pray that He, who has ever protected us and ordered all for the best, will continue to guide us and help us. This past one has been—after the dreadful one of '61—the most eventful of my life, as it took one (and almost the dearest one of all my children) into the dangers of a war and brought him out gloriously and safely. These feelings will ever, ever be engraven on my grateful heart.

---

[1] In the 1870's he had attacked the Monarchy and questioned whether it was worth the cost. In an elaborate republican speech he criticised the Queen. Gladstone was faced with the hard task of persuading the Queen to agree to Dilke's inclusion in the Cabinet. He recorded in his diary "Audience of Her Majesty at 3. Most difficult ground, but aided by her beautiful manners, we got over it better than might have been expected." Speaking to his constituents in Chelsea Dilke said that when first he represented them he was between 23 and 24 and was perhaps at that time rather scatter-brained.

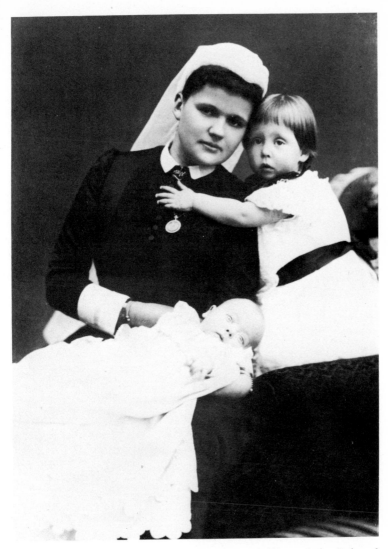

The Duchess of Albany with her children, Princess Alice and the Duke of
Albany, December 1884.

(Left to right) Grand Duke and Grand Duchess Serge of Russia, Prince and Princess Louis of Battenberg and the Grand Duke of Hesse, March 1884.

1883

OSBORNE, JANUARY 3, 1883

Two striking and shocking events ushered in the New Year—
one the hour before—poor Count Wimpfen's suicide and the
other five minutes before—the death of that clever but (I must
always think) bad, disreputable and totally unbelieving man
Gambetta. What will the effect be? I think to prevent war—
though no doubt he was friendly to England. It is not a bad thing
for his friend (a pleasant Cabinet Minister) Sir C. Dilke. You are
such an extraordinary Radical that you even appear a republican
at heart; and accept a man, who I fear, is not to be trusted entering
the Government![1] You would be cured of this if you lived here.
Abroad where there is great tyranny it may be very different.

From the Queen

OSBORNE, JANUARY 10, 1883

Now let me soothe your feelings of injustice about my "little
hit" at your being a Radical. I will yield to none in true liberalism, but republicanism and destructiveness are no true liberalism.
Where is there greater tyranny and greater oppression of religious thought and sects than in France? You say you are a pro-
gressist. Right and well—when fundamental landmarks are not
abolished and swept away, and every good thing changed for
change's sake, and that unfortunately has become the doctrine of
people like Mr. Chamberlain, Sir C. Dilke, Mr. Courtney, and
Mr. Gladstone himself as well as a good many others. Mr. Gladstone has helped to roll the stone downhill—instead of guiding
and checking it. There is the danger. If you lived here and saw and
understood all that goes on you would see that these so-called, but
not really "liberal" ideas are very mischievous.
The new Archbishop-designate—for he won't be Archbishop

---

[1] The meaning of the Queen is perhaps not clear. Dilke was a close personal
friend of Gambetta, to whom as Prime Minister of France public opinion in
England was unfavourable. The Queen means that his death (considering how
he was viewed in England) might be no bad thing for Dilke.

for another two months—came here yesterday and I was charmed with him; so agreeable—so kindly—sensible—so humble and yet with such right views—and very large-minded and charitable; his presence too—is all that can be wished; a fine, intellectual, benevolent face.[1]

You will have seen Affie and Marie; the former is not very well and very dull and depressed and rather morose in company, which distresses poor dear Marie very much.

From the Queen

What a terrible cloud has burst over the bright festivities of your dear silver wedding day! It is too sad and so unexpected! Or did you suspect any danger? I conclude that the *fêtes will take* place in a month's time. The disappointment of the Country would be too great were not this so, and the whole given up. Nothing more unfortunate could happen and the fact of his being so bad a man makes it all more dreadful.[2]

From the Crown Princess

The disappointment and confusion created by poor Prince Charles's death on the eve of a festive occasion cannot be described. A cold from which he was too weak to recover, put an end to his existence quite peacefully. The Emperor and Empress and little Fritz Leopold were present. When Fritz and I arrived—it was just over. All his Household had been most attentive and devoted to him, and were all in tears yesterday. His gentlemen, doctors and servants behaved exceedingly well.

The Emperor is deeply affected. It is his last brother and they were very intimate as you know from childhood upwards. Poor Prince Charles looked peaceful enough; and in death one forgets all that else was difficult to get over. He was most patient all through his illness.

Our Silver Wedding is now indeed quite spoiled! Of course there can be no *fête* of any kind until the end of February, and of course most of our guests will stay away. The people in the town

---

[1] E. W. Benson, Archbishop of Canterbury.
[2] The death of Prince Charles on January 21.

and from the provinces are sadly disappointed and it is very sad in every way.

From the Queen

Louischen was much upset at her grandfather's death; she said he was very kind to her and her sisters and mother. Is this so? What is the Will? Of course the Landgravine Anne will again try to get all she can.

From the Crown Princess

BERLIN, JANUARY 26, 1883

You ask about Prince Charles's Will. I do not know anything official still I suppose my information is correct. He has left all his places—Glienicke etc. to Fritz Carl and has left nine millions of marks, four to Fritz Carl, three to his daughters, one to the Order of St John and one in small legacies. His art treasures he offers for sale to the Crown. If the Crown does not take them, to the State and the money to go to Fritz Carl. The grandchildren are not mentioned. He was always very kind to Marianne, his daughters and his grandchildren (of the latter he was very fond).

We had no religious ceremony. Our Silver Wedding was mentioned a week before and Sunday last in all the churches of the Country (Catholic and Protestant).

From the Queen

OSBORNE, JANUARY 27, 1883

The dear 25th was a very fine day. I planted the tree in a nice place and Henry Hunt was there who said you planted your first tree in '46!! Therefore 37 years ago. Your picture in the dining room had a beautiful wreath of evergreen and laurestinus round it and it looked lovely. Ernest L.[1] came in the afternoon and joined our dinner; Jane Churchill who is delighted with your present—the Sydneys, Ponsonbys—Mary Biddulph—Mr. Sahl to represent Germany, J. Ely, Sir John Cowell and Captain Bigge dined with us and the others came in the evening. But the band had to be put

---

[1] Leiningen.

off. We drank your health and it was drunk by all the house; yesterday my servants had a dinner in "the hall" in honour of the occasion.

From the Queen

Is it not extraordinary of the Emperor and Empress to give a banquet (private though it is called) within a week after the former's own brother's death? I think it quite shocking! But it is always so I know. Was not poor old Prince Charles a very wicked man? Very immoral and besides were there not some mysterious disappearances of people set to his account? Fritz don't conceal his horror of him. You did hint years ago that your children would not be safe with him.

From the Queen

Poor old Prince Charles he seems regretted by no one except the poor.

From the Queen

Though I am not an admirer of babies—I must say this[1] is a beautiful child, so plump and so big with such neat little features and such a complete head of dark hair.

From the Crown Princess

You will have heard that there was some little disagreeableness here—between Louis and the Baden family. I will not touch upon it because it is no business of mine. I only think that they were a little hard on Louis, and I felt very sorry for him. I hope all feeling of annoyance will soon pass off on all sides.[2]

---

[1] Princess Alice, Countess of Athlone, daughter of Prince Leopold.
[2] The Baden family had hoped that the Hereditary Prince of Baden could marry the daughter of the Grand Duke of Hesse (Louis). Their hopes were not fulfilled. The Hereditary Prince's mother was the daughter of the German Emperor and Empress.

From the Queen

Your account of the affair about Ella is just mine who know all from Louis who deeply regrets it.[1] But it is most unjust to accuse Louis of want of openness. The only chance was to wait—instead of which Louise and Fritz[2] hurried it on, and Louis could not in justice to his child help telling her that others had wished to marry her—when she declared she would not accept poor Fritz of B. junior. Perhaps he did not make himself agreeable or make his wishes very evident? A Russian marriage would be very painful to me and it is not wished by Louis, anyhow none is to be wished for at present. I can't do anything about Irene. I am sure that would not either be likely.

Bertie is returned greatly pleased to have been to Mr. Boehm's today and saw the two monuments of our two beloved friends—the two Deans. They are beautiful and so like. But it is most sad to see and feel that they are gone on to our real homes.

From the Queen

The terrible blow which has fallen so unexpectedly on me—and has crushed me—by tearing away from me not only the most devoted, faithful, intelligent and confidential servant and attendant who lived and, I may say (as he overworked himself) died for me—but my dearest best friend has so shaken me—still quite helpless as I am—prevented my writing on Wednesday last.[3] I missed Saturday the 17th on which day I meant to with my accident; and then on Wednesday the 23rd I was not able to write much—nor on Saturday as my day was so disarranged—and on Sunday again, when my dear, faithful friend's illness began to cause us great alarm—I was incapable of writing almost.

He had an attack of the same horrid erysipelas at Baveno four years ago but got over it in six days, just about the same time of

---

[1] Her possible engagement to the son of the Grand Duke of Baden.
[2] The Grand Duchess and the Grand Duke.
[3] John Brown died on March 27. The Queen was suffering from the effects of a bad fall.

year, and then we thought it was a sting which caused it—and it is an illness people are often so very ill with that, though very anxious, we were never at all hopeless; he took plenty of nourishment and it never spread to the scalp. On Tuesday we were so much happier about him and Sir William Jenner who knew him well and is never over-sanguine or ever misleads you told me that evening at 10 o'clock I need not be so much alarmed, that his pulse was better and he took plenty of nourishment and the eruption had not spread! An hour after, all was over in his sleep! The shock—the blow, the blank, the constant missing at every turn of the one strong, powerful reliable arm and head almost stunned me and I am truly overwhelmed.

The sympathy is universal—the appreciation of his noble, grand and yet simple nature—true and great—which is soothing. To be tied to my chair, not able to go and see after him while he was ill or go about now from one chair to another even, has greatly added to the cruel suffering and sorrow.

It is such a shock to see strength and support—promising to last at least one's lifetime—struck down; and to be left powerless, helpless. And this time again when all leant on him I, gentlemen and servants and they knew I was safe when he was with me. God's Will be done but I shall never be the same again in many things.

From the Crown Princess

BERLIN, APRIL 4, 1883

I am thinking so much of you with the most loving sympathy as I am sure you are sad and worried and depressed and miss one who has served you faithfully for many years! You must excuse if my letter is incoherent, but I am half wild with a neuralgia in my forehead and eye the consequence of a violent influenza.

From the Crown Princess

BERLIN, APRIL 6, 1883

Indeed it was most kind of you to write to me. Indeed I did not at all expect it, but you need not fear to worry me with speaking of what is uppermost in your mind! You know how deep my sympathy is with all that suffer and that mourn, how much greater with my own dear Mama! I grieve so much to think of you depressed and cast down and sore in heart. I wish I could do anything to cheer you and help you or be of any use to you at a moment when you feel the want of comfort and affection. I have read all the articles you mention and can well imagine that they gave you pleasure, giving evidence as they did of kindly feeling.

From the Queen

WINDSOR CASTLE, APRIL 8, 1883

I am crushed by the violence of this unexpected blow which was such a shock—the reopening of old wounds and the infliction of a new very deep one. There is no rebound left to recover from it and the one who since '64 had helped to cheer me, to smooth, ease and facilitate everything for my daily comfort and who was my dearest best friend to whom I could speak quite openly is not here to help me out of it! I feel so stunned and bewildered and this anguish that comes over me like a wave every now and then through the day or at night is terrible! He protected me so, was so powerful and strong—that I felt so safe! And now all, all is gone in this world and all seems unhinged again in thousands of ways!—I feel so discouraged that it requires a terrible effort to bear up at all against it.

From the Crown Princess

BERLIN, APRIL 11, 1883

I am so very sorry for you to think of the *abattement* you are still in and which of course cannot so quickly disappear, and must often come over you at times with double force in spite of the endeavour to rise superior to it. I am sure dearest Beatrice must be a great comfort to you.

From the Crown Princess

BERLIN, APRIL 15, 1883

I am so distressed that your leg is still so weak and that you cannot stand yet. It must be doubly trying for you just now! When you are at Osborne I suppose you will have a can of half-warm sea water poured over it every morning. It is supposed to be wonderful both after sprains and for rheumatism.

From the Crown Princess

We left Berlin as you know on the 23rd had a cold journey to Munich and found it cold there. We spent a day there and then went on to Trento. The top of the Brenner was covered with deep snow and it snowed all the time. Trento was mild and agreeable. It is such a beauty spot. Anything so sad as the terrible destruction that has been wrought by the inundations I never saw! The lovely fruitful valleys—where there were orchards, kitchen gardens and vineyards—are buried in a mass of mud, sand and stones—walls—roads—banks all broken and destroyed. It is a grievous sight, but worse far in the beautiful, wild glen between Trento and Bassano through which we drove in a carriage—the houses in some of the villages are literally cut in two by the force of the flood and the boulders which were carried along. A place that has been bombarded or destroyed by the eruption of a volcano or an earthquake could not be more utterly wretched. The Val Sugana through which we drove is too beautiful, wild and magnificent. I wish you could see it. We passed a night at Bassano which is beautifully situated, and then visited the curious old towns of Castelfranco and Treviso on our way here. We were reminded of Napoleon's march and battles in these places. We went to see a house called the Villa Mazer. It is celebrated for its frescoes and its history as having been built for an ancient Venetian family. But it is much spoiled and modernised.

From the Queen

Our kind, good Dean Connor who had been somewhat ailing since the beginning of the year—but seriously unwell since the last two months—got very rapidly worse and as it were faded away, and expired this morning! It is too dreadfully sad and a great loss to us all. He was an old, true, kind, tender-hearted friend, and just when he settled in the Deanery not three months ago he has been taken. Windsor is indeed a tomb to me! All my greatest sorrows have taken place there!

From the Queen

Little Alice is not like anyone in particular at present. What I do know is that she is a very fine as well as a very pretty child with enormous blue eyes—which we hope will be brown—and is dark. She is a particularly good child.

My going over to Venice or travelling much in future is I think very problematical. I must get much stronger and better before I can think of that. Venice would not, at any rate excepting just for a day or two, ever have suited me for I can't take long walks or go much sightseeing and rather dislike going on the water and most particularly living on board. So you see that that would not do. My knee makes very little progress, and I am very rheumatic. I am generally weak and much shaken. My troubles and sorrows I know well I must bear alone.

Good Dean Connor's death is most sad in every way. I have just been seeing his very amiable daughter. I have appointed in his stead the son-in-law and right hand of the late Archbishop as well as the right hand of the present one (Chaplain and Secretary) Mr. Davidson, a young man of 34—but full of experience and knowledge of men—most sensible and agreeable, with excellent judgement, and singularly kind and sympathetic which is what I want so much. He is charming and I hear she is most agreeable too.

From the Crown Princess

HOTEL GRAND BRETAGNE, FLORENCE, MAY 14, 1883

Because I say little on the subject it is not that I do not constantly think of you and feel the greatest distress at your being sad etc. "The heart knoweth its own bitterness". Since knowing as I do that this is so and that I can say nothing to cheer or comfort you I almost think it is a better proof of sympathy and affection to be silent.

Amongst the people I know and have met here are—Sir James Hudson, Sir James Lacaita, the Duc de Dino—M. Morelli, Mr Robinson, Mr Malcolm and Mr Mitchell. My friend Marie Dönhoff and her charming Mama are expected this evening.

From the Crown Princess

I am staying here for a very few days to see the "Salon", do a little shopping and go to Mr Evans, not a pleasure for poor Vicky—who is in great want of having her teeth put right. The air does seem so heavy after Italy and the light of Portofino and Baveno made even a Paris sky look dull.

From the Crown Princess

NEUES PALAIS, JUNE 2, 1883

All seems to have gone off well at the Coronation but I fear the state of Russia is not more reassuring notwithstanding! The Emperor does not seem to intend granting a constitution, and the people are sighing for the simplest form of liberty—and this gives nihilism its strength. It would have died out long ago whereas now it is kept up by the discontent of the well-meaning and sensible fraction of society.

From the Queen

BALMORAL CASTLE, JUNE 11, 1883

That book[1] of Uncle E.'s must be stopped for if he contradicts what Sir T. Martin wrote we will contradict him and bring forward proofs. If you would speak in my name to Hermann as I have neither time or bodily strength to undertake all these things and you and Hermann could do it so well in my name.

I never told you that Willie painted me a plate representing part of the bombardment of Alexandria and wrote very kindly about it all. But I must copy the ending of his letter as it is too funny. "I spent a short and delightful time at Prague where I saw the Crown Prince and whom I found in high spirits on account of the approaching happy event which shall enlarge his Household".

From the Queen

BALMORAL CASTLE, JUNE 12, 1883

You had not heard of good Lord Rokeby's death. Poor Lily Wellesley's cup is very full. It is an awful sweep of everything.

---

[1] Presumably his memoirs, published in 1888, on which he was working at this time.

She is exceptionally unselfish and in her grief spoke so kindly of me and made one very true observation which is "We can hide ourselves away in our grief, but you never can therefore it is so far harder".[1] I have always felt this in all sorrows and trials! I sit on "such a cold pinnacle".

From the Queen

Though I told the Duchess of Roxburgh to write I write a line to say I hope to hear from you that something has been done to stop Uncle Ernest's book. As you so truly say in your last letter of the 9th he will only do himself more harm than he has already done—and I fear the scandal at Gotha is beyond everything. It is too awful—dear Aunt is really very much to blame in all this.

From the Crown Princess

NEUES PALAIS, JUNE 20, 1883

I can quite understand that not feeling well etc. you should not wish for visitors and not be able to receive us this year. We would not be in your way for the world. Our two little ones are going to Bournemouth while we are at the manoeuvres this autumn, because the doctor wishes it, and all other coasts nearby are too cold at that time. Should circumstances allow I was thinking of joining them and perhaps paying Bertie a visit but of course that would in no way interfere with you—and I hope you would not object to that! I should feel it very much indeed if that annoyed you.

From the Queen

WINDSOR CASTLE, JUNE 25, 1883

You are, I see, pleased at the engagement of Victoria of H. with Louis Battenberg. I thought she would not have married at all—nor would she if she had to leave her poor father (as she said) but as she will not have to do that I am so glad she has found a person, kind, good and clever and whom she knows thoroughly well. Of course people who care only for "great matches" will not like it.

---

1 The widow of Gerald Wellesley, Dean of Windsor, was the daughter of the last Lord Rokeby. Her husband, son and father had all recently died. (See *A Scrap Screen* by Alice Buchan, Hamish Hamilton, 1979.)

But they do not make happiness and Louis says they will be quite comfortable.

I cannot give a good report of myself at all; my leg improves but I feel weak and exhausted and dreadfully sad on returning here. I could not well have little Feo here as I am unfit for anything and require quiet as much as possible.

Though I asked Lenchen some time ago to tell you that as alas! everything was so changed and my plans uncertain I should no longer be able to carry out my intention of receiving you at Balmoral this autumn, I think it but fair to yourself to tell you so myself. I grieve to have to disappoint you but I must ask you to postpone any visit to Scotland or England to another year, as it would be most painful to me to know you are over here and be totally unable to receive you which alas! I am.

From the Queen

WINDSOR CASTLE, JUNE 30, 1883

I am very sorry indeed to be obliged to repeat what I said in my last letter viz. that I must ask you to postpone any visit to England this year to another year. I must ask it out of consideration to myself, and beg you not to propose paying a visit to Bertie this year, as to know you with him and not to receive you myself would be most painful to me, besides causing remarks to be made from which I have suffered before. Nothing but the very shaken state of my nerves and health would have made me write this to you, dearest child, and ask you to give up coming here. I shall indeed be disappointed if I find that you do not agree to make that sacrifice for my sake. I am much grieved to have to say all this but think it best to prevent all misunderstanding.

From the Crown Princess

NEUES PALAIS, JULY 3, 1883

Here the newspapers have as usual found an opportunity for abusing England in which the public heartily join—i.e. the cholera in Egypt which is attributed to British selfishness and will, it is said, spread to Europe through England's fault.

As regards my coming for the autumn your letter leaves me no alternative—and I will say nothing more—though you will understand that I feel much hurt.

P.S. I send you three pamphlets showing Mr E. Cazalet's scheme for the Euphrates Valley Railway and I hope, dearest Mama, you will be able to look at them. It seems to me an excellent idea and I trust will some day be taken up as a national interest. At present it would not even be good—if government were to take it up it might rouse the attention and awake the jealousy of other Powers.

The scheme is an old one as you know—has been put forward and dropped and modified again and again, and never been carried out.

Lord Stratford de Redcliffe took an interest in it, Mr Layard has ideas of his own on the subject (that has nothing to do with Mr Cazalet's plan) but the idea is mainly the same. It seems to be like M. de Lesseps idea of the Suez Canal—a thing that would be very useful in future in spite of all the doubts that can be raised. At any rate it is well worth your attention. Then I was going to observe that so much is spoken now about armaments here in Germany. English troops are supposed to be badly armed on old-fashioned principles much inferior to the Germans. A new rifle has now been invented here on the principle of a "revolver" said to beat everything yet known. It has been invented by Mauser who already invented the newest improvement.

Fritz is going to see a trial on Saturday. 600 have been distributed and Fritz is to see a battalion use it. It is no business of mine, but should not Uncle George find it worth his while to enquire into it—one does not like hearing that the British troops are at such a disadvantage on account of their firearms.

Pray excuse my mentioning this and please burn this postscript of mine directly. I must also add that our huge guns on board the ironclads are supposed to be inferior to the Germans because they are shorter and consequently cannot have so long a range.

For all the money England spends on these things and the great perfection to which so many of their arrangements are carried we ought to have the best guns on our ships I think. I suppose all these technical specialities are well known at the Admiralty and War Office and that I am only telling a very old story.

From the Queen

WINDSOR CASTLE, JULY 18, 1883
[Princess Beatrice was going to Aix-les-Bains for treatment for rheumatism.]

Her absence is of course a great trial to me as for 22 years she has only been absent for 10 days once.

I don't know if I told you that Miss Pitt (who is forty) is going to be married to a sedate clergyman a widower, with seven children; a worthy man but I think she would have done just as well without him and I am very sorry to lose her. She is succeeded by Lady Southampton's second daughter a nice girl only too tall. Wally Paget's daughter makes what the world calls a great "*parti*", for Lord Windsor is immensely rich. He is a relation of Lord Bridport's and a nephew of Lord Bradford.

From the Queen

WINDSOR CASTLE, JULY 23, 1883
Many affectionate thanks for so kindly sending me little Fritz Wilhelm's photograph which is very nice. What a very extraordinary name Eitel is. Not pretty. I like fine old names like Sigismund, Waldemar, Adalbert also Ferdinand. Why choose such an ugly one I wonder.

From the Crown Princess

NEUES PALAIS, JULY 28, 1883
What I wanted to say about Russia was this; the old idea of the Russians possessing themselves of Constantinople is by no means abandoned, what has been the definite policy of Russia for 200 years continues to be so still, though the present Emperor has said it was not opportune to pursue it hotly or openly now, the time would come when that would be easier. The Russians wish to keep a firm hold on Bulgaria for this reason, and to prevent this State from developing itself independently or its ruler from establishing himself well and having a secure position. They use him merely as a mask to conceal the fact that they wish to govern Bulgaria and reign supreme there which they are striving to do by every means of intrigue in their power—using the Greek religion for a means etc. They will throw off that mask at the moment which is the most convenient to themselves and push on to Constantinople whenever there is a good opportunity.

To be anti-Russian in principle is absurd and unjust, but to remember Russian interests and English interests in the East are and must be antagonistic, is a fact never for a moment to be forgotten. The more the Russians are closely watched the more readily the danger of having to resist them by force can be avoided. Fritz imagines you know all this in England better than we do here, still the great advance Russia is striving to make in the East often makes us anxious. They have the Shah of Persia completely in their power; they are massing large forces on the Persian frontier. They will never invade India, but they will succeed—if not prevented—in persuading all the inhabitants of the surrounding countries that the Czar is the greatest Power in the world. They are half savages themselves and they know how to get round the people of the East. They may spread this belief in India and any dissatisfaction may make the Indians ready to listen to the voice of so cunning a charmer, and what a danger that would be!! Fritz thinks that if England, Austria, Italy and Germany could combine to help and support Bulgaria and watch that she be the real barrier to the Russian progress towards Constantinople it would be the best policy; also that Bulgaria should try to be on as good a footing as possible with the Turks—as they have to a certain degree the same interests.

Here it is believed that the Russians will shortly be in Asia Minor and that they mean to take as much of it as they can, and much wonder is felt at England allowing quite quietly what is so much against her interests. Of course all this is nothing new and British statesmen have no doubt given it thought and attention but to us the danger seems very evident. I for my part am dreadfully sorry that England has lost all influence over the Sultan as it might have been used to such good account! At present the Germans are the only ones trusted in Constantinople as they are supposed to be the only disinterested friends. Bulgaria must extend and grow—in time— and [I am] sure the Turk aided, guided and protected by England ought to be in Asia Minor and not the Russians who will try to diminish British influence everywhere in the East.

How does it stand with the Euphrates Valley railway scheme? Poor Mr E. Cazalet who had taken it up so warmly is dead, I am sorry to say.

Good-bye dearest, beloved Mama, hoping my letter will not bore you too much.

From the Queen

I had a long visit from Tennyson yesterday with which I was much pleased, and he was so very kind to me and felt for me. His is a great and good mind. But he thinks the world darkened and I can't deny it is—though I have faith it will come right.[1]

From the Queen

In my last letter I forgot to say how amused I had been at your selling fruit and flowers and Vicky cigarettes. Did this not shock the natives?[2]

From the Queen

I am indeed greatly shocked and grieved at the good English nurse being sent away—and the German one taken instead (by Willie and Dona). About these sorts of things my children never were obstinate and I think it very wrong and very foolish in two young people to pretend to know anything about the management of young children. One must depend so much upon one's nurse. Lenchen is very indignant and Christian too.

From the Queen

The heat is intense since Saturday, and tires me very much. I am however getting on and I hope "Charlotte"[3] whom Beatrice swears by will finish the rest.

---

[1] Tennyson spoke despairingly of the irreligion and socialism pervading modern life. In reply the Queen quoted from "In Memoriam": "Oh yet we trust that somehow good will be the final goal of ill". *Tennyson* by R. B. Martin, Clarendon Press and Faber, 1980.

[2] This was a fancy fair held in aid of various Potsdam charities on July 24. Writing to her mother on July 19 the Crown Princess says, "the children are going to appear in peasant costume and to sell flowers in stalls". On July 25 she says, "William had charge of the fireworks and we gave the supper. It was great fun for the young people, who only regretted no time was left for dancing...."

[3] A masseuse.

(Children in ascending order) Princesses Marie, Alexandra and Victoria Melita of Edinburgh. (Left to right) the Duchess of Edinburgh, Queen Victoria, Princess Victoria of Prussia, the Crown Princess of Germany, Princess Beatrice, September 1884.

Queen Victoria with (left to right) Princess Victoria of Wales, Princess Victoria of Prussia, Princess Victoria Melita of Edinburgh, and the Crown Princess, September 1884.

From the Queen

I have told Victoria to tell her dear Papa all—and also all about Sandro's waiting. As regards Bulgaria we know that the Russians are behaving shamefully. I heard from Lord Granville who maintains Sandro is not popular which I cannot entirely believe—Louis B(attenberg) said they were indifferent. Lord G. further says "If Germany and Austria were willing to make representations in order to carry out the spirit of the Treaty of Berlin as regards the independence from foreign influence of the small states, Lord G. will be ready at once to propose to Mr. Gladstone and the Cabinet to join in such representations". Now can't you and Fritz get the Great Man who forced Sandro to accept—to do something of the kind? I am sure if Germany and Austria are ready to do this we should at once join. Do try.

From the Queen

"Charlotte" is a regular trained masseuse and doucheuse—by the real good Drs. (as there are 2 very clever ones at Aix) who does everything most carefully—and though fatiguing I feel what good it will do. She is such a nice, homely person—very clever and with a thorough knowledge of anatomy—nerves etc. and yet a simple French *paysanne* with a nice white cap and apron, which she walks out in, knitting. She is a widow about 44 or 45 I should say, and is so kind and zealous. "Ma bonne Majesté" she always calls me. She must have been very handsome.

From the Queen

I fear young Charles of Portugal will be far too lively for me. That is what I cannot stand at all now. Pedro and Louis were a great deal too much for me even formerly and dear Papa had to restrain them. My spirits have become more and more unable to bear noise and high spirits of young people.

Mr Gladstone's journey well deserves blame. But can you imagine that he is so ignorant of what is going on that he never knew till the pilot told him when they were on the way to Copenhagen that the Emperor of Russia was there? He trusts

Russia, hates Austria and don't like Germany. Republican France and Italy are all he cares for. I should think the last exhibition in France must have somewhat disenchanted him. I share your anxiety about politics in general and especially with such a very dangerous unaccountable man as the "Grand Old Man" is, as our Premier.[1]

From the Queen

BALMORAL CASTLE, OCTOBER 30, 1883

Let me now say a word upon the projected visit to Spain.[2] That this should take place by and by I think quite right and natural, but just now in such a hurry will I think not be of use to the King of S., and put him in a worse position still with France, for the whole will then look really like a political act. Forgive my saying this but I do hope for the very sake of that peace which Fritz is so anxious for it may be delayed.

Uncle E.'s conduct is perfectly monstrous and I must blame Aunt very much. They have not written to me yet—but when they do I shall have to write very strongly.

I was not aware that Louis had yet mentioned to you my possibly going to Darmstadt for dear Victoria's marriage. It must depend on how I am and if my lameness does not improve I fear I hardly could go. Anyhow it would for many reasons be a painful and great effort; but it is merely as the poor dear children have no mother and have been so much for that very reason like my own that I ever thought of coming at all. But I look on it as a duty! For all such ceremonies are most painful to me. I am anxious it should not be spoken of at present.

---

[1] Mr. Gladstone was on a cruise to the Western Isles in the *Pembroke Castle* as the guest of the owner, Sir Donald Currie. Tennyson was among the guests and urged that they should cross the North Sea for Denmark. They arrived at Copenhagen where there was a great family party with the King and Queen. After a dinner at Fredensborg, the Emperor, Queens and Princes visited the *Pembroke Castle* and Mr. Gladstone proposed the health of the Emperor after he had proposed the health of the Queen. After luncheon the "senior imperial and royal personages", as Gladstone called them, crowded in a small cabin to hear Tennyson read two of his poems. The story of the voyage and of the Queen's vexation is in *Gladstone* by Sir Philip Magnus, John Murray, 1954.
[2] By the Crown Prince. The King of Spain, visiting Paris on his way back from Berlin, had been very badly received, so that the French President had to make a public apology. The Crown Prince in fact went to Spain, and stayed for a fortnight in Madrid.

From the Crown Princess

One hears the affair at Coburg much talked about. Many people, while admitting all we know, regret that the Ball was given. It is so difficult to defend poor Uncle Ernest, who is his own enemy, still I always think that the family must not show up his faults and stand by him as much as they can as alas! through his extraordinary ways, he has so few friends.

Anyhow it is most disagreeable for Alfred, and Coburg society, that for once all sides against Uncle Ernest (by his own fault), will I am sure be delighted. You have always been so kind and generous and forgiving to Uncle Ernest, and even in dear Papa's lifetime always tried to smooth over difficulties and shield him from the consequences of many an imprudent word or act, that I am sure he will listen to what you say. The whole thing is most painful.

From the Queen

BALMORAL CASTLE, NOVEMBER 6, 1883

It is very trying to be able to walk so very little out of doors; ten minutes or a quarter of an hour is the outside I can do but the colder weather does me good. You never will take in, how infirm and shaken I still am. I think as you don't wish to believe it you won't, and never allude to it!

About Uncle Ernest it is most grievous but really this could not be avoided; Affie and Marie had to do something and the antecedents of these two ladies (?)[1] are so bad that they are cut by everyone; and for Affie to give up his Ball would never have done. Society are very thankful to him for his firmness. As my name has never been brought into the dispute I have as yet done nothing. If I write I must do so very strongly.

I am very sorry about the Spanish journey. It is a mistake I do think. Why unnecessarily irritate France which is in such a state?

From the Crown Princess

NEUES PALAIS, NOVEMBER 16, 1883

I should be wretched if I thought you fancied I had not enough

---

[1] The question-mark is the Queen's. Presumably the Duke and Duchess of Edinburgh refused to ask the Duke of Coburg's ladies to the Ball.

sympathy about your health. I wonder to whom your health, life and happiness could be more precious than they are to me but I am the one always away, I never have a chance hardly of showing all the love and devotion I feel! And letters can say so little. There is not a day I do not think of you and how you are getting on, and wish I could be of some use in restoring you to your former strength and activity; which I so anxiously and fervently hope will return in time. It is just a year now since I last saw you.

Would you believe that William has never taken any notice of us since the 29th of September? Not a line, a message or a telegram, and simply forgot to take leave of me when he left for Austria on that day. That I should feel hurt is not extraordinary.

From the Queen

WINDSOR CASTLE, NOVEMBER 21, 1883

I don't for one instant doubt your love and affection and interest in me, for I know your warm, loving heart, but I only wish you to know and understand that I really am much shaken and unfit for exertion, before we meet D.V. at Darmstadt, a great, great trial for me and one which I still must look on as uncertain. I consider it however a duty.

From the Queen

WINDSOR CASTLE, NOVEMBER 28, 1883

Our troops were never going to leave Egypt altogether, but merely Cairo and a certain number to leave and the rest to go to Alexandria and elsewhere. Sir E. Wood told me and everyone that he said before (for now everyone says all must remain at Cairo) our troops might leave Cairo but—if Egypt was to be for the Egyptians 3,000 British troops must remain for an indefinite period—and for very long—or the French and Italians would take possession, and I am also very strongly of this opinion.

Little Alice was also here and is a dear, very merry, healthy, little thing; the eyes (fine large ones with black lashes) are becoming quite brown which is what I so much wished—as since the Stuarts we have had no brown eyes in the family.

From the Crown Princess

The dear little children[1] must be a great pleasure to you, and to see the nice tidy nursery with the excellent nurse at the head, and the children so well cared for and prettily dressed. All that is spoiled now at the Marmor Palace; it will be very trying to see it all in that condition and not be allowed to say a word—but what can I do? Victoria says the children are hers and she will do what she likes with them and will not be interfered with. This is all quite fair—only she does not do as she likes but as Countess Brockdorff likes. You will remember how we were interfered with, how the Emperor always stopped the journeys that were arranged, how I was not allowed to take Willie over to England in 1859. We should never dream of interfering with William and Victoria in that way, and forbidding them from taking their children with them on a visit. In fact we let them do exactly what they please; but the consequence is, alas! that they quite ignore and forget our existence and think it unnecessary to take any notice of us, and always ask the Emperor and Empress about everything, take all their orders direct from there, and we are not even informed of what they mean to do, or consulted. Countess Brockdorff writes to take the Empress's orders through her ladies; Willie goes daily to his Grandpapa for all he wants and cuts his Papa, because it is a great deal more convenient for them but for us it is most painful and disagreeable. Please keep this to yourself, dearest Mama. I am not complaining of them but, our life and position which never was easy at Berlin has only become more difficult and more complicated in consequence, and I dread going back there very much.

From the Crown Princess

May I send you this little pamphlet?[2] Of course you will have

---

[1] The Duke of Connaught's children who, with Prince Leopold's daughter, were staying at Windsor.
[2] This concerned the housing of the working-classes in London. The Queen said in a letter to Gladstone: "She can not but think that there are questions of less importance than this, which are under discussion, and might wait till one involving the very existence of thousands—nay millions had been fully considered by the Government." (See *Letters of Queen Victoria*, Second series, Vol 3, page 452.)

had it already. Should you not have seen it do cast a glance over the sad and dismal pages. How much good it would do if the people knew you wished everything to be done to change and improve this state of things. Can you not order a special inquiry to be made, a special report to be drawn up for you! Surely Sir H. Ponsonby must have heard a great deal about it lately.

I can imagine how dear Papa would have taken it up—and stirred people up and put his shoulder to the wheel as he always did. I am so glad this question is being discussed in all the papers. One ought not to let it rest! The "19th Century" is full of interesting though intensely painful articles on the subject. May the attention and energies of everyone who means well, is rich, or has influence, be roused in this good cause, and things not be left another day in the state they are in now. I hope my feeling so strongly may plead as an excuse for touching on the subject at all. I feel that if you and Bertie came forward and insisted on knowing what is going to be done it would do so much good.

From the Queen

WINDSOR CASTLE, DECEMBER 5, 1883

Now let me answer you shortly (but Sir Henry [Ponsonby] shall write fully to you) about the "Bitter Cry of London". I have seen it and read some of the letters in the D. Telegraph, which are in fact the same [as the pamphlet], and at once wrote strongly to Mr. Gladstone about it who communicated with Sir William Harcourt and Sir C. Dilke; and everything is being very fully enquired into with a view to seeing what can be done to remedy the evil which however is not worse now than it has been, and is exaggerated in this pamphlet. But it is the horrid middle men who make profit out of these poor wretched creatures. I also talked to Sir R. Cross about it who is thoroughly conversant with the subject and who has done a good-deal in the way of building houses. I also spoke to Sir C. Dilke (for the first time) about it last week. Sir Henry shall write to you what is being done.

I think dear Alice's short "Life" will be very useful and I think much would not have been known had it not been published. I only lent extracts from my letters otherwise I have had nothing to do with it but I think Lenchen has done it with great refinement and feeling.

You don't touch upon Ella's engagement. I was told it was to be a secret and then some were told who let it out. It is a real sorrow to me and the less I say about it the better.[1]

From the Queen

WINDSOR CASTLE, DECEMBER 12, 1883

The news from Egypt causes much anxiety. I see Fritz is going to Rome! They seem to order him far too much about. Italy seems to be a second home. I expect you will settle there some day.

You will I think be pleased at my wonderful success at the Cattle Show. I have carried all the best prizes. I am especially glad for young Tait who had so suddenly to succeed his excellent father a year and seven months ago—but the whole was saddened by the feeling that the two who would have cared and rejoiced the most were not here to enjoy it. How many bitter drops there are in life! What "stabs", what trials, which no one can know, one silently suffers. What an inner life is lived—next to the outer one—which no one but God knows besides ourselves.

The stupid calumnies about Carlos's reception have all been contradicted and disputed but it annoyed him very much. He came on Monday and took leave yesterday. I like him very much and so do we all. What you say about Serge is a little bit of comfort to me but I can't get over it—for these poor children have been like my own since their darling mother's death, and I feel like an old hen when her ducklings go on the water.

From the Crown Princess

BERLIN, DECEMBER 15, 1883

I can quite well picture your feelings to myself about Ella's marriage—Serge will captivate you when you know him I am sure. There is something quiet and gentle, in fact rather melancholy about him, and his appearance and manners have something high bred and *distingué* which one misses in some of his brothers.

Fritz was more than astonished, "struck all of a heap" and "flabbergasted" as the servants would say, at being sent to Rome and I think the Emperor no less. It was decreed by Jupiter—from

---

[1] Her engagement to the Grand Duke Serge of Russia.

the Olympian Heights. I do not quite see or know why. Fritz
wanted to be allowed to go to Lisbon, but it was not permitted.

From the Crown Princess

I am much relieved to think that things in Bulgaria are doing
better, and I only hope that Fritz may be disposed to overcome his
repugnance to the idea, and that if he does, his parents and Prince
Bismarck may not be too adverse to poor Vicky's wishes. She has
not yet dared to speak to her Papa again, nor have I said anything
more. Letting a thing rest often does good.

1884

From the Queen

I do always pray for strength, patience and courage to "fight on", for life does become sadder and sadder and harder. And there are many breakers ahead to make one very anxious; India, Egypt (very serious) Ireland and difficulties at home all enough to make everyone anxious. I was pleased and touched by all you say to me about my trials and difficulties and sorrows.

I send you today a private copy of my book—which will be published in about a month with only a very few curtailments.[1] It will I hope interest you both and I will send Fritz a copy also if he likes.

From the Queen

OSBORNE, JANUARY 5, 1884

I also omitted in my last letter saying that I was very glad to hear that Elizabeth of Hesse is going to make a good marriage as the poor thing is not happy,[2] but I regret that you have not got him *en réserve* for Vicky if her fond hopes cannot be realised. Perhaps they may.

From the Crown Princess

BERLIN, JANUARY 8, 1884

Indeed the nihilistic murder at Petersburg is too dreadful.[3] Alas! the Emperor does nothing to satisfy the just demands for reforms and more liberty, and for changes etc.—not one wise concession to public opinion and modern times has been made. The King of Italy and King of Spain understand their times and their countries

---

[1] *More Leaves From The Journal Of A Life in the Highlands 1862–82.*
[2] Elizabeth of Hesse-Cassel, granddaughter of Prince Charles of Prussia. On May 26, 1884, she married the Hereditary Prince of Anhalt-Dessau. He died in 1886.
[3] Colonel Soudaikin, the energetic head of the Secret Police, was drinking tea with his nephew, in a house on the Nevsky Prospect. Both men were killed by Nihilists.

better. This does not excuse this hideous nihilism and its desperate deeds—but it does swell their ranks with disappointed and unhappy people who despair of seeing things amended by lawful means.

I feel very much for the Russian people who are by nature so quiet and good natured and suffer from an awful regime of corruption, tyranny and iniquity of all kinds. The Emperor is a kind, well-meaning and honest man but I should think not intelligent and large-minded enough to grasp the situation and rise superior to all the bad advice that is given him; he is indolent by nature and does not like a change, and then I suppose he is very obstinate and so angered by all the horrible deeds that have been committed that he will not make anything like a concession even there, where they are most necessary and harmless. How curious it is that the Russians have always money at their disposal for intrigues, that Nelidov at Constantinople is an arch-intriguer, and bribes the pashas with any amount of money and has most of them in his pocket. He means very ill towards poor Sandro. I wish Louis knew that and could tell his brother. I believe Bulgaria to be in a better state even now than Russia is.

From the Queen

That murder in St Petersburg is awful and the people are not caught and it took place quite near the Anitchkoff Palace.[1] It is madness not to do something to terrify the people.

The Sudan and Egypt affairs cause me great anxiety. We don't do what we ought. Lord Granville is become so indolent and don't answer telegrams and despatches which is terrible for those who are employed.

From the Queen

As regards the Pagets[2] I don't think either at all suited for

---

[1] The Palace was on the Nevsky Prospect and was the official residence of the Empress Dowager.
[2] Sir Augustus and his wife Walpurga. He was Ambassador in Rome 1876–83. He was then Ambassador in Vienna 1884–93.

Vienna and I hear she is not likely to be well or cordially received. This is most unfortunate. He suffers from his liver and is not prepossessing or clever. He is not my choice. I am also struck with the mistake of removing the good Elliots[1] who I saw here last month who I think far superior. He has not been well-used by his party and feels it. Sir J. Lumley[2] was in despair at the "36 naked little boys and girls" that Wally has painted all over the Embassy at Rome—and even the looking glasses! He means to cover them up as else he could not hang his many very fine pictures.

From the Crown Princess

Of course I have read the continuation of your Scotch Diary, and not without profound regret at having been so many years absent from Balmoral and unable to share any of your recollections of the last twenty years in that dear place of which you describe the charms so well.

From the Queen

Les beaux ésprits se rencontrent. I had already just written to ask the Empress if I could pass a few hours (not a night as for that I would not be fit—being unable to sleep in any strange bed; I send my own to Darmstadt). And she is so delighted with the idea that she said she could not speak of it for fear it should not be realised. The Emperor I did not mention, though I of course should be delighted to see him, but I should like to be able to be alone with my dear friend after not having seen her for so long.

I am still very cripply—I can't stand except for a few minutes. I can walk for a short while out of doors—and go upstairs alone if I have a good rail to take hold of—but my own servant must always lead me downstairs and support me in getting in and out of the carriage.

From the Queen

We (thank God) not I for I have warned and warned and wrote

---

[1] Sir Henry Elliot, Ambassador in Vienna 1877-84. A strong Liberal.
[2] Sir John Savile Lumley, first Lord Savile, Ambassador in Rome 1883-8.

and cyphered without end for months, that is the Government have bungled and blundered and delayed—as I grieve to say they have everything from the time they came into office.

Mr Gladstone cares little for and understands still less foreign affairs. He is a great optimist and thinks all is doing well. Lord Granville is absolutely *passé* and *baissé* and neglects things (not answering them even) in a dreadful way. Lord Hartington is very idle and hates business! And so on. God knows what is to happen next.

We see Uncle Ernest has been with you at Berlin or at least he has been to Berlin. He can't wash himself white.

From the Queen

OSBORNE, FEBRUARY 7, 1884

As regards Sandro, when I heard from Lord Dufferin he told me that the greatest security for Sandro would be in keeping on good terms with the Sultan who is now very favourably disposed towards him and especially in small things—to avoid irritating him by any show of independence. I know this question of the Orders is one on which the Sultan is tenacious and Sandro did himself no good by offering them, at any rate at present.[1]

From the Queen

OSBORNE, FEBRUARY 18, 1884

I send two letters asking you to send them on to poor Mariechen. I do hope she may be free from her dreadful husband.[2] If you have not ordered the picture don't do so as I really think he has been so brutal to his poor wife.

From the Queen

WINDSOR CASTLE, FEBRUARY 20, 1884

You have written me a very political letter of the 16th but I can

---

[1] In 1883 Prince Alexander had been awarded by the Sultan the Osmanje in Diamonds, but the Sultan made it clear that he did not wish Alexander to form a Bulgarian Order. Nevertheless Alexander went ahead with his plans and founded an Order.
[2] Prince Fritz Carl.

well understand your anxiety.[1] I will try and answer some of your questions though affairs have advanced and do advance so as to be changed before you get my letter. Affie's squadron is not going to the Red Sea—but is in the Mediterranean ready when required.

We have a first-rate and most energetic, brave and clever man in Sir William Hewett who I know well.[2] General Gordon is a most extraordinary man and certainly has a wonderful power over these half savages. He writes full of confidence for Khartoum. Troops being sent to Suakim and Tokar.

Though I know it don't interest you much, it will still gratify you to hear that the enthusiasm and affectionate sympathy with which my book has been received is most touching and gratifying. There have been some 30 or 40 different articles—really beautifully written. So many from the country—county papers— such an appreciation of all I have gone through.

From the Queen

WINDSOR CASTLE, FEBRUARY 25, 1884

I must write you a line to say how delighted we were to see dear Henry again; my particular child looking well though thin, though no wonder; they had such an awful (really dangerous) passage back.[3] Thank God! they were spared—for there have been so many shipwrecks. He is as dear, simple and affectionate as ever, very fond of his profession but delighted to come home. Count von Seckendorff is as amiable and kind and handsome as ever and gives the very best report of dear Henry, how well he does his duty and how good he is. You must be very grateful for this and for having such an excellent man about him to whom Henry is so much attached.

---

[1] Once again suggesting that the British should annex Egypt. The Queen was shocked when the Crown Princess first suggested this. "It would be a most greedy action." (See *Darling Child*, page 256.)
[2] Admiral Sir William Hewett, V.C. After the defeat of the Egyptians at Tel-el-Kebir in 1882, the Admiral landed with a force of seamen and marines for the defence of Suakim.
[3] Prince Henry's cruise on the *Olga* lasted for two years and on the way home the ship nearly foundered in a violent storm.

From the Queen

Affairs in the Sudan are of course a great anxiety and trouble, and one waits anxiously almost hourly for news. Two more battalions are sent off from here but as usual everything is done in a desperate hurry and without forethought or pre-arrangement. It is distracting I can assure you. No pleasure to be at the head, and in spite of warning and writing, cyphering and speaking to see nothing done till the pistol is pointed at their breast. Never was there such shortsightedness such want of profiting by experience. Mr Gladstone is not now a bit troubled by the state of affairs, or the least about Merv.[1]

I must just say one word in answer to your very affectionate observations with regard to my book.[2] I have been nearly 45 years on the throne, I have always been fully aware of what I was doing—and know perfectly well what my people like and appreciate and that is "home life" and simplicity. I know the good, the great good it did in '68[3] and now again. The articles of all shades have expressed a kind sympathy and appreciation which very rarely falls to the lot of anyone during their lifetime. It is for others—and to show my affection for and gratitude towards those who history would perhaps not think of mentioning—as well as to describe habits and customs which are not known, that I have wished to publish these extracts. But secondly and certainly not least of all—people write about anything now and the amount of false reports, accounts and "lives" is such that it is not only better but absolutely necessary to give the truth simply and only as much as is thought desirable. This is now believed and known—and the false biographies and lives (endless ones have been published of me) then fall into the background and vanish altogether. Let me now hope and trust—that you will understand this and trust me, with 45 years experience in future; for it is very painful when there is universal satisfaction that my own children do not share it.

Never mind about Fritz Carl's picture. It is a very fine one and I shall always be glad to have it. I need not hang them[4] up together.

Let Lenchen see this letter as I can't write to her. So much—

---

[1] An important town in Afghanistan occupied by the Russians.
[2] Seemingly this letter has not survived.
[3] The year when the first volume was published.
[4] Husband and wife.

alas! since my terrible loss falls upon me that I feel quite overdone and overworked and ill—and the amount of writing is as they say at Balmoral "just terrible".

From the Queen

We are very anxious today—as the battle between my brave troops and these savage, fanatical Arabs will [be]—and is probably—taking place. It is always a cause of intense anxiety when anything of this kind takes place and one knows it beforehand. Really it would be far better not.

From the Queen

The second great but very bloody victory of Tumassi[1] (I write it wrong I think) was most brilliant and has I trust done good but I fear we have not yet crushed the spirit of these wild, but splendid fanatics. I feel very anxious about General Gordon. The Government said they trusted him implicitly and must support him— and yet in spite of repeated, earnest demands for *what* (viz: the sending of Zobehr[2] to Khartoum) he, backed by Sir E. Baring— considered as absolutely necessary—has been refused.

I know there were great difficulties but what were they in comparison to the refusal of what the man they sent out with full powers said was absolutely necessary to be done? He asked again and again and Sir E. Baring used the very strongest language, and I said everything in the world I could, to urge it but in vain. And I tremble for the result.

I am glad to hear Serge speaks so nicely of me. I think we shall get on very well, though he is a Russian and carries off my grandchild, which I always felt about my sons-in-law and my own daughters. But he looks so thin and delicate in his photographs that I am quite alarmed at it. It's a very thoughtful, nice countenance.

---

[1] Tamassi, where General Graham won a hard-fought battle against Osman Digna fighting on behalf of the Mahdi.
[2] Or Zebehr Pasha, a slave-trader, appointed Governor of the Sudan by the Khedive.

From the Queen

I have just seen Lieut. Lloyd (younger brother of Mr C. Lloyd) who brought me the flag taken at Tokar[1] and which Sir G. Graham has sent to me. He also showed me a shield and a spear, the former a strong round thing of buffalo hide just like what is represented in the illustrated papers. The spear which is dreadfully sharp is very like the assegai of the Zulus only longer and larger and sharper. Lieut. Lloyd says he was in the Zulu War and says these men are not near such fine men as to physique as the Zulus but are fanatics and therefore rush single-handed at you, which the Zulus did not; they are more savage than the latter who are brown—while these are quite black with short but straight hair which stands up.

From the Queen

CLAREMONT, MARCH 29, 1884

Dearest Child, this is an awful blow.[2] For him we must not repine; his young life was a succession of trials and sufferings though he was so happy in his marriage. And there was such a restless longing for what he could not have; this seemed to increase rather than lessen.

From the Crown Princess

BERLIN, APRIL 4, 1884

It will ever remain an additional grief to me to have been separated from you in these hours of pain, and even more so the feeling that my presence would have been painful and hurtful to you instead of useful and soothing which I had fondly hoped it might have been; I have been through adversity enough myself—to know how sensitive one is, and how much rest and quiet are a necessity to the shaken and excited nerves to force myself upon those in sorrow, or be in the way when calm and repose is needed.

---

[1] Surrendered by Egyptian troops under Valentine Baker at the end of February but recaptured by General Graham at the beginning of March.
[2] Death of the Duke of Albany in France. The Queen had gone to Claremont to be with the Duchess.

From the Queen

And let me now thank you for your dear, affectionate letter of the 4th which I received this morning. Many, many loving thanks for it. Do not think your dear presence would have been painful, but I felt I should be so upset at a fresh, affecting meeting and at seeing your grief that as I had to keep up for dear Helen and my sakes I was obliged to avoid all fresh and additional emotions. Dear Fritz, whom I was so pleased to see, will tell you all and on Wednesday I will send you some newspapers in which the descriptions are admirable. He will tell you how beautiful and touching the procession up to Windsor and the Albert Chapel was on Friday—the dear coffin and the simple gun carriage, with that most beautiful March by Chopin (which he wished for) once alternated by Beethoven's splendid one—and it was most affecting how admirably those fine Seaforth Highlanders—covered with medals—did their sad work.

The Albert Chapel looked heavenly with its innumerable wreaths and crosses—the gardenias, roses and other richly scented flowers giving a perfume which rose like incense. The dear remains were placed first beyond dear Papa's cenotaph covered with the Union Jack, his dear Highland bonnet and claymore upon it—as well as a wreath of mine which had gone with it from the station, and a large one of violets from the poor Empress Eugénie which had gone on the gun carriage and then we all placed wreaths and crosses. After the short service, at which all the family were, we drove up to the Castle. At half past three, poor dear Helen arrived so touchingly resigned and calm—and at a quarter to five I drove alone with her down to the Memorial Chapel and took her in. It was an awful moment but she bore it like an angel. Her whole behaviour is beyond praise.

WINDSOR CASTLE

I finish this here. The next day dear Helen went down alone to the Memorial Chapel to take her last look for some time as she can't go into the vault till after her confinement. At half past eleven we drove down to St George's and here the service was very touching and beautiful. The Princes and Gentlemen were all in uniform. The word of command given in the church while the singing was going on had a very fine effect. While "Lead Kindly Light" was being sung I, with the Princesses, left and I felt quite crushed but I struggled on and went to dear, gentle but most courageous and truly deeply resigned Helen.

I am very tired though not ill at all—but sadder and sadder and I little needed that.

From the Queen

NEUES PALAIS, DARMSTADT, APRIL 17, 1884

Arrived here this morning at ¼ to 9. I write these few lines to say that the journey has passed off very well—tho' the passage was not a good one—and the being on board the "Osborne" quite dreadful.[1] I felt strange in a new ship and I particularly dislike at all times, since '61 being on board, which was additionally so now, when the right hand for everything concerning my comfort, safety etc. was also wanting.

The railway was a pleasant change—for the passage besides was a long and disagreeable one. A great deal of rolling so that I had (as is generally my fate) to be the whole time without moving by which means I escaped sea-sickness but could only lunch at five.

From the Queen

NEUES PALAIS, DARMSTADT, APRIL 22, 1884

I am sure that your child's happiness must be your first object— but unless she has enough to live comfortably no marriage is happiness. I have seen what the reverse is and it does not answer.[2] I am devoted to the Empress—but I cannot understand her views about marriage. They are too incomprehensible.

From the Queen

WINDSOR CASTLE, MAY 15, 1884

I wish also to thank you for your dear letter of the 13th received this morning and to say that the whole affair is at an end and that dear L. has promised in writing never to see or write to her (but keep this to yourselves) without Bertie's or my sanction; and that the divorce will be effected as soon and as quietly as

---

[1] The *Osborne* had brought back the Duke of Albany's body from France. The *Victoria and Albert* was being refitted.
[2] The Queen is referring to Princess Victoria and the difficulties of her engagement with Prince Alexander Battenberg.

possible.[1] Dear Louis is so really good, and has such a chivalrous feeling towards Countess Czapaska but his eyes are opened and he knows that others believe the worst of her. He cannot bear to hear her violently abused to him, for if a man is much attracted to a woman and thinks she is attached to him and has been deceived as to her antecedents he cannot in a day hate her. That conviction of her depravity must come gradually. We are very anxious to know whether now, as Louis is doing all we wish to get out of it all, if—before others—Fritz will be kind and civil to him at Philippsruhe—where he almost feels bound to go for the wedding as head of the family—for else either he better not go there or Fritz could perhaps avoid going there.[2] I should hope however that as it is now known that the whole affair will be annulled, F. would be brotherly and kind towards poor dear L.—who has suffered much—and has committed no sin. He is much better now.

Would you telegraph "all right" if F. will be friendly when they meet in public or "he cannot" if he intends the contrary. Louis will be leaving probably on the Tuesday 20th and it is important to know before.[3]

From the Crown Princess

NEUES PALAIS, MAY 16, 1884

Alas! we have had to go through many disagreeables on account of poor Sandro. I will tell you all, dearest Mama, knowing how safe I am in your hands and how you will burn everything

---

[1] The Grand Duke of Hesse had fallen in love with the divorced wife of a Russian diplomat. The Queen and a large contingent of European Royalty were at Darmstadt for the marriage of Princess Victoria and Prince Louis of Battenberg. The Queen's private secretary wrote home to his wife "we are in the midst of love matters". On the evening of his daughter's wedding the Grand Duke married morganatically Madame de Kolomine. On the next day the German Empress ordered the immediate return of all the members of the Prussian royal family from "this contaminated court"—the description is from the Queen's private secretary. On June 3 Madame de Kolomine signed an Act annulling her marriage on the payment of 500,000 marks from the Grand Duke. She was a descendant of Luther's friend Ulrich von Hutten; her maiden name was Countess Czapaska. Those who enjoy romantic fiction, told without discretion, might care to read *A King's Second Marriage* or *The Romance of a German Court* by Ary Ecilaw, translated from the French and published in London in 1892.
[2] The marriage of Elizabeth of Hesse-Cassel.
[3] The reply has not survived.

directly if I implore you. They have put paragraphs in the newspapers about Vicky and him which have been very disagreeable
to us and there was great excitement here in court circles and the
garrison, at the Emperor's etc. etc. Willie behaved most unkindly
and spoke in terms of Sandro which made it difficult for his Papa
to keep his temper. He said he could not imagine how such a
person could dare to think of his sister—the Emperor's grand-
daughter—how impertinent everyone thought it, and then he
repeated all the usual accusations and when Fritz said they were
unfounded as he knew from Sandro himself William said—how
can one believe a word S. says—Prince B. and the Foreign Office
know the truth and Prince B. had snubbed him as he deserved. I
own I could hardly contain myself. Then I had the same story
over again from Henry and from Charlotte. They quite cut poor
Vicky; and range themselves on the Emperor's side. I own it is a
great comfort that Fritz has taken a liking to Sandro and is not
angry with Vicky. He admitted to me that when he once is
Emperor he will allow it rather than make her unhappy—but at
present he must abide by the Emperor's decision.

I am so sorry for him [Sandro] as it must be very wounding to
his feelings. Though as he has never really and formally proposed
he has never had a refusal, and he knows Vicky's feelings and
mine, and I trust we shall succeed in overcoming the difficulties in
time, but it is a sore trial to me and I have no one here to whom I
can turn or who would help me.

From the Queen

WINDSOR CASTLE, MAY 21, 1884

This affair of poor Sandro is indeed very painful and trying.
But I think you need not despair. I saw him yesterday (he came to
Ludwig quite incog. and alone and therefore it will not appear)
and he spoke of all you wrote to him about, of the distress you
were in, and how grieved he was to be the cause of all this family
feud. But it is shameful of your three eldest children to behave as
they do. It seems Bismarck said if he lived as a retired Prussian
General there would be no difficulty and no objection to his
marrying Vicky but not as Prince of B. Whereas the Empress
who launched out in a letter, quite uncalled for, to me that on
account of the parents she and the Emperor would never consent
to such a marriage. I have not yet answered but shall say when I

do I can't enter into this as I entirely differ from her, and have the highest opinion of Sandro.

Affie brought Paul here today who I thought particularly nice and pleasing, more so (to me) than Serge.[1]

From the Queen

I read with much interest the proceedings at the laying of the foundation stone of the church on my poor old birthday which seems to have been very nicely done.[2]

You must let me now just say a little word privately to you about a person who I saw was there and took some part in the proceedings, viz. Mr J. Shore.[3] I know him well; he is a clever and very plausible man and took me and others of the family very much in. But he is very pushing—designing and rather a vulgar-minded man and all the clergy of different views dislike him. He likes to be with people of rank and title and boasts of never having had to do with the poor. He can preach very well and has short services very much liked for children. But both Alix and Mary Teck have seen through him and the children dislike him, out of lessons, particularly. I thought it my duty just to warn you—as Louis also found him out about the Alice Hospital. Of course be civil to him—only beware of him.

From the Queen

I am grieved at all your annoyances about Sandro and Vicky. But pray be patient. Don't talk about it to Vicky and don't let her write about it to anyone and not to Beatrice, nor to talk to her about it for I don't wish her to be mixed up in it.[4]

---

[1] "He is always monosyllabic, always shows a discontented countenance and is the only one [of the Grand Dukes] who in my case has never passed beyond the most frigid politeness." *My Early Life* by William II of Germany, 1926.
[2] St. George's Memorial Church in Berlin, which was a pretty, English church on the north bank of the Spree.
[3] The Reverend Teignmouth Shore was Chaplain in Ordinary to the Queen. He was incumbent of the Berkeley Chapel, Mayfair, and editor of *The Children's Bible*.
[4] Probably because the Queen realised that Princess Beatrice had fallen in love with Sandro's brother Prince Henry of Battenberg.

From the Queen

BALMORAL CASTLE, JUNE 10, 1884

You will have heard from me now in answer to your letters but I am so powerless—the Ministers are so weak and obstinate that I have no hopes of any kind. To be a sovereign and to be unable to prevent grievous mistakes is a very hard and ungrateful task. This Government is the worst I have ever had to do with. They never listen to anything I say and commit grievous errors.

Louis and the lovely Bride (whom I do not envy and whose marriage grieves me) and the rest arrived safely on Sunday at Peterhof.[1]

From the Queen

BALMORAL CASTLE, JUNE 17, 1884

I am glad you see what a deplorable, short-sighted Government we have and what a terribly discouraging task mine is. I have written and written—and telegraphed and spoken for months and months all to no purpose. Mr Gl. says they are very sorry when they can't agree with me. He loves France and trusts Russia—and Lord Granville is as weak and sweet as *eau de rose*. I assure you when I have to fight all these questions with no hope of success and with a sad, bleeding heart besides I often long to lay my head down and join those dear ones who are "not lost but gone before" and where "the wicked cease from troubling" and "the weary are at rest".

From the Queen

BALMORAL CASTLE, JUNE 20, 1884

We leave on the 24th. Today is the 47th anniversary of my Accession. It seems incredible I should have borne this heavy burden so long.

I must end. We (Beatrice and I) are very sad! And for me pleasure has for ever died out of my life. The sense of doing good to others is the only thing which still remains.

---

[1] Princess Elizabeth's marriage to the Grand Duke Serge.

From the Queen

We arrived here at 9 this morning having left dear Balmoral at 2 yesterday, and coming straight through without getting out at Perth which we have not done for the last five years in the summer as it is so heating to stop there for dinner. When we return in the autumn we always stop there for dinner.

I am tired and sad. Everywhere when one moves from place to place one hopes to find one's dear ones who are not lost but gone before; and alas! never does.

I cannot understand Lord Ampthill. He writes to Lord Granville in the greatest admiration of their present alas! miserable mistake about Egypt and hopes they'll have a good majority. Is it not too bad?

From the Queen

WINDSOR CASTLE, JULY 9, 1884

Let me now thank you for your dear letter of the 5th as well as for the other one, telling me that it was the Empress and not the Emperor who stirred up the latter and Bismarck against poor Sandro—which is really very annoying. I fear affairs are going very badly there. I am very sorry for it and pity poor Sandro very much.

We have got rather a crisis here today. The House of Lords have rejected the Franchise Bill not on the ground of lowering the franchise—but on that of its being unsafe without the Redistribution, which the Government won't bring in till next year. I have offered to mediate. If they can't agree I think they should dissolve.[1]

---

[1] The Franchise Bill, passed in the House of Commons earlier in the year, extended the Franchise to about 5,000,000 electors. The Conservatives in the House of Lords were extremely hostile to the Bill and proposed that a Redistribution of Seats should be passed first. The cry, invented by Chamberlain and Morley about the Lords, "Mend them or end them" was echoed throughout the country. Eventually, as the Queen says, she was successful in bringing together the two antagonists.

From the Crown Princess

BALMORAL HOTEL, EDINBURGH, SEPTEMBER 12, 1884
[The Crown Princess was driving back from Balmoral to Braemar.]

We became rather hungry and, as it was too damp to get out and sit by the side of a road, we knocked at a farmhouse which seemed occupied by a rather untidy-looking lady—whom we have found to be a Mrs Hutchinson (née Miss Codrington) cousin of Macdonald Gattsberg (General Gattsberg as you know was with Fritz in the war '70). This lady had been staying at Kassel with the Gattsbergs while the boys were at school there and saw a deal of them, so of course we had plenty to talk about. She gave us some oatcake which we ate in her room with the excellent luncheon you had so kindly provided for us—and which the careful, nice footman served to us.

From the Queen

BALMORAL CASTLE, SEPTEMBER 20, 1884
I send you today the photographs which are very amusing and—excepting poor Vicky—not at all bad. In the large group (in which Beatrice says I look oppressed by my family) Vicky comes out well.

From the Queen

BALMORAL CASTLE, SEPTEMBER 22, 1884
I had a letter from Lorne yesterday in which he expressed such a wish that L. and he could stay with you quietly for a while that I wish you could ask her to join you when you go to the Tyrol or Switzerland. Only you must not make her do the third part of what you can do. You would beat anyone at walking with your incredible activity. Not one in a thousand could do what you do in the way of walking and sightseeing.

From the Queen

BALMORAL CASTLE, NOVEMBER 5, 1884
In home politics I am more hopeful. I have worked very hard to try and bring about a meeting of the two sides in which I have

Alexander, Prince of Bulgaria, "Sandro" of Battenberg, a portrait from the 1880 Almanach de Gotha.

Louise Margaret, Duchess of Connaught, in her wedding dress, March 13, 1879.

Helen, Duchess of Albany, in her wedding dress, April 27, 1882.

The wedding of Princess Beatrice to Prince Henry of Battenberg, July 23, 1885.
(Left to right) Back Row: Alexander, Prince of Bulgaria, Princess Louise of
Wales, Princess Irene of Hesse, Princess Victoria of Wales, Prince Franz Josef
of Battenberg. Middle Row: Princess Maud of Wales, Princess Alix of Hesse,
Princess Marie Louise and Princess Helena Victoria of Schleswig-Holstein. Front
Row: Princesses Victoria Melita, Marie and Alexandra of Edinburgh, Princess
Beatrice and Prince Henry of Battenberg.

succeeded so that they may try and come to an agreement upon these difficult reform questions.

From the Queen

You will be shocked to hear that poor Lord Londonderry died suddenly yesterday and also poor blind Mr Fawcett the Post-master-General—a clever and an honest man.

From the Queen

We had two heavenly sunsets yesterday and the day before which were beautiful [and] brought very frosty days. We had driven into the hills toward Gairn Shiel, but to the left close to the Gairn to see an old woman the aunt of the Browns, sister of their dear old mother. How I wish you could paint her in her regular close, white cap and shawl such a handsome old woman, very like her dear sister and with all the dignity which the Highlanders have. She lives in a regular, little, old Highland cabin, with a fire in an open hearth—no grate. She would have made a splendid picture.

The sun had set and as we drove down, the mountain ledges were pink and lilac with an afterglow, the sky golden and pink blending upwards into blue. Range above range of hills rose up as we descended the Shiel and it was splendid.

Poor old Willie Blair the fiddler who had played at all our Balls since '48 and long before, is just dead aged 90 having played at my last Ball here (I shall never go to another) two years ago. Another link with the past is gone.

From the Queen

These lines are to wish you every possible happiness in this world and in the next with which we are so inseparably bound up! God bless and protect you, beloved child for many a long year, in health and happiness with all those dear to you and guide and support you in everything.

We[1] have heard from General Gordon up to the 4th of November; which is wonderful and all well and able to hold out 40 days more. Our people must get on as fast as they can. I hope also that political matters at home are brighter.

From the Queen

I must write you a line from this dreary, gloomy old place—to wish you again joy of your dear birthday, which makes me think much of former days and of your birth on a dark, dull, windy, rainy day with smoking chimneys, and dear Papa's great kindness and anxiety—though he was disappointed you were not a boy.

From the Queen

It is dreadful to see how they [the Ministers] go on. Mr Gladstone openly avowed to me that he wanted to get out of Egypt as quickly as possible, but to do it—as he has done by yielding to the French—is dreadful. I can't say what I feel—and oh! what would my darling Leopold have felt? All your brothers are furious and I must try and get Mr Seeley's book on the expansion of the British Empire.[2]

Dear Helen is wonderfully well and so good such an example to all, I do love respect and admire her, poor darling—always a kind, sweet smile on her poor, sad face and cheerful and always thinking of others and not of herself. But it is heartbreaking to see her and still more almost, the dear innocent pretty merry little children. Little Alice is very intelligent and such a healthy child.

From the Queen

One line to thank you for your dear letter of the 26th with the interesting enclosures and to tell you that after all the opposition of Lord G.—your and my urgent appeals that poor Morier should

---

[1] The Queen is not writing of herself or the family but of the Government.
[2] J. R. Seeley's *The Expansion of England* had been published in the previous year.

not be passed over again have prevailed, and he is to go to St Petersburg, Sir E. Thornton going to Constantinople.

He will do very well there and be of great use and we must all caution him and her to be conciliatory. Lord Carlingford and Lord Derby spoke strongly in his favour also.

From the Crown Princess

These tiresome reports about Ella being divorced etc. are all over the place; and in everyone's mouth. I think it would be very good to have them contradicted.

From the Queen

The Service at the Mausoleum was very touching and impressive. This year it was again as usual but at a quarter to one on account of its being Sunday and the choristers could not have come. That piece by Gounod is one of the most beautiful things I know. It has been sung there several times and so has "Wachet auf". We were all there and poor, dear Helen (a black veiled figure) so alone. But though much affected she was quite calm. But her courage, her wonderful gentle, unmurmuring resignation and gratitude to God for what is left to her and her courage to struggle on, fill me daily more and more with love, admiration and respect.

It is too absurd about Ella. She is quite happy.[1] They (the Battenbergs) go to Kent House on Monday where Ludwig's third brother is coming to them for a few days. I thought I had told you in the summer that I was going to take Victoria back to Windsor for the event in February.

From the Queen

The Empress avoids all subjects which were painful and her letters are short and rather empty as letters always are when one has to avoid subjects—but very kind. She complains of being very tired.

---

[1] That is doubtful.

I will write for Christmas again. Oh! it will be a sad one. Ever since '61 it has been clouded over and totally altered. '78 casts fresh shadows and now again since last year and this year all is terribly changed so that I have altered much. I cannot do many things again.

> "The Yule log sparkled keen with frost,
> No wing of wind the region swept,
> But over all things brooding slept
> The quiet sense of something lost."[1]

From the Crown Princess

BERLIN, DECEMBER 23, 1884

I think it a great shame that the German flag has been hoisted in New Guinea.[2] I do so wish we[3] had taken the whole three years ago, before colonising had become the rage and fashion here. People are too foolish here about it and will make a fine mess of their so-called colonies as you will see. The Emperor is very much excited about the Reichstag and very cross.[4] He began with great violence about it to me at dinner but as it was in the middle of a conversation and on other subjects I did not at all understand or in what to answer—so I remained silent. Yesterday he wrote a very rude letter to Fritz asking him why I read no newspapers and was so ill-informed. It is strange how the old despotism and tyranny comes out sometimes. The Emperor Nicholas's way of thinking.

From the Queen

OSBORNE, DECEMBER 24, 1884
CHRISTMAS EVE

How provoking and really distressing it is about Willie and foolish Dona. I had a very ungracious letter from the Empress again.

---

[1] *In Memoriam* LXXVIII.
[2] The Imperial Government in London had decided in the autumn that there should be only a limited Protectorate over New Guinea. Consternation was roused in both England and Australia when the German flag was hoisted over the northern portion of New Guinea.
[3] England.
[4] After the October election Bismarck had suffered a series of defeats in the Reichstag.

From Princess Victoria of Prussia

BERLIN, DECEMBER 24, 1884

You are ever and constantly so loving and kind to me. It is such a comfort to have at all events one Grandmama who loves me and to whom one can tell everything. This is the first Xmas I spend melancholy. My thoughts are not here to-night but far away where they always are. You know where dearest Grandmama. Oh if I can but only get a glimpse of him, so low in spirits I am and there seems no hope. If beloved Mama were not there to rouse me up perpetually really I don't know what would become of me.

From the Queen

OSBORNE, DECEMBER 27, 1884

I am so grieved at Willie's politics which are very foolish.

This German colonisation and hoisting of German flags has perfectly enraged our Colonies who protest in every direction.

Emily A. is at Woburn. I sent her an enamel I had purposely made for her of dear Odo and a card and she is much touched by it.

From the Crown Princess

BERLIN, DECEMBER 30, 1884

Your dear health has rather improved than otherwise, and the sad imbroglio at Darmstadt, which was indeed a trial and grief, has taken a better end and a better turn than was to be feared which is not a little due to your efforts.

From the Queen

OSBORNE, DECEMBER 30, 1884

I fear my letter will only reach you late on New Year's Day— but I could not manage to write this morning having a Council besides many telegrams to write. Let me now wish you all possible happiness in the New Year—which we are about to commence. These two have been full of sadness and anxiety to me though I am not unmindful of the blessings still remaining and of God's help and support in those dreary hours of grief and trouble.

I pray God to help and protect us in the new one, and to protect you, dear Fritz and your children and grandchildren.

Lenchen and Beatrice have both written to you, and the former has told you of the pain it has caused me that my darling Beatrice should wish (which she never did till she had lost her dear brother) to marry, as I hate marriages especially of my daughters, but as I like Liko very much and as they are both so very much devoted to each other, and she remains always with me, I cannot refuse my consent. Nothing was settled until yesterday and I could have said nothing before as all was uncertain.

1885

From the Queen

My health is better, and I can walk and stand much better, but I fear I shall never walk for any great length of time again. Still I can stand much better within the last 3 weeks and also can walk more than a mile at a time, for which I am thankful.

Your second letter pleased me as I saw you take the right view of darling Beatrice's engagement with Liko. But you who are so fond of marriages which I (on the other hand) detest beyond words, cannot imagine what agonies, what despair it caused me and what a fearful shock it was to me when I first heard of her wish! It made me quite ill. For long I could not hear of it and hoped against hope that it would not be! But alas! she was so determined that her health would have suffered if I had not relented. It was her dear brother's death which determined it. She looked to him for advice.

From the Queen

JANUARY 7, 1885

I have two very dear letters of the 3rd and the 4th to thank you for, which have touched me very much as you feel for me.

I am surprised at myself—considering the horror and dislike of the most violent kind I had for the idea of my precious Baby's marrying at all (never personally against dear Liko) how I should have been so much reconciled to it now that it is settled. But it is really Liko himself who has so completely won my heart. He is so modest, so full of consideration for me and so is she, and both are quietly and really sensibly happy. There is no kissing, etc. (which Beatrice dislikes) which used to try me so with dear Fritz. But the wedding day is like a great trial and I hope and pray there may be no *results*! That would aggravate everything and besides make me terribly anxious.

Now I must tell you how very unamiably the Empress and even dear Fritz have written to me. I think really the Empress has no right to write to me in that tone. I send you copies of her letter and my rather stern answer but I cannot swallow affronts.

Please return them to me and ask Fritz to let you see what I wrote to him, for his letter was very cold and not what it should be to me.

Dear Fritz speaks of Liko as not being of the blood—a little like about animals. Don't mind my saying this.

This colonisation mania is really too bad and foolish.[1] I am sure I have not the slightest objection but quite the contrary to the Germans having colonies—but I think the way in which it has been done is foolish and absurd. We have our eyes well open to the very question you mention.[2]

Lord Derby (as I foresaw) has made dreadful messes. He is a terrible Minister, for he won't do anything to prevent wars and complications.

One thing I do feel strongly in this marriage of my beloved child it is a security and a relief to me for the *future*! When I see them so happy my heart sinks within me! May they be spared trials and sorrows and rending of the heartstrings. The marriage is immensely popular here and the joy unbounded that she, sweet child, remains with poor, old, shattered me.

From the Queen

I have to thank you for your letter of the 6th in which you tell me of the extraordinary impertinence and insolence, and I must add, great unkindness of Willie, that foolish Dona—and of Henry, who had before "*l'ordre de Mufti*"[3] telegraphed very kindly to Beatrice and Liko. It is most impertinent and I shall not write to either. As for Dona, a poor, little, insignificant Princess raised entirely by your kindness to the position she is in, I have no words.

Lord Granville very truly said with respect to the extraordinary behaviour of the Emperor and Empress (but much more of the

---

[1] The German Colonial Empire is generally dated from 1884 though the ground had been prepared for two or three years before. Gladstone had welcomed it—though he was certainly not speaking for the country generally when he said "he looked with satisfaction, sympathy and joy upon the extension of Germany in these desert places of the world". The Queen probably means that founding the Colonies for trade and as coaling-stations for shipping was "absurd".

[2] In her letter of December 30 the Crown Princess had urged that the strength of the Navy should be maintained and she quoted Lord Odo, that British diplomacy ought to be organised like the Prussian Army or the Society of Jesus.

[3] The interpretation of Canon Law pronounced by the Mufti.

latter) and your naughty, foolish sons that if the Queen of England thinks a person good enough for her daughter what have other people got to say? Think if I was to do such a thing! No other sovereign in the world would do such a thing. All have telegraphed so kindly. I own I do resent it. And I do feel angry with dear Fritz too though I know I can not quite understand his point of view.

I think Liko the handsomest of the three handsome brothers.

From the Queen

Don't fear that I should be angry with dear Fritz—for I know his attachment to all of you. But your children or rather sons' behaviour and Dona's impertinence I do resent and shall do so. I had intended writing to both but shall not do so and wish that they should know why I do not do so. I had got a present for Willie's birthday. Shall I send it to him or not? I shall certainly not write to him.

From the Crown Princess

BERLIN, JANUARY 15, 1885

The Vicomte de Beaucaire, who is at the French Embassy here, has written a most interesting book about Eléonore D'Olbreuze (Duchess of Brunswick). It contains nothing new but the details the letters etc. are most interesting. The Vicomte de B. descends from the same family, and has made me a present of the book, and I said I though he might send you one too, as I felt sure it would interest you. I hope I have not done wrong?[1]

I could not help smiling at the exact similarity of the Empress's attitude with that of the Princesses of the Hanoverian family of those days. How they ill-treated and insulted this unfortunate lady because she was not a princess! I am afraid George I behaved very badly. The fate of the Duchess of Brunswick and her poor daughter Sophia Dorothea are most touching and melancholy and the whole story most curious and sad. Please do read it when you get it. I am sorry I cannot read it to you. It is quite short.

---

[1] Eléonore d'Olbreuze, mother-in-law of King George I, and therefore ancestress of the Hohenzollern family. She was a Huguenot, but not of royal blood. The book is *Une Mésalliance aus dans le maison de Brunswick* by the Vicomte H. de Beaucaire.

From the Queen

OSBORNE, JANUARY 17, 1885

I should be delighted to receive that book about the
D'Olbreuze written by that French gentleman and perhaps you
could send it to me? It will interest me immensely and I shall read
it at once when I get it—as I never heard much about her and
always wished to do so.

I was very audacious and answered the last letter of the Empress
full of hints and insinuations about the origin of the family which
she supposed I did not know and that I did know and that the
character of the young man and his brother and sister which was
so excellent was what I considered first, and then that I could not
understand how she could object so much to the family when
she remembered that the father of her own son-in-law and his
brothers and sister were the children of a Fraulein Geyersberg,[1]
a very bad woman, and that they had been acknowledged by the
whole of Europe as Princes of Baden. Then that if one enquired
into the history of all the royal and princely families I feared
many black spots would be found—and finally, that if no fresh
blood was infused occasionally the races would degenerate finally
—physically and morally—for that almost all the Protestant
Royal Families were related to each other and so were the
Catholic ones!

I also said morganatic marriages were unknown in England and
if a King chose to marry a peasant girl she would be Queen just as
much as any princess. I said (all in a friendly tone) that as she was
quite open to me I should be the same to her. I am very curious
what she will say by tomorrow's messenger. I would never have
continued the argument but that I thought really I could not
swallow all she said.

From the Queen

OSBORNE, JANUARY 24, 1885

The Battle of Abu Klea[2] was most brilliant and really shows
what British troops are—but our loss is heavy! Poor little Eddy
Gleichen passed safely through it—but what a *baptême de feu!* Poor

---

[1] Fraulein Geyer von Geyersberg, afterwards Baroness von Hochberg. The
Queen was correct about this lady's history which will be found in *Secrets of the
Gotha* by Ghislain de Diesbach, Chapman and Hall, 1964.
[2] The first heavy fighting of the Nile Campaign intended to aid General Gordon
in Khartoum.

— *180* —

Colonel Burnaby I am sorry for. He was a strange man but so brave and enterprising! Well he died the death every brave soldier must covet.

From the Crown Princess

I see there is nothing to be done. Poor Vicky sees it too—and deeply as she is attached to Sandro she will not stand in the way of his interests. He must think of his country and as Prince Bismarck insists on swelling out the question to one of high political importance and has told the Emperor and Fritz it cannot be, for many highly important reasons we must think of it no more.

It is really too sad but the sooner Louis and Liko tell their brother so—the better. Up to two days ago I thought one could still see one's way out of it but now since the articles in the Moscow Gazette and all Prince B.'s steps there is nothing left but to drop it. I would not advise Sandro asking again formally, as it is so intensely painful to have to give a formal refusal, when one's wishes and inclinations are to say the reverse. His only chance would be that of giving up his throne and position—and then when Fritz is Emperor he might probably consent but would do so unwillingly as the question of rank and position would then come to the fore and you know that Fritz is unusually touchy on this subject.

From the Crown Princess

Private To Be Burnt[1]

Yes I have no doubt you are quite right in what you say. I was too sanguine—and took too much responsibility upon myself. I wished for the best and did for the best. I see that S. cannot wait and must not do so.[2]

Vicky again told her Papa how deeply attached she was to Sandro, and he again said that as long as his father the Emperor

---

[1] The Queen kept it apart from the general correspondence of the Crown Princess, and evidently did not destroy it because of the importance of anything concerning the Battenberg family at this time.
[2] This letter has not survived.

lived he would not be able to get her the permission, and even then he foresaw great obstacles. I have no means of communication with Sandro—and I dare not write, would you undertake to let him know the truth? It is not my fault that matters have taken this bad turn and it is not his. I feel sure that he would not turn round upon me and betray me when he knows how earnestly and zealously I am working in his cause and stuck to him through thick and thin for my child's sake and for his. I have always found him so thoroughly gentlemanlike and honourable—full of tact and good feeling that I am sure it was not his wish to spoil all in this rough way. Prince Bismarck then brought forward his reasons against such a marriage. They were purely political! You know them already—not one word about rank etc. was even breathed and his objections are not on this score.

In a little while you, dear Mama, must write her a little word and preach to her to have courage and hold her head up.

Every word you say she listens to and your influence on her is so very great—because she loves you so devotedly.

From the Queen

OSBORNE, FEBRUARY 7, 1885

This is dreadful news but we are determined (though Mr. Gladstone—the old sinner—does not feel the least what we do!!!) to show a bold front, and full powers have been given to Lord Wolseley to do what he thinks best and to make no retrograde movement.[1] We were just too late as we always are and it is I, who have, as the head of the nation, to bear the humiliation. Most people think Gordon is alive! No stone shall be left unturned to ascertain the truth and to rescue the brave and heroic man who this Government sent out on a mission and never supported!

Poor dear Moretta[2] I am so sorry for her! I fear, dearest Child, I cannot ask you to the wedding—for Sandro is coming and it would never do for you to meet so soon with the excited feelings existing at headquarters. Much as we shall regret not seeing you here. The wedding is to be here in Whippingham church—half

---

[1] News of the catastrophe of Gordon's death and the fall of Khartoum reached England on February 5.
[2] Princess Victoria.

state uniforms and evening dresses, but no train, and Beatrice will have no train or train bearers—but eight of her nieces as at dear Alice's marriage when she had her three sisters and poor Anna.

From the Queen

If Gordon's demands and entreaties had been listened to—he would be alive and none of all this bloodshed necessary. The culpability of this miserable Government with the motto "Too Late" is wicked and dreadful. On their heads rests the precious blood of Gordon and thousands!! Imagine my feelings—though my conscience is clean! I warned, urged without ceasing all in vain. Mr. Gladstone don't take interest in it. He will be for ever branded with the blood of Gordon that heroic man. Now it is become a crusade of the 19th Century.

Your letters shall be burnt—but you go too far. Why distrust me as I think my discretion and the safety of what I have locked up can never be doubted.

From the Queen

OSBORNE, FEBRUARY 13, 1885

As for Willie that very foolish, undutiful and—I must add—unfeeling boy I have no patience with, and I wish he could get a good "skelping" as the Scotch say (flogging) and seriously a good setting down. It is very wrong of the Empress to spoil him so much. The atmosphere he lives in is very bad for him.

From the Queen

OSBORNE, FEBRUARY 18, 1885

Your letters are burned and I burn many a one which speaks of people which might be disagreeable hereafter. All I do is to keep them for a few days.[1]

From the Queen

WINDSOR CASTLE, MARCH 11, 1885

How I wish there could be a coalition. It must come to that

---

[1] Most of the Crown Princess's letters for 1885 were evidently destroyed.

but in the meantime the misrule is most terrible. The Cabinet all pull different ways—and Mr. Gladstone writes such confused reports—so contradictory—and then decisions are so disastrous that I am in great trouble and distress.

The system (now totally different to Lord Palmerston's, Lord Aberdeen's and Lord Clarendon's) is never to support their agents abroad, and they are now hampering Lord Wolseley giving him and Sir E. Baring, who must be the best judges, no answers. I can assure you my life is one of incessant anxiety.

Victoria is most carefully watched and can commit no imprudence. She has been kept so quiet, has seen not a soul but just one or two of my ladies in the last two or three days. It is a fortnight today and she is sitting up a little bit in her armchair. No one under my care and with my experience would ever commit an imprudence.

From the Queen

WINDSOR CASTLE, MARCH 16, 1885

I scribble a few hasty lines to say that contrary to all what I expected and to my great satisfaction I have been able to appoint dear Emily Ampthill my lady-in-waiting which I know will delight you.

Only imagine that odd little woman Lady Abercromby resigning—in a huff as (what I constantly have to do) I had to change her waiting!! She is very odd, but I had thought her much attached to me. She hated half my people and was very rude to many of my Maids of H. and Gentlemen whom she took antipathies to—particularly to some of the nicest—so that there is a general sensation of relief at her resignation. But we were always on very good terms though she was singularly unsympathetic.

From the Queen

WINDSOR CASTLE, MARCH 25, 1885

Just as I am writing I received the news that dear Arthur is appointed to a Divisional Command and ordered to Pindi and can't come back. The disappointment and trial are fearful. I am so alone. I need him so much. But I can't blame him or refuse. I don't forget I am a soldier's child, and a soldier's mother and proud of the name and that others are now suffering far more than I am from fearful anxiety for their husbands and sons in the Sudan. That is a dreadful danger.

The fighting on Sunday was terrific and the loss of the unfortunate animals of transport is as dreadful as it is serious. The rush was so sudden and unexpected from the nature of the ground that they had not been secured as is generally done and they ran loose and it is wonderful that all were not killed. But the wonderful steadiness of my brave soldiers, especially of the Berkshires on whom the heaviest fighting fell is beyond all praise, and on all occasions we are victorious but alas! at the expense of much life.[1]

Very energetic measures are being used—very late but I hope and think not too late to be at hand to help the Amir and to resist the Russians.

Numbers of native princes and nobles in India have offered help in troops and money both for the Sudan and against Russia.[2]

The nasty newspapers at home see fit to attack my dear and most brave Sir J. McNeill who is considered one of our best soldiers without knowing the true state of the case. These Arabs are really like bees and swarm and attack—utterly regardless of life.

I must end, and am well nigh worn out with all I have to do. A little rest I must have or I fear to break down entirely. Anxiety, trouble and grief are all I have now—with nothing to cheer or brighten my sad life of constant and incessant labour!

From the Queen

WINDSOR CASTLE, MARCH 28, 1885

We are going with Helen to the Evening Service (which I never like) at St. George's but we are going to have a fine, appropriate anthem, and play Chopin's March by poor Helen's express wish.

From the Queen

AIX-LES-BAINS, APRIL 15, 1885

I feel much your kind words about darling Beatrice's birthday. We both felt the last unmarried one very much and to me the

---

[1] On March 22 General Sir J. McNeill was surprised by a formidable Arab attack on Suakim.
[2] The Queen is here speaking of Afghanistan.

thought was too dreadful. I count the months, weeks and days that she is still my own sweet, unspoilt, innocent lily and child. That thought—that agonising thought which I always felt, and which I often wonder any mother can bear of giving up your own child, from whom all has been so carefully kept and guarded—to a stranger to do unto her as he likes is to me the most torturing thought in the world. While I feel no girl could go to the altar (and would probably refuse) if she knew all, there is something very dreadful in the thought of the sort of trap she is being led into.

I can't help saying to you what has cost me always so much and what in poor, darling, gentle (and not very strong) Beatrice's case almost tortures me! However we must trust in a higher power.

We took a very long drive up to the Col du Chat quite into the mountains. There are no tombs at Chambéry but at Haute Combe there are. Unfortunately the old Abbey is comparatively modern and in bad taste. Forty Princes and Princesses of Savoy are buried there and there are sixteen monks—Cistercians who live there and take charge of all. We went across in a steamer, and all the monks who wear white, came down to receive me and showed me about. And they gave us some cakes and wine and we sat down together with three of the principal monks. Such a curious scene. The order is very strict—a branch of the Trappists but not quite so severe. Still during weekdays they do not speak.

From the Crown Princess

I omitted yesterday mentioning a subject which I hope you will not be vexed with me for bringing before your notice. It is about the vacant post of Director of the Science and Art Museum of Edinburgh. Professor Archer, as you most likely know, has lately died; and I have heard a gentleman named whose nomination by many would be considered most excellent. It is Colonel Murdoch Smith of the Royal Engineers, now in charge of the Persian Telegraph at Teheran.

It is to him that the Kensington Museum owes its very complete and unique collection of Persian art objects. He is a Scotchman, a diplomatist, an artist and an administrator. As much as I know, the people at the South Kensington Museum would strongly advocate the Edinburgh post being given to him. I happen to know that poor Colonel Murdoch Smith has during his long residence at Teheran lost his wife and all his children so that he is most anxious to come home.

I also believe Lord Carlingford knows about him, and thinks him a suitable candidate for the place; no doubt there is a long, large list of names to choose from.

It is because I think it would be of real benefit to the Edinburgh Museum and also an act of personal kindness well-deserved that I venture to ask whether you would kindly mention his name to Lord Carlingford which I do not feel I have the right to do.

From the Crown Princess

BERLIN, APRIL 14, 1885

Prince George of Saxony is going to bring his son here in a few days. Poor young man! It is a pity he is so ugly—and ungainly and awkward for the future King of Saxony and speaks such broad Saxon that it is impossible to keep serious.

From the Queen

AIX–LES–BAINS, APRIL 22, 1885

Let me now thank you for two very dear letters of the 14th and 19th received this morning. The latter did me good for I know you felt for and understood my terrible suffering at the thought of my darling Baby's marriage, and my feelings at any young girl's marriage. But what you say is quite true. I felt it and feel it, but still the struggle is awful! You write so well that I am always in admiration of it.

I will write better from Darmstadt for I should like to answer it fully. I can't say I look forward to that visit as much as I would if the dreadful engagement of Beatrice was not in existence and if I didn't know how unwittingly I was deceived about it there. But she is so good that I feel quite angry with myself to vex her and yet I can't help my feelings.

From the Crown Princess

BERLIN, APRIL 24, 1885

The Empress gave a great *soirée* last night, and appeared in a lemon-coloured gown covered with flowers. Turquoise blue—and sea green—with roses and water lilies she wears very often. I haven't the courage to wear such youthful colours.

From the Queen

We drove back and at half past one there was a family *déjeuner* here.[1] And at 4 (the room having been cleared out), the Christening took place in the same room. She was christened by good old Binder, who just 22 years ago came over to christen Victoria at Windsor on this day and I held their little one as I had then held her mother and Prince Alexander was again one of the sponsors. Louis, Ella, Princess Battenberg and Marie Erbach and myself being the others and she was called Victoria *Alice* Elizabeth Julie Marie and will be called Alice.[2]

I have asked Serge to assure the Emperor of my pacific intentions and hope that we may both be able to avoid war but I don't see how exactly. Serge (who I like much better) looked sad and preoccupied about it and is most anxious to avoid it. I have not spoken but written to him about it. They seem quite happy and comfortable together but Ella is looking thin and pale—which however they say is caused by the heat.

From the Queen

NEUES PALAIS, DARMSTADT, APRIL 27, 1885

I omitted two things. The first is that I am so glad dear Amélie is with you to whom pray give my affectionate love. Tell her she should come to England to consult some good Doctor for she never tried an English one for her headaches. The other is about the Empress. She wrote several times to me about my journey to Aiz; sent Beatrice an outsïze Easter Egg, and wrote kindly about Ernest Ludwig's confirmation.

You will be shocked to hear that the Emperor and Bismarck both wrote most unkind and insulting letters to poor Sandro just lately which have hurt him very much, saying he must obey Russia and never pretend to think of obtaining the hand of a Princess of Prussia!! He has been cruelly used.

---

[1] The Queen and members of the family had been to the Schloss Kirche for the confirmation of Prince Ernest Louis.
[2] Princess Alice was mother of the Duke of Edinburgh.

From the Queen

WINDSOR CASTLE, MAY 6, 1885

I cyphered to you yesterday and I send you here merely a précis of what is the state of the case to which should be added that Penjdeh is to be neutralized during the transactions of the Commission. The unfortunate thing is that Sir P. Lumsden has—though a brave, honest soldier—not done his work well and that he has had several times to correct his previous statements, and that Lord Dufferin knows and has privately informed me that the Afghans were the aggressors and that he could not fight about this; and this is the opinion of many calm and well-informed people. We shall and must not relax in our preparations for of course if the boundary is not satisfactorily settled or there is any hitch we may have to fight after all.[1]

From the Queen

WINDSOR CASTLE, MAY 20, 1885

I am so frantic about our disgraceful policy about the Sudan and the readiness (I grieve to say) to please Russia that it makes me ill. I wish I could show you all the remonstrance of the civil and military authorities in Egypt against the parade of announcing the abandonment of our policy in the Sudan and the violent hurry of rushing away and leaving the fine province of Dongola to utter ruin and anarchy. How I have written, and cyphered and spoken and warned and all in vain. I will send you some to show in confidence (to Fritz) for it comes between me and my peace.

Lord Rosebery is going on Friday for a few days to Berlin and I wish you would see him and talk to him for he is very clever, and very unprejudiced. Let him hear all he can.

---

[1] This concerned a dispute between England and Russia over the Afghan border. The negotiations were carried on in London, and during the negotiations Penjdeh was attacked, and the Russians drove the Afghans from the town. Popular feeling in England was inflamed but war between Russia and England was avoided through the diplomatic skill of the Viceroy—Lord Dufferin. He said that a war between the two European powers would be a combat between a whale and an elephant.

From the Queen

I am so thankful that you do see the blind folly and weakness of my present Government and that you saw and were pleased with Lord Rosebery, for I like him, and dear Leopold liked him very much. He is quite the rising politician of the day and is always very respectful and anxious to please me. He is very happy with Hannah who is a kind, good person and has four pretty, nice, little children. He was so nice and attentive to his dear old step-grand-mother, Lady Waterpark's sister.[1]

From the Queen

WINDSOR CASTLE, JUNE 17, 1885

What has not happened since I last wrote. Many affectionate thanks for your dear letter of the 12th received before we left dear Balmoral yesterday, and the long one with the sad details of poor Fritz Carl which I have just received. There is something so indescribably sad in such a death when the nearest can only be relieved by the departure of one, to whom she had been bound by the nearest ties and who hated him.[2] What a terrible recollection! Poor Fritz Carl. To see that iron will and tyrannical disposition—powerless in death—has also something very affecting and very striking. I am so thankful that the relations between you both and him were so satisfactory. It is so pleasant now. Alas! I fear his nice boy has no pleasant recollections of his poor father.

My reason for naming Emich[3] was—as he was a near relation of mine. But I can quite understand his being too young and not of high enough military rank. I have now deputed Louis as my son-in-law and a great friend of Fritz Carl's to represent me. It looks more respectful to have a special representative—there was no time to send anyone from here else I would have sent Sir J. McNeill.

I think such a hurried funeral most indecent. Even if the coffin had to be closed the second day—it could and ought to have

---

[1] Anne Margaret (died 1882), daughter of Lord Anson. "She who has loved me longer, and whom I loved tenderly." Lord Rosebery in his diary when she died quoted in *Rosebery* by Robert Rhodes James, 1963. Lady Waterpark was extra Lady of the Bedchamber to the Queen. Hannah Rothschild was Lord Rosebery's wife.
[2] Marie Anne, 1837-1906. Daughter of the Duke of Anhalt.
[3] The Hereditary Prince of Leiningen.

remained till the end of the week and it should have been delayed for Arthur and Louischen. None of my carriages will appear on the course tomorrow and Bertie would do better not to go.[1]

From the Queen

WINDSOR CASTLE, JUNE 20, 1885

I will not deny that I was hurt and shocked at the repeated refusals to me as Queen of England and the absurd (forgive me using the word) pretensions that the rules of the Prussian Court (which are not the case at the other German Courts) should govern every other mark of respect on such an occasion. And I must openly say that I think you ought to clear all these prejudices about rank and mediatised princes and other princes away when you come to the throne. It was not so formerly and will end in preventing many to come to Berlin. I can't understand it all—but fear beloved Fritz is rather fond of all these restrictions which give pleasure to no one and are a great trouble.[2]

From the Queen

FROGMORE GARDENS, WINDSOR CASTLE, JUNE 24, 1885

I have been terribly bothered and troubled till matters could be adjusted and only yesterday morning could the difficulties be surmounted. However all is satisfactorily arranged now—though the difficulties for Lord Salisbury are very great. Sir M. Beach is a determined man and by no means over-conservative but the reverse and he has backbone.[3]

You call Sir S. Northcote (who is now Lord Iddesleigh) "so old". I thank you for the compliment as he is my age or one year older! Mr. Gladstone is too old for he is 75. Lord Randolph Churchill is not a bit worse than Sir C. Dilke (and Lord R. never spoke against the Royal Family as the latter did) and he will be kept in bounds by his Council at home and by Lord Dufferin and the Council in India, and his language will be kept in due bounds.

---

[1] To Ascot.
[2] It is difficult to say why the rules of the Prussian Court prevented the Grand Duke of Hesse from representing the Queen. In fact the Queen was represented by the British Ambassador, Sir E. Malet, sitting, as the Crown Princess says, "in a special place—apart as representing you".
[3] Gladstone and his Government resigned on June 9. They were brought down by divisions in the Cabinet and Party.

From the Crown Princess

NEUES PALAIS, JUNE 24, 1885

About your representation here at the funeral I can assure you in this case it would really have been impossible otherwise, Arthur and Louise can explain to you that it would not have done. I quite agree that my own dear husband (like the Empress) attaches too great an importance to etiquette but rules there must be, and though of course the other German courts are at liberty to have what rules they like for themselves, yet the Emperor's will always be the first. I think there is great room for improvement etc, but the Empress thinks me a perfect heretic and I own it is very difficult. The Emperor of Austria's rules are much more stringent still.

From the Crown Princess

NEUES PALAIS, JUNE 27, 1885

I beg your pardon for calling Sir Stafford Northcote "old". I thought he was a vast deal older than you say he is, as he has something a little feeble about him.

From the Queen

WINDSOR CASTLE, JUNE 27, 1885

[The Queen is discussing the Household changes.]

It is hopeless for me now to have people of my age. They would now be as you call good Lord Iddesleigh (Sir Stafford) "so old". All my Ministers, who don't look young, are excepting Lord John Manners, the Duke of Richmond and Lord Cranbrook younger than me, and my Prime Minister nine years younger. How old I feel and I am old.

From the Queen

WINDSOR CASTLE, JULY 1, 1885

How distressed I am to hear you felt so ill but I am sure you need not be alarmed or that there is anything really the matter. You are so much the strongest of the family excepting Bertie. You could do more than anyone I know.

From the Crown Princess

NEUES PALAIS, JULY 2, 1885

The Empress wishes William to go to Coblentz.[1] Alas these visits never do any good. She flatters him and twists him round her finger, and it does not make him easier to deal with. I am sorry to say! the influence she has over him is not a good one.

From the Crown Princess

NEUES PALAIS, JULY 7, 1885

Well Prince Bismarck is going to lunch with us today. It will be ten years at least since such a thing has happened as he never accepts invitations.

From the Queen

WINDSOR CASTLE, JULY 8, 1885

I did not wish and never have wished to touch the subject but I cannot help alluding to the tone of Fritz's letter to Arthur. It is very offensive and though I shall certainly not bear him any ill will for it, I do resent it and think it very unkind. My people here are most indignant including my Ministers present and past—that any other sovereign should dictate to me in my family and Court. Liko will be naturalised immediately after the marriage, and the title I give him as my son-in-law is for England and not for Germany where the absurd laws about rank etc. will keep people from going there.

You need not fear that Liko and Beatrice will ever hurt Fritz's dignity by going to Berlin as I am sure they will never go there. At Darmstadt naturally he would not go before his father and brother.[2] I do not forget how rude they were to Papa when I went to Brühl and how bitterly I resented it—though the King was very kind afterwards. If the Emperor is so all-powerful at his Court it is the more rude and unkind to deny to the husband of

---

[1] The Residenz schloss at Coblentz was the favourite residence of the Empress.
[2] With the rank of Royal Highness, he would not have had precedence over the Grand Duke who was made Royal Highness by a decree of the Queen just after his marriage to Princess Alice. As the Queen says he naturally would not have taken precedence over his father or Prince Louis of Battenberg. Good manners would have taken the place of pretension and rank.

the daughter of the Queen of England a position of courtesy on account of their relationship. You told me Fritz was so frantic at the idea of Liko becoming Royal Highness and getting the Garter, long ago but I did not think he would venture to try to prevent it. I am sure it must pain you to see him act thus.

From the Queen

Now let me thank you for your dear letter of the 11th. I quite understand your explanation. That is—I know exactly what you mean, though I own I cannot understand it really for I think an exception should be made. I thought Fritz's memorandum so objectionable and threatening that I felt it my duty to bring it before my Government and send you here Lord Salisbury's answer and also a strong opinion of Lord Granville's.

And now I send you the copies of a letter or rather enclosure in a letter from the Empress and my answer. I am sure you will be indignant. The rudeness of asking me to give such a message to my guest, the brother of my daughter's bridegroom, on the occasion of a wedding visit is really outrageous and it seems to me as if she was bent on persecuting and insulting this family now so nearly allied with me and you, and insulting me. I am really very indignant and after this our long-standing friendship has become very cold which I am sincerely sorry for—and the more so as I was her truest and best friend.

"23 July. The marriage of H.R.H. Princess Beatrice with Prince Henry of Battenberg celebrated at Whippingham Parish Church, Isle of Wight, in the presence of the Queen, the Royal Family, and a distinguished party of English Nobility; no representatives of the German reigning dynasties attended." *The Annual Register*, 1885.

The statement about the German dynasties is probably correct except that the Grand Duke of Hesse was naturally there as a relation of the bridegroom, and the Crown Princess would, of course, have been present except that the Queen thought that it would be impossible to ask her in view of all the difficulties over the engagement of Prince Alexander of Battenberg and Princess Victoria of Prussia.

In her journal the Queen wrote: "A happier-looking couple could seldom be seen kneeling at the altar together. It was very touching. I stood very close to my dear child, who looked very sweet, pure, and calm. Though I stood for the ninth time near a child and for the fifth time near a daughter, at the altar, I think I never felt more deeply than I did on this occasion, though full of confidence. When the Blessing had been given, I tenderly embraced my darling 'Baby'."[1]

From the Queen

OSBORNE, JULY 25, 1885

I bore up bravely till the departure and then fairly gave way. I remained quietly upstairs and when I heard the cheering and "God Save The Queen" I stopped my ears and cried bitterly.

---

[1] *The Letters of Queen Victoria*, Second series, Volume 3, John Murray, 1928.

INDEX

This index gives a brief description of only those people who are not already identified in the text, the footnotes, or the list of familiar names.

ABERCROMBY, Lady (1858-1915), wife of the 4th Lord, 184

Aberdeen, George, 4th Earl of (1784-1860), 184

Albany, H.R.H. Prince Leopold, Duke of (1853-84), 3, 12, 40, 46, 71, 76, 97, 104, 111, 112, 117, 118, 134, 151, 162, 164, 172, 176, 177, 190

Albany, H.R.H. the Duchess of (1861-1922), 3, 111, 112, 118, 162, 163, 164, 172, 173, 185

Albert, H.R.H. the Prince Consort—passing references throughout

Albrecht, Prince. See Prussia

Albrecht, Princess. See Prussia

Alderberg, General Count Alexander, 91

Alice, H.R.H. Princess. See Hesse

Alice, H.R.H. Princess, Countess of Athlone (1883-1981), 134, 139, 150, 151, 172

Alfred, H.R.H. Prince. See Duke of Edinburgh

Amélie, daughter of Prince Augustus of Saxe-Coburg, 188

Amir, 185

Ampthill—See Russell

Anderson, George (1819-96), M.P. for Glasgow, 24

Anhalt-Dessau, Hereditary Prince of (d. 1886), 153

Annual Register, The, 32, 34, 195

Aosta, Prince Amadeo, Duke of (1849-90), 55

Arabi Pasha, 122, 124, 125

Archer, Professor, 186

Aristarchi Bey, Turkish Ambassador in Berlin, 103

Arthur, H.R.H. Prince. See Duke of Connaught

Aumale, Duc d' (1823-97), son of Louis Philippe, 83

Austria, Emperor Francis Joseph of (1830-1916), 68, 70, 79, 192

Austria, Empress Elizabeth of (1837-98), 68, 92, 93

Austria, Crown Prince Rudolph of (1858-89), 68, 70, 125

Austria, Crown Princess Stephanie of (1864-1945), 68, 70, 125

Aziz, Abdul (1830-76), Sultan of Turkey, 103

BADEN, Grand Duke Frederick of (1826-1907), 135

Baden, Louise, Grand Duchess of (1838-1923), wife of the Grand Duke and daughter of the Emperor, 135

Baden, Frederick, Hereditary Grand Duke of (1857-1928), 134, 135

Baker, Colonel Valentine (1827-87), 162

Baring, Sir E., 161, 184

Barker, Nicholas, 77

Barnard, C. T., Chargé d'Affaires at Coburg, 34

Barrington, Lady Caroline, Woman of the Bedchamber to Queen Victoria, 125

Bassano, Duc de, 44, 46

Bassano, Marquis de, 46

Battenberg, Prince Alexander of (1857-93), Prince of Bulgaria, 19, 43, 44, 98, 103, 147, 156, 158, 164, 166, 167, 169, 181, 182, 188, 195

Battenberg, Princess Alice of (1885-1969), mother of H.R.H. Prince Philip Duke of Edinburgh, 188

Battenberg, Prince Henry of (1858-96), 19, 167, 176, 177, 178, 179, 181, 193, 194, 195

Battenberg, Princess Henry of. See Princess Beatrice

Battenberg, Prince Louis of (1854-1921),

Battenberg, Prince Louis of—*cont.*
19, 43, 44, 141, 147, 156, 165, 166, 173, 181, 193
Battenberg, Julie (1825–95), Princess of. Born Countess von Hauke, 18, 102, 188
Beach, Sir M., 191
Beaconsfield, Earl of (1804–81), 2, 5, 6, 7, 23, 24, 42, 73, 75, 78, 79, 98, 99, 100, 101, 118, 121
Beaton, Mr., Clerk of the Works at Balmoral, 52
Beatrice, H.R.H. Princess (1857–1944), Princess Henry of Battenberg, 3, 4, 8, 41, 44, 46, 75, 76, 79, 87, 97, 107, 116, 137, 144, 146, 167, 168, 176, 177, 178, 183, 185, 186, 187, 188, 193, 195
Beaucaire, Vicomte de, 179
Beckford, William, 123
Bedford, Duchess of (d. 1897), wife of the 9th Duke. Mistress of the Robes to Queen Victoria, 76, 103
Belgium, King Leopold II of (1835–1909), 27, 68, 70
Belgium, Marie, Queen of (1836–1902), 27
Belgium, Princess Stephanie of, 68, 70, 125
Bell, Doyne (1830–88), Permanent Secretary to H.M.'s Privy Purse, 59
Benson, Edward White (1829–96), Archbishop of Canterbury, 131–2
Beresford, Lord William, V.C. (1847–1900), 52
Bibliothca Lindesiana, 77
Biddulph, Mary. Wife of Sir Thomas Biddulph, 133
Biddulph, Sir Thomas (1809–78), Keeper of the Privy Purse, 27, 125
Bigge, Arthur John, afterwards 1st Lord Stamfordham (1849–1931), 56, 133
Binder, Mr., the Chaplain at Darmstadt, 188
Bismarck, Herbert, son of Prince Bismarck, 112
Bismarck, Prince (1815–98), 1, 8, 39, 49, 50, 62, 63, 64, 76, 79, 80, 94, 96, 108, 109, 112, 114, 115, 147, 153, 154, 166, 169, 170, 174, 181, 182, 188, 193
Blair, Willie, 171
Blake, Robert, 78
Blakiston, Caroline, 90
Blücher, Countess Madeline Dallas, 51, 125
Boehm, Sir Joseph Edgar (1834–90), sculptor, 135
Boni, Giacomo (1859–1925), Italian architect, 58
Botticelli, Sandro, 123, 126, 127
Bradford, 2nd Earl of (1789–1865), 144
Bradley, George, Dean of Westminster (1821–1903), 105
Braun, Herr, Court photographer, 108
Bridport, 1st Viscount (1814–1904), 144
Brockdorff, Countess, 151

Brown, John, personal servant to Queen Victoria, 2, 3, 8, 135, 136, 137, 171
Brunswick, Duchess of. See Eleonore d'Olbreuze.
Buchan, Alice, 141
Buller, Sir Redvers (1839–1908), General, 53
Burke, Thomas, (1829–82), Under-Secretary for Ireland, 119
Burnaby, Colonel Frederick (1842–85), 181
Byng, Miss, 37
Byron, Lord, 54
Burton, F. W. (1816–1900), Director of the National Gallery, 59

Cambridge, George, 2nd Duke of (1819–1904), 23, 47, 69, 71, 107, 143
Carey, Captain Jahleel Brenton (c. 1847–85), 52
Carlingford, 1st Baron (1823–98), Liberal politician, 187
Caroletta, Princess, 112
Castelbajac, M. de, 46
Cavendish, Lord Frederick. Chief Secretary in Ireland, 119
Cavendish, Lady Frederick, niece of Mrs. Gladstone, 119, 120
Cazelet, Edward (1827–83), 143, 145
Celebrities Under Fire, 42
Ceteywayo (d. 1884), Zulu Chief, 124
Chamberlain, Joseph (1836–1914), Statesman, 78, 131, 169
Charles X, 114
Charles Kingsley; His Letters and Memories of his Life by his Wife, 102
Charlotte, a masseuse, 146, 147
Chelmsford, Frederick Augustus, 2nd Baron (1827–1905), 2, 45, 52
Chichester, Dean of, 106
Churchill, Lady Jane, daughter of 2nd Lord Conyngham (d. 1900), Lady of the Bedchamber, 133
Churchill, Lord Randolph (1849–95), 6, 191
Clarendon, Earl of (1800–70), Foreign Secretary, 57, 184
Clark, Sir James (1788–1870), Queen Victoria's doctor, 125
Clary, Mme., 46
Coghill, Nevill, Lieutenant, 85
Connaught, H.R.H. The Duchess of (1860–1917), daughter of Prince Frederick Charles of Prussia, 3, 23, 27, 52, 122, 126, 133, 191, 192
Connaught, H.R.H. Prince Arthur, Duke of (1850–1942), 23, 27, 33, 35, 36, 52, 107, 122, 125, 126, 127, 129, 184, 191, 192, 193
Connor, George Henry (1822–83), Dean of Windsor, 138, 139
Conroy, Sir J., 99
Corbould, Edward Henry (1815–1905), water-colour painter, 93

Corry, Montagu (1838-1903). See Lord Rowton
Corvisart, Dr., 44
Courtney, Leonard Henry, 1st Baron (1832-1918), Politician and writer for *The Times*, 131
Cowell, Sir John (1832-94), Master of the Household, 97, 133
Cranbrook, 1st Earl of (1814-1906), Conservative statesman, 192
Crewe, Mr., 34
Cross, Sir R., 152
Cumberland, Duke of. See Hanover
Currie, Sir Donald, 148
Czapaska, Countess. See Madame de Kolomine

Dante (1265-1321), 123, 126, 127
Davidson, Randall (1848-1930), Dean of Windsor, afterwards Archbishop of Canterbury, 139
Denmark, King Charles IX of, 148
Denmark, Queen Louise of (1817-98), 148
Denmark, Princess Thyra of (1853-1933), married Duke of Cumberland, 27
Derby, 15th Earl (1826-93), 121, 178
Dickens, Charles, 39
Diesbach, Ghislain de, 180
Dilke, Sir Charles (1843-1911), 24, 78, 130, 131, 152, 191
Dillon, Irish politician, 119
Dino, Duc de (1813-94), Son of the Duc de Talleyrand and the Duchesse de Courland, 139
Disraeli, 78. See also Beaconsfield
Dodson, John, afterwards Lord Monk Bretton, 130
Dolgorouka, Catherine (1840-1922), morganatic wife of Czar Alexander II, 81, 82, 91, 92
Dönhoff, Marie, Countess, stepdaughter to Marco Minghetti, the Italian Prime Minister, 139
Dr. Routh, 102
Drummond, Mrs., probably the daughter of "Conversation" Sharp who died in 1891, 105
Dufferin and Ava, Marquess of (1826-1902), 97, 158, 189, 191

Ecilaw, Ary, 165
Edinburgh, H.R.H. Prince Alfred, Duke of (1844-1900), 27, 34, 35, 65, 77, 81, 104, 105, 107, 117, 129, 132, 149, 159, 167
Edinburgh, H.R.H. The Duchess of (1853-1920), daughter of Alexander II of Russia, 3, 27, 34, 57, 65, 77, 81, 97, 99, 104, 107, 126, 132, 149
Edinburgh, H.R.H. Prince Philip, Duke of (b. 1921), 188
Eliot, George, 39

Eliot, T. S., 11
Elliot, Sir Henry (1817-1907), Ambassador at Vienna, 103, 157
Elphinstone, Sir Howard (1829-90), Major-General, 48
Elvey, George Job (1816-93), Organist at St. George's, Windsor, 31
Ely, Lady (d. 1890), wife of 3rd Earl, 45, 46, 133
Embassies of Other Days, 41, 105
Erbach-Schonberg, Princess Marie of (1852-1923), nèe Battenberg, 188
Erroll, 19th Earl (1823-91), 102
Esher, 2nd Viscount (1852-1930), 2
Eugénie, Empress of the French (1826-1920), 2, 44, 45, 46, 47, 48, 49, 56, 57, 163
Eulenberg, Count Philip (1847-1921), 86, 114, 115
Evans, Mr., the Queen's dentist, 140
Ewart, Colonel, 128
Expansion of England, The, 172

Farquharsons of Invercauld, the, 90
Fawcett, Henry (1833-84), Politician, 171
Figner, Vera Nikolaevna (1852-1942), Author of *Memoirs of a Revolutionary* (7 volumes), 97
Frere, Sir Bartle (1815-84), 42
Frere, Lady, wife of Sir Bartle, 42, 44
Freycinet, Charles (1828-1923), Premier of France, 117
Forbes, Archibald (1838-1903), correspondent of *The Daily News*, 41, 42
Fowler, H. W., 10

Galliera, Duchesse de, 56, 59, 60
Gambetta, Léon (1838-82), French statesman, 131
Gardiner, A. G., 95
Gattsberg, General Macdonald, 170
Genoa, Duchess of (b. 1830), married the brother of King Victor Emanuel II, 55
Geyersberg, Fraulein Geyer von, afterwards Baroness von Hochberg, 180
Gladstone, William Ewart (1809-98), 2, 3, 5, 6, 7, 8, 24, 42, 70, 73, 74, 75, 76, 78, 79, 83, 84, 88, 89, 98, 105, 106, 119, 121, 123, 126, 127, 130, 131, 147, 148, 151, 152, 158, 160, 168, 172, 178, 182, 183, 184, 191
Gladstone, Mrs., wife of the above, 105, 120
Gleichen, Lord Edward (b. 1863), Major-General, 180
Goddard, Father, 48
Gonzales, Otero, Spanish assassin, 61
Gordon, Charles George (1833-85), General, 159, 161, 172, 180, 182, 183
Goschen, George Joachim, 1st Viscount (1831-1907), Liberal Unionist, 84, 103
Graham, General Sir J., 161, 162
Grant-Duff, Sir Mountstewart Elphinstone (1829-1906), 54, 55, 84

Granville, 2nd Earl (1815-91), 75, 79, 88, 89, 90, 121, 147, 156, 158, 168, 169, 172, 178, 194
Greece, Queen Olga, wife of King George I, 126
Grey, General (1804-70), 125

HAMILTON, Princess Mary of Baden, Duchess of (d. 1888), 117
Hamilton, 13th Duke of (1845-95), 122, 123, 126, 127, 128
Hammond, J. L., 6
Hanover, Ernest of, Duke of Cumberland (1845-1923), only son of the last King of Hanover, 23, 27, 37, 69, 70, 78
Hanover, King George V of (1819-78), 36, 71
Hanover, Princess Frederica of, 36, 37, 69, 70, 71, 76, 78
Harcourt, Sir William (1827-1904), Liberal leader, 152
Hartington, Marquess of and later 8th Duke of Devonshire (1833-1908), 41, 75, 88, 158
Hatherley, William Page-Wood, 1st Baron (1801-81), 54
Helena, H.R.H. Princess. See Schleswig-Holstein
Helfmann, Jesse, 97
Henforth, H. W. (1852-81), 35
Hermann, 140
Hesse, Prince Alexander of (1828-88), 18, 19, 188
Hesse, Grand Duchess of (H.R.H. Princess Alice), (1843-78), 1, 18, 19, 23, 24, 26, 28, 29, 30, 31, 32, 33, 34, 54, 69, 72, 73, 82, 110, 152, 183, 193
Hesse, Princess Alix of (1872-1918), 23, 24, 29
Hesse, Princess Anna (d. 1865), sister of Grand Duke Louis, 183
Hesse, Prince Charles of, 38
Hesse, Princess Elizabeth of (1864-1918), married the Grand Duke Serge of Russia, 23, 26, 73, 74, 82, 111, 135, 152, 153, 168, 173, 188
Hesse, Prince Ernest Louis of (1868-1937), 28, 29, 188
Hesse, Princess Irene of (1866-1953), 29, 135
Hesse, Grand Duke Louis IV (1837-92), husband of Princess Alice, 24, 28, 31, 32, 34, 67, 134, 135, 142, 148, 164, 167, 168, 188, 191, 192, 193, 195
Hesse, Grand Duke Louis II, 18
Hesse, Grand Duke Louis III, 18
Hesse, Princess Marie of (1874-78), 33
Hesse, Princess Victoria of (1863-1950), married Prince Louis of Battenberg, 23, 28, 65, 73, 82, 111, 141, 148, 165, 173, 184, 188
Hesse-Cassel, Landgravine Anne (b. 1836),

daughter of Prince Charles of Prussia, 133
Hesse-Cassel, Princess Elizabeth of (1861-1955), married Leopold, Hereditary Prince of Anhalt-Dessau, 155, 165
Hewett, Admiral Sir William, V.C., 159
Hochberg, Baroness von. See Geyersberg
Hohenzollern, Antoinette, 39
Holland, Lady, 74
Horsley, John Callcott (1817-1903), Published Recollections of a Royal Academician, 93
Hudson, Sir James (1810-85), Diplomat, 139
Hunt, Henry, 133
Hutchinson, Mrs. (née Codrington), 170
Hutten, Ulrich von, 165

IDDESLEIGH, Earl of (1818-87), Conservative Politician, 191, 192
Ignatiev, Nikolai Pavlovich (1832-1908), Russian General and diplomat, 103
Italy, Queen Marguerite of (b. 1851), wife of King Humbert, 40, 41, 55, 72
Italy, King Humbert of (1844-1900), 40, 41, 55, 72, 155
Italy, King Victor Emanuel of, 105

JAMES, Robert Rhodes, 190
Jenner, Sir William (1815-98), Queen Victoria's doctor, 29, 31, 40, 136

KENMARE, Lord (1825-1905), Lord Chamberlain, 118
Kent, Duchess of (1786-1861), the Queen's mother, 99
Ketchwayo. See Ceteywayo
Khedive, 126, 161
King Edward VII, 96
King's Second Marriage, A or The Romance of a German Court, 165
Kingsley, Charles (1819-95), leading Anglican and novelist, 102
Kolomine, Alexandrine von (1854-193?), married Louis, Grand Duke of Hesse, 165

LACAITA, Sir James (1813-95), Italian scholar, naturalised Englishman, 139
Langham, Eva, daughter of 4th Lord Macdonald, 65
Layard, Sir Austen Henry (1817-94), Archaeologist and diplomat, 103, 143
Leighton, Sir Frederick (1830-96), Artist, 59
Leiningen, Emich, Hereditary Prince of, 190
Leiningen, Prince Ernest of (1830-1904), 133
Leopold, H.R.H. Prince. See Duke of Albany
Les Fourberies de Scapin, 107

Lesseps, M. de (1805-94), Promoter of the Suez Canal, 143
Letters of Harriet, Countess Granville, 60
Liebernau, Major von, Master of the Household to Kaiser William II, 26
Life of Sir William Harcourt, 95
Lindsay, Sir Coutts (1814-1913), 77, 79
Lloyd, Mr. C., 162
Lloyd, Lieut (younger brother of Mr. C. Lloyd), 162
Londonderry, 5th Marquess of (1841-84), 171
Lord William Russell and his Wife, 90
Lorne, Marquis of (1845-1913), afterwards 9th Duke of Argyll, married H.R.H. Princess Louise, 24, 65, 170
Louise, H.R.H. Princess (1848-1939), married Marquis of Lorne, 3, 24, 65, 78, 105, 170
Lyons, 1st Earl (1817-87), Ambassador at Paris, 1867-87, 116, 117
Lumley, Sir John Savile Lumley, Ambassador in Rome 1883-8, 157
Lumsden, Sir Peter (1829-1918), General, served in India and Afghanistan, 189
Luther, Martin (1483-1546), 165
Lytton, 1st Earl of (1831-91), Viceroy of India. As Owen Meredith wrote many poems, 42, 84

MACDONALD, Alexander (1821-81), Working Men's M.P. for Stafford, 24
Maclean, R., 116
McNeill, Sir John Carstairs (1831-1904), General. Equerry to the Queen, 38, 185, 190
Magnus, Sir Philip, 96
Mahdi, the, 161
Malcolm, Alexander (1813-93), Timber merchant at Venice, 139
Malet, Sir Edward (1837-1908), 4th Baronet. Ambassador to Berlin 1884-96, 191
Manchester, Duchess of (d. 1911), daughter of the Comte d'Alten. After the Duke of Manchester's death married the Duke of Devonshire, 107
Manners, Lord John, afterwards 7th Duke of Rutland (1818-1906). Politician, 192
Manzoni, Alessandro (1785-1873), Italian novelist and poet, 103
Marlborough, Duke of, 123
Martin, Sir Theodore (1816-1909), 140
Maynard, Frances (1861-1938), Countess of Warwick, 71
Mecklenburg, Prince Paul of, 101, 103
Mecklenburg-Strelitz, Augusta Grand-Duchess of (1822-1916), 69, 71, 74
Melvill, Teignmouth, 85
Middleton, R. D., 102
Milner, Lord, 42
Minghetti, Marco (1818-86), Italian statesman and scholar, 58

Mitchell, Mr., 139
Molière (1622-73), French dramatist, 107
Moltke, Count Helmut von (1800-91), Prussian General, 48
Monaco, Charles III, Prince of (1818-89), 114
Montagu, Lord Robert, Conservative politician, 41
Montpensier, Antoine, son of Duc de Montpensier, 60
Montpensier, Duchesse de (1832-97), Infanta of Spain, 59, 60, 61
Montpensier, Ferdinand, Duc de (1824-90), youngest son of Louis Philippe, 59, 60, 61
Morelli, Domenico (1826-1901), Italian painter, 58, 139
Morier, Sir Robert (1826-93), Ambassador at St. Petersburg, 172
Morley, John (Gladstone's biographer), 7, 169
Morris, Donald, 52
Mortimer, Raymond, 10
Most, Johann, Editor of Freiheit, 98
Mouchy, Anne Murat, Duchesse de, 46
Mouchy, Duc de, 46
Murat, Prince Joachim, 46
Münster, Count, afterwards Prince (1820-1902), 112
My Early Life, by the ex-Kaiser, 26, 167

NAPIER, 1st Baron of Magdala (1810-90), Commander-in-Chief in India, 1870-6, 54
Napoleon III (1808-73), 2, 138
Napoleon, Prince Imperial (1856-79), 2, 44, 45, 46, 47, 48, 49, 56
Nelidov, 156
Netherlands, King William III of (1817-90), 34, 118
Netherlands, Prince Henry of (1820-79), brother of King William III, 27, 34, 35
Netherlands, Princess Henry of (1855-88), daughter of Prince Frederick Charles of Prussia, 27, 33, 34, 35
Netherlands, Queen Emma of (1858-1934), 34, 112, 118
New Gleanings from Gladstone, 70
Nightingale, Florence (1820-1910), 107
Noër, Count, son of Prince Frederick of Schleswig-Holstein, 115
Noër, Countess (formerly Carmelite Eisenblat), 115
Nordenskield, Baron Nils (1832-1901), 86
Norfolk, 15th Duke of (1847-1917), 106
Northcote, Sir Stafford (see Lord Iddesleigh)

O'KELLY, Irish politician, 119
Olbreuze, Eleonore d' (d. 1722). Married the Duke of Celle. The Duke and

Olbreuze, Eleonore d'—*cont.*
Duchess were the parents of King
George I, 179, 180
Osman Digna, 161

PAGET, Sir Augustus (1822-96), Diplomat,
156
Paget, Walburga (d. 1929), wife of Sir
Augustus Paget, 41, 75, 76, 77, 78, 105,
144, 156, 157
Pallavicini, Marchese, 56
Palmerston, 3rd Viscount (1784-1865),
Statesman, 84, 184
Parnell, Charles Stewart (1846-91), Irish
politician, 119
Pawel-Rimmingen, Baron Alphonse de,
son of 1st *conseiller intime* to the Duke of
Saxe-Coburg-Gotha, 69, 70, 71
Pearson, Canon, 125
Persia, Shah of, Nasr-Ed-Din (1831-96),
120, 145
Phipps, Sir Charles (1801-66), 125
Pietri, Franchesini, attached to the Court of
Napoleon III in England, 44
Pitt, Miss, 144
Plymouth, Earl of (1857-1923), 144
Ponsonby, Sir Henry (1825-95), the
Queen's private secretary, 46, 94, 108,
133, 152
Ponsonby-Fane, Spencer (1824-1915), 25
Poynter, Sir Edward (1856-1919), Presi-
dent of the Royal Academy, 93
Portugal, Charles of, afterwards King Car-
los I, 147, 153
Portugal, King Louis of (1838-89), 147
Portugal, King Pedro V· of (1837-61),
147
Prince Imperial. See Napoleon
Pringle, Miss, 107
Prussia, Prince Adalbert of (1811-73), 26
Prussia, Prince Albrecht of, 19
Prussia, Princess Albrecht of (1810-83),
Princess of the Netherlands, 64
Prussia, Princess Albert of (known as Marie
Abbat) (1854-98), 91
Prussia, Princess Augusta Victoria (Dona)
(1858-1921), wife of Prince William, 42,
50, 61, 64, 66, 69, 70, 71, 72, 79, 90, 91,
95, 96, 97, 108, 110, 121, 122, 146, 151,
174, 178, 179
Prussia, Augusta, German Empress (1811-
90), 26, 29, 33, 38, 42, 43, 49, 55, 65, 70,
89, 91, 95, 96, 132, 134, 151, 154, 157,
164, 166, 169, 173, 174, 177, 178, 179,
180, 183, 187, 188, 192, 193, 194
Prussia, Princess Charlotte of. See Saxe-
Meiningen
Prussia, Prince Charles of, 70, 132, 133,
134, 155
Prussia, Prince Eitel Frederick (1883-1942),
2nd son of Prince William, 144
Prussia, Queen Elise of, 64, 65

Prussia, Prince Frederick Charles of (Fritz
Carl) (1823-85), 23, 27, 33, 37, 38, 39,
127, 133, 158, 160, 190
Prussia, Prince Frederick Leopold of (1863-
1931), son of Prince Fritz Carl, 132
Prussia, Elector Frederick William III
(1770-1840), 64
Prussia, Frederick William, German
Crown Prince (1831-88) (Fritz), 19, 23,
25, 27, 31, 32, 36, 37, 39, 41, 47, 49,
51, 52, 58, 62, 63, 66, 67, 72, 74, 77, 91,
92, 95, 96, 98, 108, 110, 114, 115, 118,
119, 121, 132, 134, 143, 145, 147, 148,
151, 153, 154, 155, 163, 165, 166, 170,
174, 176, 177, 178, 179, 181, 189, 191,
193, 194
Prussia, Prince Frederick William (1882-
1951), eldest son of Prince William, 121,
122, 144
Prussia, the German Crown Princess (The
Princess Royal) (1840-1901)

1878
Agrees that the name of Prince Henry's
ship should be changed, 26; comforts the
Queen on the death of Princess Alice, 30;
is unhappy at being prevented from attending Princess Alice's funeral, 32.

1879
Feels for the young widow of Prince
Henry of the Netherlands, 34; and fears
that little provision had been made for
her, 35; praises Prince Waldemar, 35; is
sad to be leaving London after the Duke
of Connaught's wedding, 36; declares
that the King of Hanover chose to become the enemy of Germany, 36-7; but
promises to help to restore the Hanoverian revenue to his family, 37; reports that
Prince Fritz Carl was not pleased by his
visit to England, 37, 38; is anxious because Prince Waldemar has diphtheria,
37; tells of his death, 38; is pleased with
Prince Alexander of Battenberg but
doubts the wisdom of his election as
Prince of Bulgaria, 43; reports the Emperor's relief that the Emperor of Russia
is not to visit Berlin, 43; is interested in
the Queen's reports of the Zulu War and
suggests some reform in military arrangements, 48-9; saddened by Prince
Waldemar's clothes, 49; feels the Franco-
German war should not be blamed entirely on the German Emperor, 49;
thinks contemporary German policy
disgraceful, 50; reports that Prince
William wishes to marry Princess Victoria of Schleswig-Holstein, 50; feels it a
release to escape from Berlin to stay in
Italy, 53; defends Mr. Grant Duff, 55; is
hurt by the Emperor's refusal to let her

Prussia, The German Crown Princess (The Princess Royal) (1840–1901) *1879—cont.*

daughters join her in Italy, 55; visits the King and Queen of Italy, 55; regrets Prince William's lack of interest in travel, 56; describes her feelings in taking off her crepe mourning, 56; agrees that the Empress Eugénie is not a fanatical ultramontane, 57; is grieved that the Crown Prince will not spend Christmas with her, 58; regrets attacks by Oxford enthusiasts on the restoration of St. Mark's, 58; suggests that national monuments and pictures in England should be cleaned, 59.

1880

Feels that Sovereigns should insure their lives against assassination, 61; is saddened by the death of the Duke of Schleswig-Holstein and fears its affect on the possibility of Prince William marrying his daughter, 62; is disturbed by Bismarck's influence over the Emperor, 63; and finds it impossible to be friends with the regime, 63; reports the Emperor's agreement to Prince William's engagement, 63; but fears his choice of bride may not be popular, 64, 67; observes that wives of the Prussian Royal Family do not receive the same loyalty as their husbands, 64–5; is thankful for Prince William's happiness, 66; discusses Russian assassins and the Crown Prince's fear that their attempts may be copied in Berlin, 66; thinks Stephanie of Belgium's engagement to the Austrian Crown Prince very sudden, 68; wishes that Prince William's engagement was not being kept secret, 68; regrets not seeing the Queen when she visits Germany, 69, 72; is not surprised by the news of Frederica of Hanover's engagement, 70; is glad that the Queen is pleased with Princess Victoria of Schleswig-Holstein but agrees that Prince William ought to see more of the world before marrying, 71; reports the congratulations received on Prince William's engagement but reflects that it is hard to forget lost loved ones, 72; finds Rome much altered, 72; appreciates the Queen's anxiety at the change of Government and reports that many in Germany are disturbed that the Liberals are in office, 74; is disappointed at the changes in Naples, 74; asks for a picture by Tintoretto for her birthday, 74; praises her daughter, Princess Margaret, 75; feels Lord Beaconsfield will be glad of rest from Government, 75; reports on Wally Paget's artistic efforts, 75, 77–8; reflects on the situation in Europe and is horrified at the thought of Germany and Russia becoming allies and feels that Bismarck is convinced that Gladstone is a friend of France, 76–7; proposes that, if Turkey is to disappear, a new state should be organised and governed by the Duke of Edinburgh, 77; is pained by the frigidness towards her in Germany on her return and shocked by the state of politics, 79–80; deplores the tendency of Russia to expand, 80–81; discusses the rumours regarding the Russian Royal Family, 81; feels Prince William is too busy with military duties, 83; and finds him chauvinistic and ultra Prussian, 85; is upset by the shooting of Prince Waldemar's cat, 86; confesses she is not proud of Prince Henry, 87; but feels she should give the Queen her frank opinion of her children's characters, 87–8; complains about the constant entertaining at the Court in Berlin, 89, 94; describes the completion service at Cologne Cathedral, 90–91; explains that Prussian princesses have three ladies-in-waiting when they marry, 91; complains of growing unsightly, 91; informs the Queen that the Emperor of Russia has remarried, 91–2; is shocked at the anti-Jewish disturbances in Germany, 93; gives her idea of a liberal, 93; and holds that the British Constitution is the best in the world, 94; puts forward a candidate for the appointment of Surveyor to the Queen's Pictures, 94.

1881

Describes Prince William's wedding ceremonies, 95–6; and complains of exhaustion, 96; is much struck by Sandro Battenberg, 98; reports that Russian news is melancholy, 99; records the curious marriage of Prince Paul of Mecklenburg, 101; and does not know what will come of it, 103; finds Wagner's trilogy dull and tiresome, 101; is not pleased by the Emperor of Russia's appeal for loyalty of his people, 102; is curious about the details of Sultan Abdul Aziz's murder, 103; is moved by Rossi's rendering of Dante, 103; is shocked by the French being in Tunis, 103; announces a visit to England, 103; and records details of the visit, 106; finds the International Electrical Exhibition in Paris very interesting, 108; is distressed that the Crown Prince was not mentioned during the proceedings in Kiel, 108; reflects that Parliament and the Crown in Germany are only shadows and is alarmed that under Bismarck there will be a rise of communism, 109; but is glad that the elections

Prussia, the German Crown Princess (The Princess Royal) (1840–1901) 1881—*cont.* returned so many Liberals, 109; is hurt that Princess Christian is to make the arrangements for a nurse for Princess William, 110; but finds that Prince William is being kinder to her, 110; wonders why Prince Bismarck's son has been sent to London, 113; describes her room, 113.

1882
Reports that the Crown Prince is horrified by the Royal Rescript, 114; and that his position gets more unbearable, 114–15; is upset that the International Hygienic Exhibition at Berlin is burned down, 119; asks to send the Queen a pamphlet on the proposed scheme for a railway through the Euphrates valley, 120; feels it will be a mistake if Germans and not English build the railway, 121; is disappointed at the name given to Prince William's son, 122; urges that the Duke of Hamilton's Dante manuscript should be kept in England, 123, 126, 127, 128; is glad that Turkey has declared Arabi a rebel, 124; describes a visit to Val d' Anzasca, 124; is pleased to see the Crown Prince and Princess of Austria, 125; describes how her bed caught fire, 127.

1883
Describes the death of Prince Charles of Prussia, 132; and its effect on her Silver Wedding, 132, 133; gives details of Prince Charles' will, 133; comments on disagreeableness between the Grand Duke of Hesse and the Baden family, 134; expresses sympathy at the death of John Brown, 136, 137; but feels silence is a better proof of sympathy, 139; suggests remedy for the Queen's rheumatism, 137; describes the journey to Venice over the Brenner Pass, 138; does not think the state of Russia improved, 140; understands that the Queen cannot receive her but proposes to visit the Prince of Wales, 141; is hurt by the Queen's request that she should not come to England, 142; sends pamphlets showing the scheme for the Euphrates River Railway, 143; informs the Queen of the new Mauser rifle being distributed in Germany, 143; writes at length on her views on Russia, 144–5; comments on Coburg affair, 149; stresses her concern for the Queen's health, 150; is distressed that Prince William consults the Emperor and Empress rather than his parents, 151; sends pamphlet about the housing of the working-classes in London, 151-2, over which she feels that the Queen and the Prince of Wales could have influence, 152; expresses her opinion of the Grand Duke Serge of Russia, 153; is relieved that the Bulgarian situation is improving and hopes it may mean that Princess Victoria's wish to marry Prince Alexander may be granted, 154.

1884
Is appalled by the nihilistic murder at Petersburg, 155-6; regrets being unable to share the Queen's recollections in her Scotch Diary, 157; is grieved to be separated from the Queen on the death of the Duke of Albany, 162; is distressed by the Prussian family's disapproval of Princess Victoria's wish to marry Prince Alexander, 166; describes a visit to a farmhouse near Braemar, 170; records reports of Princess Elizabeth of Hesse being divorced, 173; regrets the German flag is hoisted in New Guinea, 174; is criticised by the Emperor, 174.

1885
Suggests that the Queen reads a book about Eleonore d'Olbreuze, 179; reports the end of Princess Victoria's romance, 181-2; and asks the Queen to write to the Princess, 182; proposes candidate for the post of Director of the Science and Art Museum in Edinburgh, 186-7; explains the etiquette for representing the Queen at a German Royal Funeral, 192; apologises for calling Sir Stafford Northcote old, 192; feels the Empress's influence on Prince William is not good, 193; reports a luncheon visit by Prince Bismarck, 193.

Prussia, Prince Henry of, 2nd son of the Crown Princess (1862-1929), 25, 26, 87, 115, 159, 166, 178

Prussia, Princess Louise of, daughter of Prince Fritz Carl. See Duchess of Connaught

Prussia, Queen Louise of (1776-1810), wife of Frederick William III, 64, 65

Prussia, Princess Margaret of (1872-1954), youngest daughter of the Crown Princess, m. Frederick Charles, Landgrave of Hesse, 74, 75

Prussia, Princess Marianne (1837-1906), wife of Prince Fritz Carl, 27, 37, 38, 39, 133, 158, 190

Prussia, Princess Sophia of, 3rd daughter of the Crown Princess (1870-1932), married King Constantine of the Hellenes, 106

Prussia, Princess Victoria of (1866-1929), 2nd daughter of the Crown Princess, 98, 146, 147, 154, 155, 164, 166, 167, 170, 175, 181, 182, 195

Prussia, Prince Waldemar of (1868-79), youngest son of the Crown Princess, 2, 35, 37, 40, 49, 51, 86, 88
Prussia, William I, German Emperor (1797-1888), 8, 9, 29, 32, 33, 36, 43, 44, 49, 50, 55, 58, 61, 63, 65, 68, 70, 89, 91, 92, 95, 96, 103, 108, 110, 114, 115, 119, 120, 121, 132, 134, 140, 151, 153, 154, 157, 166, 169, 174, 178, 181, 188, 192, 193
Prussia, Prince William of (1859-1941), later Kaiser William II, 25, 26, 42, 50, 51, 56, 57, 61, 62, 63, 64, 65, 66, 68, 69, 71, 72, 73, 83, 85, 86, 90, 95, 96, 108, 110, 115, 121, 122, 140, 146, 150, 151, 166, 167, 174, 175, 178, 179, 183, 193

REDGRAVE, Richard (1804-88), Surveyor of the Queen's Pictures, 93, 94
Richmond, 6th Duke of (1818-1903), Conservative politician, 192
Ripon, 1st Marquess of (1827-1909), 84
Roberts, Sir Frederick, later 1st Earl (1832-1914), Field Marshal, 88, 92
Roberts, Lady (d. 1920), née Norah Bews, wife of the above, 92
Robinson, Sir John (1824-1913), Art connoisseur, 93, 94, 124, 139
Rokeby, 6th Lord (1798-1883), 140
Rosebery, 190
Rosebery, Archibald, 5th Earl (1847-1929), Statesman, 189, 190
Rosebery, Hannah (d. 1890), daughter of Baron Meyer de Rothschild, 190
Routh, Dr., 102
Rossi, Ernesto (1829-96), Italian actor, 101, 102, 103
Rowton, Montagu William Lowry-Corry, 1st Lord (1838-1903), Private secretary to Disraeli and founder of the Rowton housing schemes, 23, 100
Roxburghe, Duchess of (died 1895), Lady of the Bedchamber to the Queen, 25, 141
Ruskin, John, 58
Russell, Lord Odo (1829-84), Ambassador at Berlin, 89, 90, 175, 178
Russell, Emily (d. 1927), Lady of the Bedchamber to the Queen and wife of the above, 89, 175
Russia, Emperor Alexander II of, (1818-81), 18, 43, 65, 81, 82, 91, 92, 97, 98, 99
Russia, Emperor Alexander III of (1845-94), 82, 92, 97, 102, 145, 147, 148, 155, 156, 188
Russia, Dagmar (Minny), wife of Alexander III, 92
Russia, Empress Marie (1824-80), wife of Alexander II, 81, 82, 92
Russia, Grand Duchess Marie of, daughter of Emperor Alexander II, married H.R.H. Prince Alfred. See Duchess of Edinburgh

Russia, Grand Duke Alexis (1850-1908), Admiral, 83
Russia, Grand Duke Constantine (1827-92), 81, 99
Russia, Grand Duke Michael (1832-1901), 99
Russia, Grand Duke Nicholas (1832-1909), 81
Russia, Grand Duke Paul (1860-1919), 99, 167
Russia, Grand Duke Serge (1857-1905), 99, 153, 161, 167, 168, 188
Russia, Grand Duke Vladimir (1847-1909), 99
Rylands, George, 11
Ryleev, General, 91

SAHL, Hermann, German Secretary to the Queen, 28, 133
Salisbury, Marquess of (1820-1903), Prime Minister, 34, 54, 55, 107, 191, 194
Salvini, Tommaro (1829-1916), Italian tragedian, 101
Satarov, Count (1835-1918), Russian Ambassador at Berlin, 80
Saxe-Altenburg, Princess Alexandra of, wife of Grand Duke Constantine of Russia, 99
Saxe-Coburg-Gotha, Alexandrine, Duchess of, wife of Ernest II, 4, 66, 141, 148
Saxe-Coburg-Gotha, Duke Ernest II of (1818-92), 64, 65, 66, 68, 69, 88, 95, 117, 129, 140, 141, 148, 149, 158
Saxe-Meiningen, Bernhard III, Duke of (1851-1928), 67, 85
Saxe-Meiningen, Princess Charlotte of (b. 1860), wife of the above and eldest daughter of the Crown Princess, 38, 39, 53, 57, 67, 85, 90, 108, 166
Saxe-Meiningen, Princess Feodore (b. 1879), daughter of the above, 67, 85, 142
Saxony, Prince George of (1832-1904), 187
Scharf, Sir George (1820-95), Director of the National Portrait Gallery, 59
Schaumberg-Lippe, Prince Adolph of, 98
Schleinitz, Alexander, Prussian Foreign Minister, 50
Schleswig-Holstein, Princess Augusta Victoria of (Dona). See Prussia
Schleswig-Holstein, Princess Caroline Matilda of (Calma) (b. 1860), 50, 69, 70, 79
Schleswig-Holstein, Prince Christian of (1831-1917), married H.R.H. Princess Helena, 62, 69, 115, 117, 146
Schleswig-Holstein, H.R.H. Princess Christian of (1846-1923), 52, 69, 79, 102, 105, 110, 115, 142, 146, 152, 160, 176
Schleswig-Holstein, Adelaide, Duchess of (1835-1900), 64, 67, 69, 70
Schleswig-Holstein, Frederick, Duke of (1829-80), 62, 64, 67

Schleswig-Holstein, Prince Frederick of, 115
Schreiber, Lady Charlotte (1812-95) daughter of 9th Earl of Lindsay. A noted collector, 106
Schwabe, Madame, 74
Schweinitz, Colonel in Prussian Army, 91, 92
Scott, Mr., Clergyman at Coburg, 34, 95
Scrap Screen, A, 142
Seckendorf, Count Götz von, 159
Secrets of the Gotha, 180
Seeley, J. R., 172
Seymour, Sir Beauchamp, 122
Shore, Rev. J. Teignmouth, Chaplain in Ordinary to the Queen, 167
Singh, Dhuleep, 116
Smith, Colonel Murdoch, 186, 187
Soudaikin, Colonel-in-Chief of the Russian Secret Police, 155
Southampton, Lady, 144
Spain, Alphonso XII, King of (1857-85), 61, 148, 155
Spain, Queen Isabella of (1830-1904), abdicated 1868, 84
Spain, Queen Marie Christina of (1858-1929), 61
Spinola, Marchesa, 56
Stanley, Arthur (1815-81), Dean of Westminster, 105, 125, 135
Stanley, Lady Augusta, wife of above, 125
Strachey, Sir John (1823-1907), Indian Administrator, 84
Strachey, Lytton, 10, 11
Stratford de Redcliffe, Viscount (1786-1880), 120, 143
Suther, Thomas George (1814-83), Bishop of Aberdeen, 102
Sydney, 3rd Viscount and 1st Earl (1805-90), formerly Lord Chamberlain, 44, 45, 46, 133

TAIT, A. C. (1811-82), Archbishop of Canterbury, 4
Teck, Mary, Duchess of (1833-97), 167
Tennyson, Lord (1809-92), Poet Laureate, 146, 148
Thornton, Sir Edward (1817-1906), Diplomat, 173
Tintoretto, Italian painter, 74
Turkey, Sultan of, 84, 158

Une Mésalliance aus dans le maison de Brunswick, 179

VICTORIA, H.M. Queen (1819–1901)

1878
Discusses Princess Alice's daughters, 23; is disturbed by Ernest of Hanover's announcement of his father's death, 23; dwells on Lord Beaconsfield's qualities, 24; announces that Princess Louise and the Marquess of Lorne are to go to Canada, 24; comments on the dangers of water, 25; criticises the Crown Prince's way of signing official letters to her, 25; is half pleased at becoming a grandmother, 26; feels that Prince William should not marry too early, 26; explains Ernest of Hanover's title and engagement, 27; explains why the Crown Princess cannot stay with her after the Duke of Connaught's wedding, 27; is concerned that Russian troops have re-occupied land around Turkey, 28; agonises over the illness of the Hesse children and the death of Princess May, 28, 29; the death of Princess Alice, 30, 29; tells the Crown Princess to try to understand her mother-in-law, 29; is shocked that the Crown Prince is prevented from attending Princess Alice's funeral, 31.

1879
Comments on Princess Alice's faith, 33; and on the German Court's attitude to mourning, 33; assures the Crown Princess that the retiring British Counsellor in Coburg will be replaced, 34; expresses her views on marriage, 34; plans to visit Italy as Countess of Balmoral, 35; is grieved at the trials of the Crown Princess in Berlin, 36; is anxious over the illness of Prince Waldemar, 38; feels Prince Fritz Carl's behaviour in England shows lack of breeding, 38; sympathises at the death of Prince Waldemar, 39; is concerned over the Crown Princess's rheumatism, 40; describes her visit to Italy, 40-41; is shocked by implications that she had used her Royal Prerogative injudiciously, 41; unwilling to interfere in Prince William's marriage prospects, 42; is pleased with the visit of the Battenberg princes, 44; agonises over the death of the Prince Imperial, 44-5; and goes to comfort the Empress Eugénie, 46-7; fears that the Prince Imperial had not been sufficiently protected by British troops, 48; describes mud at the Agricultural Show, 50; sympathises with the Crown Princess in her family problems, 51; receives and decorates heroes of the Zulu War, 52, 53; explains the British position regarding the Afghan War, 54; comments that sightseeing fatigues her, 56; comments unfavourably on house parties, 57; defends the Empress Eugénie over the ultramontane party, 57.

1880
Is shocked by the Tay Bridge disaster, 61; describes Princess Louise's accident in

Victoria, H.M. Queen (1819–1901)
1880—*cont.*
Canada, 65; congratulates the Crown Princess on Prince William's engagement to Princess Victoria of Schleswig-Holstein, 65; plans to visit Darmstadt for the confirmation of Princess Alice's daughters, 67; comments that married children are often a trial, 67; is surprised by Princess Stephanie's engagement, 68; finds Princesses Victoria and Calma of Schleswig-Holstein pretty and aimable, 69, 70; announces the engagement of Frederica of Hanover, 69; and describes the wedding, 76; is seriously troubled by the election of the Liberal Government, 73, 75, 78, 79; is amused by Wally Paget's artistic efforts, 78; declares she will try and be active to the last, 80; expresses her affection for the children of Princess Alice, 82; is shocked by the morals of the Emperor of Russia, 82; is critical of Mr. Gladstone and of his Government, 83, 84, 88, 90; feels the Crown Princess has misunderstood her views on the Turkish question, 84; expresses her views on babies, 85; is horrified by the killing of the Crown Princess's cat, 87; is proud of the victory at Kandahar, 88, 92; blames the state of affairs in the East on Gladstone's muddling, 89; sympathises over Princess Charlotte's behaviour about Prince William's engagement, 90; writes to warn the Empress of Austria against visiting Ireland, 92; and stresses the alarming state of Ireland, 92, 94; seeks the Princess's advice over the Keeper of the Queen's Pictures, 93.

1881
Admires the Crown Prince's speech about Jews in Germany, 95; is horrified by the assassination of the Emperor Alexander, 97; and discusses the situation at St. Petersburg, 97; defends the annexing of the Transvaal and feels the Boers are treacherous, 98; is shaken by the death of Lord Beaconsfield, 99-100; feels Wagner's "Ring" must be overpowering, 102; corrects the Crown Princess's reference to Bishop Suther as Bishop of Aberdeen, 102; announces that Prince Leopold is to be made a peer, 104; tells the Crown Princess that she cannot receive her at Balmoral in the autumn, 104; foresees that her declining years will be very trying, 104; finds a successor for the Dean of Westminster, 105; complains of the weather, 106, 107; visits Edinburgh for the Volunteer Review, 107; agrees to the pictures at Buck-

ingham Palace being photographed, 108; feels that a Conservative Government provides security, 109; is shocked that Prince William did not consult the Crown Princess about his baby's nurse, 110; announces Prince Leopold's engagement, 1, 11, 112.

1882
Sympathises with the Countess Noër, 115; is gratified by the sympathy and affection shown after she was shot at, 116; is worried by Prince Leopold marrying while still an invalid, 117; describes her visit to Mentone, 117; sends an account by Lord Kenmare of the deplorable state in Ireland, 118; describes Prince Leopold's wedding, 118; is horrified by the stabbing of Lord Frederick Cavendish and Mr. Burke, 119; and reports Gladstone shaken by the news, 119-20; thinks too much fuss is made of the christening of Prince William's son, 120; is indignant about the situation in Egypt and Mr. Gladstone's lack of interest in foreign affairs, 121; feels that Prince William should call his son Fritz, 122; reports the bombardment of Alexandria, 122; is anxious over the Duke of Connaught's part in the Egyptian Expedition, 122; buys pictures and drawings from the Duke of Hamilton, 123; receives Zulu chiefs at Osborne, 124; rejoices at victory in Egypt, 125; is overwhelmed by the death of the Dean of Windsor and feels that many of her devoted friends have died, 125; feels that England must maintain a firm stronghold over Egypt, 126; reports that the Duke of Connaught wishes no fuss made of him, 126; receives the Commander of the Household Cavalry at Balmoral but is shocked by the defective medical arrangements in the Egyptian campaign, 128; her feelings at reviewing the troops from Egypt in St. James's Park, 128; confers medals, 129; is concerned over the publication of the Duke of Coburg's memoirs, 129; is to have Sir Charles Dilke in the Cabinet, 130; reviews the past year, 130.

1883
Comments on the death of Gambetta, 131; lectures the Crown Princess on so-called 'liberal' ideas, 131; is charmed by new Archbishop of Canterbury, 132; is distressed at the Crown Princess's Silver Wedding being spoilt by the death of Prince Charles of Prussia, 132; events at Osborne to mark the Silver Wedding, 133; is shocked by the Emperor giving a

Victoria, H.M. Queen (1819–1901)
1883—*cont.*
banquet so soon after his brother's death, 134; and comments few regret Prince Charles, 134; admires the daughter of Prince Leopold, 134, 139; comments on the possible engagement of Princess Elizabeth of Hesse, 145; is desolated by the death of John Brown, 135, 136, 137; tells of the death of the Dean of Windsor, 138; and appoints his successor, 139; says she is very rheumatic and weak generally, 139, 142; wants the Duke of Coburg's book banned, 140, 141; discusses the engagement of Princess Victoria of Hesse to Prince Louis of Battenberg, 141; asks the Crown Princess to postpone visiting England for another year, 142; comments on children's names, 144; has a visit from Lord Tennyson, 146; is shocked that Prince William has sent away the English nurse, 147; believes Russia is behaving shamefully over Bulgaria and Prince Alexander, 147; describes her French masseuse, 147; and her own infirmity, 149; cannot bear noise and high spirits of young people, 147; is indignant about Mr. Gladstone's visit to Copenhagen and anxious about politics in general, 149; advises the Crown Prince not to visit Spain, 148; declares the Duke of Coburg's conduct monstrous, 148, 149; feels it her duty to attend Princess Victoria of Hesse's wedding, 148, 150; is of the opinion that British troops must remain in Egypt, 150; is concerned about housing of the working-classes in London, 152; is pleased with the Life of Princess Alice, written by Princess Christian, 152; is unhappy about Princess Elizabeth of Hesse's engagement, 153; is pleased with her success at the Cattle Show, 154.

1884
Is anxious about India, Egypt, Ireland and difficulties at home, 155, 156; thinks the Pagets unsuitable for the Embassy in Vienna, 157; is pleased to be visiting the Empress, 157; but is still very crippled, 157; is concerned at Gladstone's lack of understanding of foreign affairs, 158; feels the Prince of Bulgaria should not have founded an Order, 158; and that Prince Fritz Carl has been brutal to his wife, 158; reassures the Crown Princess about Egyptian forces, 159; is gratified by the reception of "More Leaves from a Life in the Highlands", 159, 160; praises Prince Henry of Prussia, 159; is anxious about affairs in Sudan and Gladstone's apparent lack of concern, 160, 161; thinks she will get on well with the

Grand Duke Serge, 161; meets Lt. Lloyd who compares the fighting in the Zulu War with the Egyptian Campaign, 162; writes of the death of Prince Leopold, 162; and describes the funeral services, 163; refers to the difficulties of an engagement between Princess Victoria and the Prince of Battenberg, 164; comments on the morganatic marriage of the Grand Duke of Hesse, 164-5; promises to tell the Empress of her high opinion of Prince Alexander, 166-7; is interested in the building of the English Church in Berlin but suspicious about one of the clergy, 167; recommends patience in the affair of Princess Victoria and Prince Alexander but does not wish Princess Beatrice involved, 167; says the Government is the worst she ever had to do with, 168; comments on the 47th anniversary of her Accession, 168; expresses pity for Prince Alexander and is annoyed with the Empress, 169; troubled by the rejection of the Franchise Bill by the House of Lords, 169; warns against tiring Princess Louise, 170; is more hopeful about home politics, 170; describes the beauty of the Scottish hills, 171; is furious at Gladstone's actions over Egypt, 172; speaks of her love and respect for the Duchess of Albany, 172, 173; is satisfied over the appointment of Morier to the Embassy at St. Petersburg, 173; contradicts rumours that Princess Elizabeth of Hesse is to be divorced, 173; describes the anniversary service for Prince Albert, 173; is grieved at Prince William's politics and about German colonisation, 175, 178; speaks of the pain caused her by the wish of Princess Beatrice to marry Prince Henry of Battenberg, 176.

1885
Is thankful that her health is better, 177; and is pleased about the Crown Princess's understanding of Princess Beatrice's marriage, 177; is surprised that she is reconciled to the idea, 178; is upset by the attitude of the Empress and the Crown Prince and furious at the impertinence of Prince William and the rest of the family, 178, 179; writes to the Empress, 180; is delighted to receive the book about Eleonore d'Olbreuze, 180; reports the heavy losses at the Battle of Abu Klea, 180; agonises over the fall of Khartoum and the Government's attitude, 182; and the death of General Gordon, 183; fears she cannot ask the Crown Princess to the wedding, 182; assures the Crown Princess that many of her letters are burned, 183; longs for a coalition

Victoria, H.M. Queen (1819–1901) 1855—*cont.*
Government, 184-5; expresses satisfaction at the appointment of Lady Ampthill as lady-in-waiting, 184; is distressed that the Duke of Connaught cannot return home, 184; praises the British troops in the Sudan, 185; the agony she feels at Princess Beatrice's forthcoming marriage, 186; describes a visit to Haute Combe, 186; attends the Christening of Princess Victoria of Hesse's daughter, 188; tells Grand Duke Serge to assure the Russian Emperor of her hope that war can be avoided, 188; is annoyed at the insulting letters sent to Prince Alexander by the Emperor and Bismarck, 188; is concerned that the dispute between England and Russia over the Afghan border may result in war, 189; praises Lord Rosebery and commends him to the Crown Princess, 189, 190; deputes the Grand Duke of Hesse to represent her at Prince Fritz Carl's funeral, 190; and is annoyed that he is prevented by protocol from doing so, 191; gives details of the new Government, 191; and the Household changes, 192; is indignant that the Crown Prince should try to prevent her giving the title Royal Highness to Prince Henry of Battenberg, 193-4; describes her feelings at the departure of Princess Beatrice, 195.

Voltaire (1694–1778), 66

WAGNER, Richard (1831-83), 101, 102
Waldeck and Pyrmont, Princess Elizabeth of, 118
Waldeck and Pyrmont, Princess Helen of. See Duchess of Albany
Waldeck and Pyrmont, Princess of, mother of the above, 112, 118
Wales, H.R.H. Albert Edward, Prince of (1841-1910), 27, 36, 57, 79, 90, 96, 105, 117, 120, 129, 135, 141, 142, 152, 164, 191, 192

Wales, Princess of, 57, 79, 167
Wales, Prince Albert Victor of (Eddy) (1864-92), afterwards Duke of Clarence and Avondale, 79
Wales, Prince George of (1865-1936), afterwards King George V, 79
Walker, Sir Charles (1817-94), General attached to Crown Prince's Army in the Franco-Prussian War, 48
Washing of the Spears, The, 52
Waterpark, Lady, extra Lady of the Bedchamber to the Queen, 190
Wellesley, Colonel, 42
Wellesley, Gerald Valerian (1809-82), Dean of Windsor, 105, 125, 135, 140
Wellesley, Lily, daughter of Lord Rokeby and wife of the above, 140, 141
Werder, Count (1808-87), German General, 91
Westminster, 1st Duke of (1825-99), Master of the Horse, 76
William IV, 7
Wimpfen, Count, Austro-Hungarian Ambassador in Paris, 131
Windhorst, Ludwig (1812-91), 69
Windisch-Grätz, Marie, wife of Prince Paul of Mecklenberg, 101, 103
Windsor, Lord. See Plymouth
Winkler, Inspector of Police, 108
Wolseley, Sir Garnet (1833-1913), General. Created a peer in 1882, 52, 182, 184
Wood, Sir Evelyn (1838-1919), Field Marshal, 53, 54, 150
Wright, General von (1821-85), an Englishman who was a distinguished cavalry officer in the Prussian Army, 48
Würtemburg, Prince William of, 112
Würtemburg, Princess William of, 112

YATES, E. H., 42

ZEBEHR (or Zobehr) Pasha, a slave trader, 161
Zoubkoff, M., second husband of Princess Victoria of Prussia, 98